The Air Logistics Handboo

Why study air cargo? Consider that this sector moves only 3 per cent of the global volume of goods but a huge 35 per cent by value, reserved for the most costly and time-sensitive products. Air logistics is an economically and strategically important industry, and a rich source of opportunity for graduating students and logistics or supply chain management professionals.

Get a head start in this vital part of your business with this comprehensive and lively overview. It's the only book available to focus on the role of air freight in the global supply chain. It includes: a brief history; the functions of the various players in the industry (forwarders, airlines, airports, government agencies); regulations and restrictions; and terrorism management. It details the benefits of air transport, and weighs them against its considerable environmental impact to explore the question of its sustainability. Finally, it considers the future of the industry in a dynamic and increasingly globalized world.

Enriched throughout with real-life case studies and contributions from global industry experts, this is a ground-level introduction with a practical approach: all the student or professional will need to get ahead in air logistics!

Michael Sales is Managing Director of IMC Creations, UK, specializing in public relations and consultancy. Clients include Airports of Paris, Air France Express, Athens International Airport, Cologne Bonn Airport, ECS, Basque regional industrial promotion and Düsseldorf Airport.

Ian Martin Jones has been in the editorial business for 47 years, including a ten-year period in Fleet Street and 23 years editing publications covering air, sea and multimodal freight logistics. Having editorially covered consumer, travel, leisure and business disciplines. Jones took over as editor of *Air Cargo Week* shortly after its September 1998 launch and firmly established the globally distributed tabloid as the air logistic industry's best-read weekly newspaper, remaining in his post for 666 consecutive issues until the end of July 2012. He has been a frequent conference chairman/moderator at major aviation industry events including Air Cargo Europe, Air Cargo China, Air Cargo Americas and The Future of Air Transport. Ian Martin Jones received the John Richman Award for lifetime achievement 2012.

The Air Logistics Handbook

Air freight and the global supply chain

Michael Sales

LONDON AND NEW YORK

First published 2013
by Routledge
2 Park Square, Milton Park, Abingdon, Oxon OX14 4RN

Simultaneously published in the USA and Canada
by Routledge
711 Third Avenue, New York, NY 10017

Routledge is an imprint of the Taylor & Francis Group, an informa business

© 2013 Michael Sales

British Library Cataloguing in Publication Data
A catalogue record for this book is available from the British Library

Library of Congress Cataloging in Publication Data
Sales, Michael.
 The air logistics handbook: air freight and the global supply chain/
 Michael Sales.
 pages cm
 Includes bibliographical references and index.
 1. Aeronautics, Commercial – Freight. 2. Business logistics.
 I. Title.
 HE9788.S25 2013
 387.7′44 – dc23
 2012045508

ISBN: 978-0-415-64364-1 (hbk)
ISBN: 978-0-415-64365-8 (pbk)
ISBN: 978-0-203-08007-8 (ebk)

Typeset in Times New Roman
by Florence Production Ltd, Stoodleigh, Devon

Printed and bound in Great Britain by
TJ International Ltd, Padstow, Cornwall

This book is dedicated to Rosalind, my long suffering wife and partner.

Contents

List of figures

Contributors

Jean Francois Bouilhaguet *(right)*

Bouilhaguet is President of Sodexi, the express handling arm of Air France. He has over 20 years' experience in developing high-tech solutions for ground handling. He is also President of CIN, the Paris air freight IT platform.

David R. Brooks *(right)*

Brooks spent ten years in senior management roles at AMR Services, followed by 16 years as President of American Airlines Cargo, a division of American Airlines.

Chris Chapman *(no picture)*

Chapman is President of Chapman Freeborn, the world's largest charter broker. He has been a pioneer of the air charter industry for over 30 years and a highly respected personality within the air freight industry.

Ray Crane *(right)*

Crane is the retired owner and publisher of *Air Cargo News* since its launch, with wide experience of all aspects of the air freight industry.

Gerton Hulsman *(right)*

Hulsman is currently Managing Director of Düsseldorf Air Cargo. He is an expert in cargo handling and traffic development and has many years of experience with KLM Cargo.

Howard Jones *(no picture)*

Jones is a Canadian-based GSA in Toronto. He has remained successfully independent for over 20 years.

Ian Martin Jones *(right)*

Jones has been in the editorial business for 47 years, including a ten-year period in Fleet Street and 23 years editing publications covering air, sea and multimodal freight logistics.

Having editorially covered consumer, travel, leisure and business disciplines. Jones took over as editor of *Air Cargo Week* shortly after its September 1998 launch and firmly established the globally distributed tabloid as the air logistic industry's best-read weekly newspaper, remaining in his post for 666 consecutive issues until the end of July 2012.

He has been a frequent conference chairman/moderator at major aviation industry events including Air Cargo Europe, Air Cargo China, Air Cargo Americas and The Future of Air Transport.

Ian Martin Jones received the John Richman Award for lifetime achievement 2012.

Giles Large *(no picture)*

Large is an expert journalist and editor for different publications within the freight industry.

John Lloyd *(right)*

John has over 26 years in air cargo, joining Virgin Atlantic Cargo in 1987. He has steadily progressed throughout the company, serving in various supervisory and management positions. He was appointed as Director of Cargo in May 2000. During his time in this capacity, Virgin Atlantic Cargo has won 11 International Cargo Airline of the Year awards.

Ram Menen *(right)*

Menen was Director of Emirates SkyCargo for over 20 years, and a strong supporter of paperless cargo processes and computer systems for air freight.

Robert Quest *(no picture)*

Quest has been Manager of London Heathrow Airport Animal Reception Facility for over 20 years, and is an expert on dealing with animal quarantine and regulations.

Martin Roebuck *(no picture)*

Roebuck is a highly experienced journalist and editor in multimodal transport.

Michael Sales *(right)*

Sales has worked in the international publishing business since 1977 but moved to air freight publishing in 1990, with *Air Cargo News* and later the A-Z Group. He launched *IMC Creations* in 1995, specializing in public relations and consultancy. He handled a number of prestigious clients, including Airports of Paris, Air France Express, Athens International Airport, Cologne Bonn Airport, ECS, Basque regional industrial promotion, Düsseldorf Airport and many more.

Alexios Sioris *(right)*

Sioris has been Director of Air Cargo Development at Athens International Airport since its launch. He is an expert in airport management and traffic development.

Sally Smith *(right)*

Smith is President of the International Pet and Animal Transportation Association, and an experienced kennel owner.

Geoff Stowe *(no picture)*

Stowe is President of Redberry Software, which has provided user-friendly computer solutions to the air freight industry for over 20 years.

Des Vertannes *(right)*

Vertannes has over 40 years' management experience with airlines – British Airways, Air Canada, Etihad, followed by Gulf Air. Since June 2010 he has been Global Head of Cargo at IATA in Geneva.

Stanley Wraight *(right)*

With over 40 years' experience in air cargo sales and operations, Wraight has become one of the industry's leading experts. He has held senior positions with KLM, Atlas Air, Volga-Dnepr – now Airbridge Cargo. His own company, Strategic Aviation Solutions (SASI), founded in 2005, carries out consultancy work for many different companies.

Foreword

Sir Richard Branson

I have, for several decades with my airline and railway enterprises, been deeply involved in the transport business. When I look back over these years, I see incredible changes in society, the way we live our daily lives and how industry and commerce have reacted. The rapid and relentless increase of international trade has been frequently disrupted by disasters, terrorist attacks, bad weather and continuous increases in fuel prices. Despite all these challenges, the transport and logistics industry has managed to not only survive, but has become stronger than ever. Without the flow of goods and passengers around the world, our way of life and the development of poorer countries' economies wouldn't exist.

Over the last 28 years, Virgin Atlantic Airways has turned heads around the world. We have delivered on our promise to provide high quality and value for money, taking on giants, particularly when they seem to have taken their customers' loyalty for granted.

Air travel has transformed all of our lives and helps us experience different cultures and make new friends all over the world. However, airlines are not only about passengers. To make them work successfully, you also need to build a growing and award-winning cargo service – and at Virgin Atlantic Airlines we've done that too.

Air logistics is a phenomenal industry and has become even more important not only to the success of airlines, but also to every consumer and business leader around the world. Before aircraft, products moving between countries spent weeks at sea. Today, it takes just hours to move imports and exports from one side of the world to the other, putting air logistics at the very heart of world trade.

I am delighted to introduce *The Air Logistics Handbook* and I hope it will encourage you to explore the many career opportunities this outstanding industry offers. Air cargo needs new well-educated executives and entrepreneurs who will be tomorrow's leaders and innovators. Air cargo needs you.

I wish you every success.

Preface

Michael Sales

The transportation of goods and mail by air, which can trace its origins back to the early 1900s, has, in today's global consumer society, developed into a key component of world trade. Yet despite this important role, air freight remains a comparatively hidden business. Although handling an estimated 3 per cent of total world tonnage, it is the 35 per cent and upwards value of goods that makes it such a vital business. A very good journalist friend of mine has described the air cargo business as 'the far side of aviation', the hidden side of the airport away from the supposed glamour of the passenger business.

Aviation has always had many enemies and has suffered badly at the hands of bad weather, earthquakes, volcanic eruptions, wars, fuel price hikes, terrorism, misguided politicians and repressive regulation. Often seen by governments as an easy cash machine and a target for scoring cheap environmental points, our modern global economies would dry up without its contribution. This short book tells air freight's story in simple terms. It shows how, where, when and why it works and takes a look at its possible future. It takes the reader, chapter by chapter, through the different stages and functions of the air freight processes and demonstrates how, in order to achieve the distribution of goods, world trade depends on air freight just as it does on sea freight and road haulage.

I am eternally grateful to my various highly skilled contributors, especially Ian Martin Jones, who have given their time, knowledge and expert opinions based on years of hands-on experience working in the industry. The air logistics business has much to offer in terms of its wide range of career opportunities. We have attempted to guide the reader to selected and useful sources without including pages of obscure statistics and out-of-date references. It is my hope that more graduates from around the world will be attracted to this unique, exciting and stubbornly resilient global industry.

Introduction to the world of air freight

Des Vertannes

Des Vertannes' career in aviation spans four decades, joining IATA from Etihad, where he was Executive Vice President of Cargo since April 2007 and prior to that Head of Cargo at rival Gulf Air. Des began with British Airways in 1970 and during 14 years at the airline he held several management posts including Cargo Manager of Gulf States and Saudi Arabia in the early 1980s.

In 1984 he established and managed his own forwarding business before joining Air Canada as General Manager of Cargo in 1991, responsible for Europe, Africa and the Middle East. His next move was to ground handling company Menzies Aviation, where he served as Chief Executive at Air Menzies International (AMI) and Managing Director at Menzies World Cargo between 1999 and 2005.

In June 2010 he joined IATA as Global Head of Cargo and is based in Geneva.

* * *

I am privileged to be invited by the author to share my personal views on what makes the air cargo logistics industry a truly wonderful and exciting business in which to dedicate one's career.

For the uninitiated, the air cargo logistics industry is responsible for transporting over 35 per cent of the value of total global trade, that's in excess of \$5.1 trillion. More importantly, air cargo (or air freight as it's sometimes known) helps to catalyse economic prosperity for almost every country, stimulates business travel for all airlines and acts as a leading economic indicator for financial and business analysts.

What most people do not realize is that everything we need to sustain our daily lifestyle over the year, such as energy, communication, medication and hospitals, food, flowers, entertainment, clothes and transport depends substantially on the air cargo logistics supply chain. The general assumption is that air cargo is only reserved for high-value commodities or perishable items, so there remains a strong need to educate the world's consumers as to the value of the air cargo supply chain.

Obviously we live in a world where protecting the environment is becoming an ever-increasing priority which is shaping our behaviour and responsibilities.

So while we should take note that aviation and air transport accounts for 3 per cent of global carbon emissions, this should in no way prejudice our views or perceptions that purchasing goods that have been air transported over thousands of miles is simply adding to carbon emissions. Aviation is a source for good that connects people and facilitates trade and is the only industry that has globally committed to specific actions to neutralize carbon emission growth by 2020 and reduce emissions by 50 per cent by 2050.

So why has air cargo logistics become so vital around the world? We all know that we are in a fast-evolving global economy connected by events that impact us within hours, not days. We have seen over this past decade the emergence of developing countries – specifically the BRICS (Brazil, Russia, India, China and South Africa). As these countries and other developing nations begin to compete and attract foreign direct investment, we see their people prosper and begin to supplement the world's ever-growing middle class, and that means their appetite for branded consumer goods and various services increases global demand. Satisfying this thirst requires their own air cargo logistics chain to become more professional, efficient and reliable. The industry will therefore require many more talented logisticians to come forward and manage these critical supply chains so that their countries can maintain their attractiveness and competitive edge.

Let's not forget that security also plays a major part in air cargo and has evolved further since the terrorist attack on New York's twin towers on 9/11. Since then, various governments, in particular those of the USA and EU, have introduced extremely robust and uncompromising security directives to ensure we have a safe aviation industry and supply chain.

For many airlines, air cargo is their lifeline, not simply boosting their bottom line but in some instances contributing to the difference between profit and loss. For airlines like Lufthansa, Cathay Pacific, Emirates, Korean and Singapore Airlines, cargo can represent 20–35 per cent of their total revenues.

Let me tell you that a career in air cargo logistics will inspire you and introduce you to contacts across the globe, many of whom will become your friends for life. From my own personal experience, which spans in excess of four decades, I have been extremely fortunate to have had great mentors and leaders of substantial reputation that influenced my career, many of whom are contributors to this book, and to whom I frequently turned for advice. They have had an immense influence, as have some of my peers, including my closest competitors. That's what makes this industry such a unique, highly personal and sociable business.

We are now looking for a new generation of leaders who can build on this foundation, and I am encouraging any young person to look no further than this wonderful industry for a career of continuous challenges and excitement. Your skills, innovation and motivation will be needed to sustain and improve an industry that continues to drive world trade. You can be assured that you will be helped by a circle of global friends and acquaintances.

Why air cargo works

Ian Martin Jones

When speed of delivery over a long distance is the most important factor in the global transportation of commercially valuable cargo, then using an aircraft to move the goods is the only answer, explains air freight journalist Ian Martin Jones.

In the modern world, 'speed to market' has become a mantra with the dynamic global manufacturers who have become successful and want to remain so in the future. The ongoing process of globalization now sees commercial and consumer goods, or their component parts, being manufactured in all corners of the globe.

Often, production and assembly takes place in developing countries where low labour and land costs mean the manufacturing costs and the end price can be driven as low as possible, but this can often invite complications in maintaining a constant supply chain that is becoming increasingly complex every day.

Apple's successful iPhone, for example, may well have been designed in the US, but by 2012 its components were being manufactured and assembled by nine companies in six countries spread around the globe. Getting all the pieces together in the right place at the right time to take to the marketplace at the right price is the fundamental concept of modern-day supply chain logistics.

Every day, computers for retail sale to consumers in Europe or Latin America are assembled in China, televisions destined for the US are made in Korea and automotive parts manufactured in Poland can be bound for car-makers based in India. Also, the modern 'media-savvy' consumer demands goods and luxury items sourced from all points of the compass: fresh foodstuffs in the US are grown in Latin America, long-stem roses on sale in Europe can come from Ecuador and Ethiopia, generic pharmaceuticals made in Iceland may be required in Indonesia, meat from New Zealand is in demand all across the Middle East and fresh fish on the table in Japan can originate from the coastal waters of the Scandinavian countries. Even entrepreneurs in China, for many years the Holy Grail of low-cost production techniques, have done so well that there is a vibrant demand in the country's large cities for genuine, branded luxury items from the top European fashion houses – expensive items that have to move quickly to satisfy a time-sensitive demand from image-conscious buyers.

With the great distances involved in the production and supply of consumer goods – as well as an increasingly diverse geographical point-of-sale location – there comes a time in many supply chains when only air transportation can provide the answer in the time available.

While euphoria is often high with manufacturers who have found new low-cost areas for manufacturing and production in developing countries, the fact that the supply chain in those regions is often in a nascent state of development itself can present a whole raft of problems when it comes to shipping in raw materials or racing products to the marketplace.

As a result, the global supply chain has become a complex matter embracing market fluctuations in currencies and commodities that can happen on a daily basis. Also, conflict and human disaster scenarios have played a role in which the supply chain must remain resilient, maintaining a constant flow of goods and providing its users with the flexibility to outmanoeuvre their competitors in bringing new goods to market and providing better value for the end customer.

Categories of need

The need for speed in the delivery of goods necessary in today's modern commercial world can be driven by a range of requirements, which can be split roughly into a number of categories:

- The global implementation of just-in-time logistics practices has massively reduced the need for companies to carry vast and costly inventories of goods in their retail outlets or in independently owned and expensive to maintain warehouses that are no longer required.
- Sometimes items are required urgently to maintain the production level of an assembly line or the flow from an oil rig; both of these examples are areas where it would cost millions of dollars to suspend normal working practices for even a short period of time.
- A large shipment of modern high-tech items being moved over a long distance can be worth millions of dollars, while air freight reduces the transportation time between China and Europe, for example, from five or six weeks at sea to a matter of a few days – of vital importance to company balance sheets and cost of ownership.
- Many perishable items such as pharmaceutical products or fresh foods need to be moved quickly and within a carefully monitored temperature-controlled environment to maintain their effectiveness and freshness – as well as satisfying an increasing raft of strictly enforced regulations.
- Finally, driven by a constant pressure of television, radio, media and internet exposure, there is the way the modern-day consumer demands goods on a 'must-have' basis; a 'see today, want today' requirement. This

lifestyle expectation is pushed even harder by the increasing use of online ordering functions where the overriding demand is 'order today, delivery tomorrow'.

How air cargo moves

With modern aircraft able to fly at speeds of up to 600 miles per hour, and ocean-going vessels restricted to not much more than 30 knots, the time taken to travel the long distances involved is reduced to a matter of hours when an aircraft is used, against a transportation window measured in weeks over water. In an increasingly commercially sensitive world, this offers huge benefits to those shippers who opt to use it as an everyday component of their supply chain. Air freight has therefore increasingly become the way to move goods around the world – and there are a variety of ways to go about it.

Air cargo shipments can be transported in the bellyhold space of passenger aircraft – beneath the feet of the fare-paying customers of domestic and international airlines – or by utilizing the main-deck capacity of the world's fleet of freighter aircraft operating as either scheduled or chartered services. Some of these freighters are owned by the passenger airlines to complement their own bellyhold cargo offering, while others are flown by independent all-cargo airlines that earn their revenue entirely from providing freight-carrying services.

Almost every passenger flight carries some freight underneath the feet of its passengers and alongside their baggage. In America, for instance, the US Postal Service alone leases space on some 15,000 of an estimated 25,000 scheduled passenger flights in the air every day. There is a strong commercial incentive for airlines to utilize the empty below-deck space of their equipment, for many earn about 5–10 per cent of their total sales revenue from carrying freight – in fact, those with predominately widebody equipment in their fleet can make a lot more. SkyCargo, the air freight wing of Dubai-based Emirates Airline, complements the bellyhold space of its widebody fleet with a mid-sized fleet of freighter aircraft and notches up about 19–20 per cent of its revenue from carrying cargo. Others with larger fleets of freighters make a great deal more: Cathay Pacific in Hong Kong earns around one-third of its revenue from carrying freight; Taiwan's China Airlines around 40 per cent; and Korean Air Cargo about half of its sales earnings.

Passenger or freighter

Using the conventional method of transporting goods by air, freight is collected from the manufacturer – referred to in the logistics business as the shipper – by a trucking company either owned by or working for a freight forwarder, the commercial entity normally responsible for the organization of the whole air freight supply chain of the shipment. The cargo is then delivered by road to a cargo handler at the chosen airport of departure. All freight must then be cleared through exit Customs procedures and undergo the required security checks to ensure the safety of the aircraft, its passengers and crew – a process that is described in more depth elsewhere in this book.

If the cargo handler holds a licence allowing it to operate from its warehouse premises onto the airport tarmac, it can operate right up to the cargo doors of the passenger aircraft and load goods into the bellyhold space. Similarly, it can take a shipment to a waiting freighter aircraft on the airport tarmac. If the company does not hold the requisite licence, then it must hand over the shipment to a cargo handler that does have that statutory permission.

On arrival at its destination, the aircraft is unloaded on the tarmac by a licensed cargo handler and the shipment must then undergo the relevant Customs clearance requirements of the arrival nation, as well as any further security checks deemed necessary by the authorities of that country. The goods are then made available for collection from the cargo handler's warehouse by the trucking representative of the freight forwarder for final delivery by road to the end customer.

The traditional air cargo supply chain is therefore complex in the way that it works – some will argue that it is too complicated, while other air freight transportation providers like the global express logistics companies FedEx, UPS and DHL (generically known as the integrators because of their integrated air transportation chain) will claim that their seamless end-to-end systems cut out all of the middle-man suppliers in the transportation chain providing point-to-point delivery from the shipper to the retailer, or even in some cases to the end customer – but like everything else in life, this full-service procedure comes at a price that many shippers find prohibitive when bringing goods to market at an attractive cost.

These were the facts as of March 2013 but in such a rapidly changing industry, events may have altered some details.

Further reading

Many of the leading publications covering the air logistics industry are available online. As English is the recognized language of this industry, most of the magazines are in English. For more information about the business, take a look at these titles.

- *Air Cargo News* (UK international): www.aircargonews.net
- *Air Cargo Week* (UK international): www.azfreight.com
- *Air Cargo World* (USA, with an international edition): www.aircargoworld.com
- *Payload Asia* (Far East circulation): www.payloadasia.com
- *Stattimes* (India, plus circulation in the Gulf): www.stattimes.com

There are other multimodal publications mostly in English, as well as some in local languages.

1 The air freight supply chain

By Martin Roebuck

The movement of freight by air accounts for less than 3 per cent of global trade by volume. For obvious reasons of transport availability and cost, the great majority of raw materials used by manufacturing industries, as well as the finished products we buy as consumers, travel by ship or by road.

Any one of the massive container ships that leave ports in Korea, Japan and China many times every day on their way to Europe or North America can carry enough clothes, furnishings, car parts, toys and foodstuffs to fill 3,000 of the largest cargo aircraft in our skies, or would fill the available space in as many as 30,000 passenger aircraft where the cargo has to fit alongside everyone's luggage in the bellyhold.

Yet, when exports and imports are measured by value, rather than volume, air freight claims a very much larger 35 per cent share of the market. It is high-value, must-get-there products that fly: cut flowers, fresh food, pharmaceuticals, mobile phones, computers, medical equipment, spare parts and valuable machine tools.

Air freight traffic, measured in revenue tonne-kilometres (RTKs) – the quantity of cargo carried multiplied by the distance flown – achieved 191.4 billion RTKs in 2007, but decreased to 166.8 billion RTKs in 2009 as a result of the slowdown in global economic activity.

Despite this blip, the growth in gross domestic product (GDP), a measure of each country's output that reflects how well its industry and businesses are performing, is surprisingly consistent over longer periods of time. World economic growth is forecast to average 3.2 per cent per annum over the next 20 years.

This will directly benefit the air cargo industry. Thanks to the development of larger, more efficient aircraft with a longer operating range, in conjunction with more streamlined airport operations and the resulting emergence of a global supply chain that is more responsive to changes in demand, air cargo growth runs at double the rate of GDP growth. For 40 years now, air cargo traffic has grown more than twice as fast as global GDP.

Aircraft manufacturer Boeing, as well as its main rival Airbus, closely monitors this trend to make sure it can build enough aircraft to meet future demand. It predicts an annual world air cargo traffic growth of 5.9 per cent over the next 20 years. If its forecast is correct, the industry will have tripled in size by 2029.

Figure 1.1 Cargo Aircraft B777
Source: SASI.

The shipper's choice

To clarify the terminology along the air freight transport chain, the person or company requesting the movement of goods is the shipper (this term applies no matter whether the shipment is going by aircraft, ship, truck or train). The shipper is also known as the consignor, because they consign or entrust the goods to those who will undertake the physical transfer process.

The shipper can be the manufacturer or seller of a product, or a third-party distributor, ordering goods stored at the shipper's premises or in a warehouse to be shipped from A to B.

Next in the transport chain is the freight forwarder, who typically takes cargo to the departing airport or subcontracts someone else to do it, prepares the necessary paperwork, picks up the cargo at the destination airport and arranges onward delivery as required to the end-customer.

The airline, or carrier, flies the cargo from the airport of origin to the destination airport. There are three types of carrier. The passenger airlines, also called combination carriers, carry both passengers and cargo on regular scheduled services. Almost every passenger flight carries some freight and mail; and commercial airlines can earn 10 per cent or more of their total sales revenue from this part of their business. Major passenger carriers such as Hong Kong-based Cathay Pacific, Germany's Lufthansa and Emirates Airline in Dubai also operate all-cargo freighter aircraft within their fleets.

The second group, all-cargo carriers, operate freighter aircraft on a scheduled basis on routes where there is regular heavy cargo demand or where the potential passenger traffic is limited. As well as carriers of large cargo, airlines in this category include courier and express operators, such as FedEx, UPS and DHL. These offer a complete door-to-door collection and delivery service at an all-inclusive price, excluding duties and taxes applicable in the country of destination, usually for parcels or small packages of up to 30 kg. Some of these operators have expanded their services in recent times to handle larger consignments.

Third, charter airlines either fly ad-hoc services when there is special demand, fly to unusual destinations not offered by other types of carrier or operate scheduled services on behalf of specific customers. The space of the whole or part of an aircraft can be chartered, an area of the business usually the domain of the specialist charter broker, a company that will source aircraft availability and obtain the best price for the customer.

The ground handler is the agent at the airport that receives and consolidates outbound freight, stores and transfers it to the aircraft, and unloads and retrieves the shipments at their destination. The consignee is the receiving party to which the goods are sent, such as an assembly line, importer or retailer.

The owner of the goods may be the shipper, the consignee or a third party. Incoterms (International Commercial Terms) are used when contracts are signed to help clarify ownership and the responsibilities of the shipper, forwarder, airline and other parties in the supply chain. Incoterms also ensure that there is no ambiguity over who is paying for what and when.

Air freight can be significantly more expensive than ocean freight, but using the available speed it minimizes door-to-door transit time and is often the preferred choice for transporting higher-value goods quickly to market.

The smallest category of air freight is bagged mail, express documents and packages weighing a maximum of 30 kg, and therefore can be handled by one person and automatically sorted to destination via a conveyor belt.

On-board courier (OBC) or hand-carry services are sometimes used for very urgent or valuable documents and small goods. A dedicated courier picks up the shipment, flies with it on the same aircraft as a passenger, handles Customs procedures along the way and delivers it in person to the recipient or consignee.

Where mainstream freight shipments are concerned, the airline's rate calculation is usually based on the weight of the goods. Above a certain weight-to-volume threshold set by the International Air Transport Association (IATA) – currently six cubic metres per tonne – the volume instead determines the rate. For example, shipments of electronic goods or pharmaceuticals, protected by lightweight filling material such as expanded polystyrene beads or bubble wrap, will be more 'volumetric' than heavier, denser cargo such as machine parts or books. Different weight-to-volume ratios apply to ocean shipping, as well as to rail and road transport.

Cargo requiring special handling of any sort, including dangerous, chilled or perishable goods, live animals and outsize shipments that do not fit in standard containers, will usually attract extra charges.

Aircraft types

About 25 per cent of all cargo flown is carried on commercial passenger aircraft and the remainder on freighter aircraft. Specific aircraft types are described in more detail in a later chapter, but in brief summary, passenger airlines transport cargo alongside the personal baggage beneath the passengers in the so-called bellyhold space of the aircraft. This cargo, also described as lower-deck capacity, is packed into a specially shaped aluminium container called a unit load device (ULD). A familiar sight at airports when being towed out to the waiting aircraft, these containers come in various sizes and have angled corners to fit the fuselage shape.

Freighter aircraft that carry no passengers offer main-deck cargo capacity, where freight can be side-loaded through a large cargo door or nose-loaded, where the hinged front end of the aircraft can be opened. The latter method is especially suitable for large and extra-long loads, where the whole nose lifts up to enable easy access. A third variation, combi aircraft, carry fewer passengers, with main-deck cargo space provided behind the passenger area as well as in the bellyhold space.

The amount and weight of cargo that can be carried also depends on the fuselage dimensions of the aircraft. Widebody jets (also called twin-aisle because the seats are in three blocks with two gangways between them) carry many more passengers and thus have more cargo space than narrowbody or single-aisle jets.

Regional, short-haul aircraft have almost no cargo capacity when in passenger configuration, but charter airlines use a number of small, specialized

Figure 1.2 ULD
Source: general press photo.

Figure 1.3 Nose-loading aircraft B747

Source: Air France, reprinted with permission from Air France: Air France Collection. DR/Air France Museum Collection.

freighters with capacities from two to ten tonnes to make same-day or overnight deliveries of small, urgent consignments.

The air freight process

In the world of ocean transport, large-volume customers may book direct with the shipping line, but in air freight a forwarder is almost always involved as an intermediary. The only common exception to this rule is if a large shipper is looking to charter an aircraft for a special one-off shipment. It can still do this via a forwarder, but may alternatively approach a specialist charter broker which will locate a suitable aircraft and operator.

The air freight forwarder's primary job is to identify the best route, negotiate the space and price with a carrier, present the shipment ready for carriage in the appropriate packaging and with the correct documentation. The forwarder will also ensure that the goods arrive at the right place, at the right time and in the required condition.

When goods are ready for transport (RFT) – that is, correctly packed, labelled and with the right documents – the road transport company or forwarder will give the shipper a proof of acceptance (POA).

Road transfer to the airport can be negotiated on an ad-hoc basis, or a larger forwarder may operate its own consolidation service from larger cities, together with a parallel delivery service in the destination country. Airlines or their handling agents also operate road feeder services (RFSs) to cover airports that they do not serve by air, and it will subcontract specialist road hauliers for this purpose. Some of these services are allocated an airline flight number.

Forwarders typically offer three levels of service:

1   Priority, for time-critical shipments, based on the next direct flight or fastest available connection and with a transit time of 1–2 days.
2   Standard, with 3–4 days of transit time.
3   Economy, with a transit time of 5–6 days from departure airport to destination airport.

Large forwarders will pre-book capacity in bulk with the leading airlines to achieve a more economical rate via a consolidation service, which means selling to multiple clients happy to have their goods shipped to the same destination on the same day. Customers can specify the pick-up and delivery options such as door-to-door, airport-to-airport, door-to-airport and so on.

In addition to core transport services, the freight forwarder will offer insurance, assistance with documentation and, in many parts of the world, will arrange and oversee Customs clearance. In some countries, however, licensed Customs agents and brokers still operate independently from the forwarders and are responsible for Customs clearance of imported goods when they arrive at their destination airport or seaport. The air freight transaction is managed by the air waybill (AWB), traditionally a paper document but now moving towards an electronic system.

In addition to the base price by weight or volume (the chargeable weight), additional charges that the forwarder will pass on to the shipper will include charges for export goods, airline terminal handling fees, fuel and risk surcharges, Customs data entry requirements and shipment screening under new security rules. Duties and taxes are also payable on import goods, additional to the forwarder's standard service fees.

Buying and selling space

Airlines know from their future schedules how much cargo space they will have on passenger aircraft and offer a percentage of this several months in advance as 'allotted capacity'. Forwarders, anticipating their likely volume requirement on given routes, can bid for this space. Typically, 50–70 per cent of available bellyhold space will be sold to customers through a 'hard' block space agreement (BSA) at a negotiated price, a 'soft' block permanent booking (PB) or other forms of capacity purchase agreements.

Two to four weeks before departure, the freight forwarders confirm their actual requirements and the remaining capacity is put on free sale. Airlines then use complex revenue management techniques to sell the remaining space at the highest rate.

Capacity will be sold at different rates, depending on whether the airline is offering a standard service or is aiming at shippers of time-sensitive goods or cargo requiring special handling. It will want to reserve some capacity for high-margin customers, and at departure will look to load a good mix of urgent and general cargo, as well as a mix of dense and volumetric cargo to optimize the use of space in the cargo hold.

More space is often sold than is physically available, because airlines expect that a certain amount of booked cargo will not show up or a forwarder on a PB will not take up its full allocation. Forwarders do not provide detailed information on exactly what is coming until they present an AWB with the cargo a few hours before departure.

If too much cargo arrives at the last minute or there are other unforeseen circumstances, some general cargo is 'bumped' from the flight or held over until a later departure.

Airline obligations

Two international agreements, the Warsaw Convention and the Montreal Convention, govern the international carriage of goods by air and define the legal and contractual, as well as the loss and damage liability, obligations of the airline, freight forwarder, shipper and other parties in the supply chain.

Airlines accept freight on the basis of a limited airport-to-airport contract and cannot be held directly responsible for delays in consignments reaching their destination (although those with a lower reliability record can expect to find themselves losing out commercially in the long run).

Nor are airlines responsible for paying compensation for the full value of goods that are lost or damaged. This should be covered by insurance, but even here standard insurance cover will not extend to protecting consequential loss, such as a financial loss incurred by the shipper if a consignment is delayed en route.

Security

Security requirements relating to air freight movements have become more tightly regulated in recent times following terrorist incidents and attempted attacks against aircraft or specific targets at destinations. The rules differ by country of origin and destination, but in most countries air freight consignments must either originate with a government-accredited 'known shipper' or will have to be screened before being loaded onto an aircraft.

A unit of cargo (a single indivisible package) or a consolidated shipment of multiple units, such as a pallet or ULD coming from a known shipper and accompanied by a cargo security certificate, is deemed safe to fly. This type of cargo benefits from a more streamlined security process, though it will still have to be X-rayed again for shipment to certain destinations, such as the US.

Air freight presented by unknown shippers – by definition 'unknown' cargo – undergoes a more rigorous security process, such as physical inspection or X-ray screening. This has to be done by a regulated freight forwarder or other approved agent. If the forwarder is unable or unwilling to carry out this task, it will become the responsibility of the airline's handling company at the airport to X-ray or physically open and hand-search the cargo.

In this case, the acceptance or 'cut-off' time, after which shipments for a particular flight can no longer be accepted by the handler or airline, is set earlier to allow extra time for the completion of the statutory security procedures.

Companies trading inside the EU, or with transit through EU countries involved as part of an international supply chain, can apply for Authorized Economic Operator (AEO) status. This internationally recognized certificate signifies that a company's Customs processes are secure and reliable, but the security procedures outlined above must still be followed.

Documentation

More than 20 documents are needed at various stages of the air freight transport process. These include:

- the invoice, packing list and letter of instruction;
- certificate of origin and dangerous goods declaration if required;
- master air waybill (MAWB), the contract between the shipper and airline;
- house waybill, the contract between the shipper and the agent/consolidator for a specific shipment;
- cargo manifest (detailed list of goods);
- export, import and security declarations;
- Customs exports release, import release at destination – and many more.

To help make the air freight process more efficient and reduce the amount of paper carried, the IATA is converting many of these documents to electronic format through its e-freight programme.

Handling

State-owned airports may carry out their own ground handling, normally understood to include ramp handling and cargo handling, although some have opened up these services to commercial operators.

Ramp handling covers services provided to the aircraft between arrival and departure, including guiding it to its parking bay, cleaning, refuelling, de-icing, passenger baggage handling and transfer of passengers and crew.

A single ground handling company or agent (GHA) may provide an airline with all its handling at a given airport, or this work can be divided between up to four subcontractors handling passenger and baggage check-in, cargo reception, transfer from the cargo facility to the aircraft and loading.

Figure 1.4 Air waybill
Source: trade document.

When the forwarder has delivered cargo to the cargo terminal at the airport of departure, or to the airline's own dedicated depot, the handler will inspect it, check whether anything is damaged or missing against the accompanying documents, prepare the documentation for exit Customs procedures and carry out any required security procedures.

Cargo that may have been in short-term storage in the air freight handling facility is transferred from wooden storage pallets or skids onto metal aircraft pallets or into ULDs. Newly delivered cargo is combined with transit cargo (arriving from another airport and now switching flights) and taken to the aircraft for loading.

Other transport modes

While air transport offers speed and reliability, most intercontinental freight goes by sea, which is considerably cheaper.

Dry cargo movements by ship, excluding bulk commodities such as oil, metal ore and grain, totalled approximately 16.9 trillion RTKs in 2009. These movements include project and heavy lift cargo, such as industrial plant, generators, wind turbines, military equipment – anything too big or too heavy to fit into a container. Also included here is the 'wheeled cargo' category of new cars, buses, trucks and construction equipment, usually carried on specialized roll-on, roll-off (ro-ro) vessels.

Break-bulk cargo, typically material stacked on pallets and lifted into and out of the hold of a vessel by cranes on the dock or aboard the ship itself, has declined dramatically worldwide as containerization has grown.

Container ships, giving a better like-for-like comparison with the type of goods that are air freighted, were responsible for about 6.2 trillion RTKs in 2009 against 166.8 billion RTKs of air freight, so accounted for more than 97 per cent of international trade movements when measured this way.

The adoption of standardized 20 ft and 40 ft sea containers from the late 1960s onwards allowed handling to become more efficient, replacing a large element of traditional manual dock labour. Generically termed as a TEU (20 ft equivalent unit), these containers can be lifted automatically from trains, trucks and barges onto ships and vice versa in so-called multimodal freight movements.

The advent of containerization gave forwarders the opportunity to develop warehouse-to-warehouse and door-to-door services. These are usually categorized as full container load (FCL) cargo and less than container load (LCL) or groupage. The same designations are also used by road transportation companies.

Containerized cargo includes everything from car parts, machinery and manufacturing components to frozen meat, seafood, fruit, vegetables and the full range of consumer goods. The next generation of container ships will be able to carry up to 9,000 standard 40 ft containers at a time, but they can call at only a limited number of deep-water ports with the very largest cranes and handling facilities.

Shorter intra-regional journeys are made by much smaller container vessels, typically carrying 200–1,000 containers and capable of calling at many more ports. Ro-ro vessels carry either complete trucks, with a driver also making the journey, or unaccompanied trailers that are dropped off by the driver at the port of embarkation and picked up by another at the destination port. Combination con-ro vessels can accommodate a mix of shipping containers, wheeled cargo and truck trailers.

Sea–air movements

Air freight can be combined with ocean freight in a service often described as 'twice as fast as sea transport and half the price of air transport'. Cargo can make the initial sea journey cheaply and is either stored awaiting demand from the final customer, or repackaged immediately in a cross-docking operation and flown to the destination.

The concept works best in locations halfway between the larger regions of manufacture and consumption, and where a large seaport and international airport are in close proximity, allowing rapid transfer. Hubs that have established a reputation in the sea–air market are Dubai and Sharjah, positioned between manufacturers in Asia and consumers in Europe, and Vancouver and Seattle, between Asia and destination markets in North and South America.

Road and rail transportation

For speed and flexibility, road transport is the most common way of moving goods around, particularly on the well-developed road systems of Europe and North America where it has almost completely replaced air transport for domestic and regional freight movements. Very little cargo now flies internally within those two continents, except express packages and mail, and even this time-sensitive traffic goes by road where practicable.

Road transport is either used as a single mode of transport for door-to-door delivery, or for transferring goods into long-haul air or sea transport networks.

Larger container trucks, or curtainsiders, containing palletized goods deliver to and from warehouses, consolidation centres and to airports and seaports. Smaller trucks and delivery vans look after the 'final mile' delivery to retailers, small businesses and, an increasingly important market segment, to households and home workers who have ordered goods online.

Rail transport can be cheaper than other modes, particularly for moving bulky goods such as steel, wood, coal, stone and sand over long distances. Trains can also carry large quantities of dry containers or chemical tank containers to and from seaports.

The main disadvantage of rail freight is its lack of flexibility, which is why it fails to compete with road transport, especially where fast-moving consumer goods are concerned.

Infrastructure is an issue, especially in Western Europe, where bridges and tunnels can be restrictive and freight trains have to share track with faster-running passenger services. Containerized rail transport, including double-stack trains, is more familiar in locations, such as the US, where these constraints are not faced to the same degree.

The global supply chain

As transport services and electronic information systems evolved, retail customers for a wide range of consumer goods, together with their wholesale suppliers, saw an opportunity to get clothing and electronic products more quickly to market without increasing their stock of locally held inventory.

Just-in-time (JIT) philosophy enables a fashion retailer that may once have had spring and autumn collections, or at most four seasons per year, to change its offering every week. In a similar way, a car manufacturer can call parts to the assembly line from a third-party supplier literally an hour before they are needed in the production process.

With companies increasingly outsourcing non-core activities, forwarders have essentially taken control of this process, expanding beyond their traditional roles to manage the end-to-end supply chain. They have rebranded themselves as third-party logistics (3PL) providers, offering a one-stop shop service that integrates transport with several value-added services, including:

- cross-docking – immediate onward transport without intermediate storage;
- warehousing;
- pick-and-pack – where the required items are drawn from storage and possibly reformatted, repackaged or relabelled;
- tracking and tracing – knowing where the goods are at any time during the delivery cycle; and
- final to-door delivery.

Inventory management represents a further evolution of the 3PL service and can extend to vendor managed inventory (VMI), a business model in which the contracted third party takes full responsibility for order management and even suppliers' own production schedules.

The much misunderstood term of fourth-party logistics (4PL) relates to companies, often specializing in IT, logistics, transportation and supply chain management, which do not directly provide their own transport, warehousing or delivery services but act as neutral consultants to help determine the most appropriate solutions for the client.

Sometimes, accidents and natural disasters highlight the dangers of lean operation, and in particular the over-reliance on one source of a particular component or product – the eruption of the Eyjafjallajökull volcano in Iceland that forced closure of north European airspace in 2010 is a prime example of how the supply chain can suffer in such cases.

A fire in a US semiconductor plant in 2000, even though it was put out in less than ten minutes, disabled two of the plant's four all-important clean rooms. One major customer of the facility, mobile phone manufacturer Nokia, made immediate plans and effectively bought up most of the world's alternative supply of microchips. A competitor, Ericsson, had no such contingency plan, lost billions of dollars and was forced out of phone production a year later, only keeping its place in the market by entering a joint venture with Sony.

The Japanese earthquake and tsunami in March 2011, and the radioactive crisis that followed, disrupted global supply chains on a much larger scale, especially in the automotive sector. The average car contains approximately 20,000 parts. Owing to the complexity of the automotive supply chain, if one of these parts is unavailable, the final product cannot be assembled. Thousands of manufacturers work in a pyramid of up to five tiers, each tier supplying sub-assembly manufacturers in the tier above. More than 100 suppliers to Honda were located in the affected areas. The earthquake forced Toyota to suspend production of parts in Japan that were destined for overseas plants. General Motors (GM) had to halt production of vehicles at several plants.

The factories of two Japanese companies that between them control 90 per cent of the market for a specialty resin used to bond parts of microchips that go into smart phones and other devices, Mitsubishi and Hitachi, were damaged in the earthquake. The ensuing scramble for alternative suppliers of microchips and car components forced prices up. Companies with larger buffers of inventory managed the crisis better than those operating JIT systems, suggesting that whatever sophisticated management techniques emerge, traditional rules of supply and demand will always apply.

International air freight forwarders

The freight forwarder or forwarding agent organizes shipments on behalf of a company in order to ensure that goods are delivered quickly and in good condition to a foreign destination or consignee. The forwarder will take responsibility for the goods, ensure they conform to the international regulations for transportation by air of items such as dangerous goods, and will hand them over to a cargo ground handler at the airport of departure after having arranged for their delivery by truck to the departure point.

At the destination airport, the corresponding forwarder, either a branch of the same company or a designated agent, will ensure the delivery of the shipment to its final customer. A competent forwarder will be an expert in supply chain management and will have the necessary contracts in place with global carriers in order to transport the shipments. This may involve a change in the normal routes flown by the airline or even involve routing the shipment via multiple airlines when necessary.

The forwarder prepares and processes the documentation, including Customs and export declarations, dangerous goods, AWBs and the other required documentation. In some cases there may be as many as 30 paper documents prepared for a single air freight shipment. That is why every effort is being made by the authorities, such as IATA, to convert the documentation to paperless electronic processing.

In some countries, freight agents may also act as Customs brokers and may need the relevant government licence. In the case of the very large forwarders, or logistics services providers, registration and licensing with the national government may be mandatory.

Growth of the forwarder

The first freight forwarders emerged during the mid-eighteenth century and their original function was to arrange the transport of customers' goods by contracting with the carriers of the day. Today, forwarders still carry out the same basic task. In some cases, the very large multinational freight forwarders may operate their own flights in order to consolidate freight accumulated from various clients.

Although the exact order may vary from year to year, the leading multimodal forwarders include DHL with Exel USA; Kuehne + Nagel; DB Schenker; Panalpina; UPS; Sinotrans; Ceva Logistics; Expeditors; SDV + Bolloré; DSV; Nippon Express; Kintetsu; Agility Logistics; Hellmann Worldwide; Logwin; Geodis; and Yusen.

Freight forwarders receive payment by way of the fees charged to their clients. With the addition of fuel surcharges and other special costs, these transactions may involve complex calculations. By using electronic processing systems (see Chapter 14), forwarders are able to prepare cargo manifests in advance, a legal necessity in many countries, they can track the shipments – or enable their clients to do so – and calculate the final invoices.

The cargo accounts settlement system (CASS) is an IATA initiative that provides a neutral settlement system between the airlines and the freight agents. This method of settling accounts is now in operation in 70 countries.

As many of the world's huge number of freight forwarders are independent, a number of organizations have grown up to support them, and in some cases represent their interests to government bodies such as the Customs authorities.

Fédération Internationale des Associations de Transitaires et Assimilés/the International Federation of Air Freight Agents (FIATA) was founded in 1926. This non-governmental organization currently represents around 40,000 forwarders and logistics companies employing some ten million people in 150 countries. It cooperates closely with many government and international authorities in the field of transport, including IATA.

Associations and networks

Due to the global nature of the air freight industry, and indeed transportation in general, over 200 countries have their own national freight forwarder associations. Their task is to represent their members, organize conferences and training courses and represent them in international matters. A few examples of these are: AICBA, the Association of International Customs and Border Agencies in Ottawa, Canada; CIFA, the Chinese International Freight Forwarders Association of Beijing, China; HAFFA, the Hong Kong Association of Freight Forwarding & Logistics; JAFA, the Japan Air Freight Association, based in Tokyo, Japan; ACN, Air Cargo Netherlands in Amsterdam; NTC, the National Transport Committee, Riyadh, Saudi Arabia; SAAA, the Singapore Aircargo Agents Association; NAFL, the National Association of Freight and Logistics in Dubai; and BIFA, the British International Freight Association in the UK.

For independent freight agents there are various solutions for working with a network of other similar agents in other countries. Some private networks organized by the agents themselves function efficiently, but great care is always needed in choosing a partner in another country due to the possibility of fraud or malpractice.

A number of networks have been set up with paid membership, where the aim is to represent their members within the international market as a combined partnership able to compete with the global giants of the freight forwarding world. Examples of these are: EFFA, the European Freight Forwarders Association; the FFSI, FETA Freight Systems International, Global network in Hong Kong, which has members in 68 countries; GLA, the Global Logistics Associates of the Netherlands; the Security Cargo Network in Denver, US; the Bangkok-headquartered WCA Family of Logistics Networks with over

3,000 members in 170 countries; PCN, the Project Cargo Network, with members in 465 worldwide offices across 81 countries; and WWPC, the Worldwide Project Consortium network.

Further references

OAG Cargo publishes data for forwarders, including real-time rates, route planning and operational data: www.oag.com
Also, the A–Z Worldwide Airfreight Directory can be found at info@azfreight.com
IATA publishes a wide range of information on air freight at www.iata.org

2   The viability of air freight

Why choose air freight?

The decision to select the appropriate transport mode to move goods or packages from their place of origin to the final destination involves a combination of complex calculations and considerations. This is true whether it is for comparatively local deliveries or to a long-distance destination on the other side of the world. Transport accounts for a high proportion of the final cost of the product, in some cases around 40 per cent. Due to the varied factors involved, international consignments clearly demand a careful and detailed approach. The choice of transport mode will depend on the type of goods, the urgency of delivery and the destination. The choices of transport mode are ocean freight, river or canal, rail, road and air. Frequently, there will be a combination of some or all of these to eventually form a major component of the total supply chain. Intermediate warehousing, repackaging and partial assembly may also be part of the process.

The eventual choice will be based on several of the following main factors:

- value of goods
- urgency
- cost of transport
- vulnerability of goods and product life
- place of manufacture
- weight and density
- whether the goods are classed as hazardous
- accessibility of the point of delivery
- existence of severe local conditions, such as war, famine, natural disasters or poor transport infrastructure.

Although price plays a big part in the decision, it is not always the critical factor. For example, if the cargo is for disaster relief or urgent medical intervention, the deciding factor could be urgency or life and death, while if it concerns high-value equipment, such as a consignment of jet engines or the transportation of a touring music group's set and equipment, then a safe and reliable on-time method of transportation is the most important factor – regardless of cost.

Value

Despite the modern-day drive to restrict environmentally damaging emissions, vast quantities of goods need to be delivered to worldwide customers. If the global economy continues to expand, the rapid transport of goods and spare parts must be efficient. When the goods are high-value, low-weight items, such as mobile phones, electronic components, fashion goods or optical products, the fast, safe and reliable choice of air freight is clear. This is in order to meet customer requirements by offering a fast service, to keep down inventory size and to ensure a rapid return on capital investment.

When the goods are of medium value but still lightweight, such as toys or automotive parts, air freight would also be viable but the transport price would be more critical. When the value fluctuates due to time sensitivity, as in the case of seasonal flowers or fruits, the pressure falls onto the carrier to reduce the price. In this case, the shelf life of the product is the deciding factor. The flower trade is a perfect example where very long distances are involved – for example, South America to Holland or Thailand to London. If the quantities are large enough to fill a freighter aircraft, an economic tariff may be negotiated with the carrier. Unfortunately for many freighter operators, modern passenger aircraft, such as the B777, can easily carry up to 25 tonnes of cargo in their bellyhold space. The passenger aircraft operators thus have a strong price advantage and in some cases almost give away the space. This subject will be discussed in several chapters of this book.

In extreme cases of weight to bulk comparison, such as with coal or ore shipments, then clearly air freight would not normally be considered. However, exceptions always exist, as in cases such as humanitarian relief flights or the urgent delivery of emergency machinery, generators and so on. These goods come in the heavy lift category for which special equipment is employed. For a case study on an extreme exception, see the Berlin Airlift in Chapter 3.

The companies sending the goods (shippers) seek fast delivery so they may gain quick return on their money. The entire logistics chain is driven by this factor. Also, companies today do not hold large stocks of goods for sale (inventory) so just-in-time (JIT) delivery obliges the manufacturer or supplier to respond rapidly to these demands. Often, a third-party logistics (3PL) company may be involved, holding the goods in a warehouse and distributing them on demand.

Urgency

Alongside value is urgent delivery. At the extreme, life-saving body parts for transplants and vital vaccines, which are now routinely flown around the world, must arrive on time irrespective of cost. The same would apply to urgent documents required for critical business and government decisions. Perishable products, such as flowers, fruits, vegetables and seafood, need to get to market fast to maximize shelf life. However, here cost plays a major part in determining viability. Some products are in season for a very short time and must get to market fast (for example, cherries from the west coast of America, or mangos from Pakistan). In countries such as Greece, by contrast, the daily delivery of newspapers by plane to the islands is a basic commercial need – a daily paper arriving one day late is almost worthless! A replacement part for a broken drilling platform could cost millions of dollars in down time when the drilling activity is halted awaiting a vital part. These are referred to as 'time-sensitive goods' – see also Chapter 6. The choice of air freight in these instances is fundamental for long distances, but within a continent such as Europe or the US, road transport can be a quicker and much cheaper choice. The old enemy of air freight, time spent on the ground, can often negate the benefits of speed in the air. The main reason for the initial success of integrated express delivery company FedEx was the fast door-to-door service which eliminated the lengthy ground handling procedures. In addition, the highly competitive online market, which demands rapid delivery, feeds the air freight industry, forcing the adoption of faster, more time-efficient systems. Electronic cargo processing is pushing efficiency in competition with the integrators, such as FedEx, DHL and UPS.

Cost

The final cost of all the combined air logistics factors will, in most cases, determine the viability of sending the shipment by air. In Chapter 3, it is shown that the availability of considerable government subsidies made the development of airmail services feasible in the first place. Ever since those days of mail experiments there has been the balancing act between the weight and value of the cargo and the operating cost. During the last 20 years, many freighter operators, large and small, have gone out of business because they were unable to make the figures work. While airline cargo rates are negotiable, a number of airlines have been heavily fined for operating price cartels, which are seen as restrictive and illegal, especially in the US. The shipper, together with the forwarder, usually makes the decision on cost viability, while the forwarder will also negotiate the best routes and prices possible (see Chapter 1). The calculation of real costs of air freight is a complicated mixture of dozens of factors including handling, trucking and fuel surcharges. Thus the actual charge for air freight rates is far from the final price. Of course, other transport modes also incur a similar raft of costs.

Weight

The largest proportion of air freighted goods is flown in the bellyhold space of passenger aircraft beneath the feet of the paying public. In this case, high-value and reasonably lightweight items are ideal. At the other extreme, loads of up to and over 100 tonnes would require specialist freighter aircraft. The biggest aircraft in regular commercial use today is the Antonov AN-124. Based

Figure 2.1 Antonov AN-124 loading heavy construction equipment
Source: VIA.

on a robust Russian military transport aircraft, this plane can carry a payload of over 120 tonnes, depending on size and range, and is used frequently for heavy industrial goods, such as oilfield drilling equipment, steel structures or diesel locomotives. These shipments are invariably of very high commercial value in terms of meeting production schedules and in most cases there are no real alternatives. The Antonov AN-225, with a payload of 150 tonnes, is in fact the biggest aircraft in service. Used for the launch of the Russian satellite, it has a very limited and specialized application and is not normally a commercial option. Perishable cargo, which has become a very important part of the air freight business, requires great care in the choice of transport. The decision to fly aircraft full of vegetables, which can be heavy with a moderate value, must be balanced against the willingness of the end users – the consumers who pay the price on the high street – to pay for expensive shipping. Some of the bigger supermarket chains in Europe and the US have their own farms in producing countries and strike tough contracts with suppliers to ensure regular supplies and prices. Bulk is also a factor, as often the weight could be very low but the bulk high, as is the case of the packaging of some electrical goods. In Chapter 12, there are examples of exceptional loads that are carried by air.

Vulnerability

Some goods are too delicate to load onto a ship, where rough handling of sea containers can harm the goods and where the temperature may damage and even destroy the product. Sea freight is clearly the best solution for many types of bulk shipment, such as raw materials, vehicles, heavy construction equipment, textiles, machinery and slow-ripening fruits like bananas. Electronics, telecom equipment, high-fashion goods and delicate optical or medical devices are typical air freight products. Often the choice may even be between scheduled passenger flights and dedicated courier or integrator services, i.e. the combination of high value and the need to control capital.

Manufacturing convenience

The practice of manufacturing and assembling goods in countries with cheap labour, such as Brazil, Mexico, Vietnam, Cambodia and China, has created a high demand for transport both by sea and air. Toys, clothing, shoes, garden furniture, etc. are products that can be made far cheaper in these countries, even with the shipping costs taken into account. The low cost of these manufactured items is usually a fraction of the equivalent cost in Europe or the US. Often, when a product is damaged on delivery or the customer complains, the faulty goods are discarded as the return cost to the manufacturer in China, for example, is prohibitive. Some changes are occurring which are beginning to change the economic world balance. Due to the increasing labour cost in successful manufacturing countries like China, plus ever-increasing fuel and insurance prices, some manufacturing is shifting away from suppliers in long-haul destinations to more home-based or 'nearshore' sources. If European or American manufacturers, by using advanced high-tech equipment and highly skilled staff, were able to make goods efficiently, they may well gain a greater share of their own domestic, as well as world, markets. Also, success in growing out-of-season vegetables and fruits in heated greenhouses means less reliability on expensive imports from other climate zones.

In reverse, many European, Japanese or American companies have established factories in South America, Africa or India but continue to supply many of the key components from their home bases. As they become more affluent, developing countries are setting up their own modern factories to produce cars or telecoms equipment, which eventually diminishes the volume of inbound air freighted goods.

Dangerous goods

In recent years, there have been restrictions and outright bans on a wide range of goods, some of which are clearly hazardous, such as gas canisters, lighter fuel and wet cell batteries. Many other not so obvious products may contain hazardous elements; for instance, some cosmetics and perfumes and even some types of pharmaceutical products and certain types of cancer medication. The declaration and correct packaging of these products is clearly defined by IATA. Their suitability for air transport must be assessed before they may be accepted. Very high penalties exist to punish offenders. For further details see Chapter 5.

Easy access

Most countries offer modern, well-equipped airports which can handle all kinds of aircraft. Some may be restricted by runway length and there are often night curfews which severely limit the operation of long-haul freighters. Some specialist airports, known as 'cargo-friendly', welcome night-time freighters and integrator flights. In addition to dedicated ground handling facilities, fast and efficient road feeder networks are an integral part of the air freight process. It is the time the cargo spends on the ground that is the area in need of constant improvement, as time spent airborne is relatively low. At the other end of the scale, in some countries within Africa or South America for example, the airport facilities are often limited or very primitive. When exporting perishable produce – fish, flowers or fruits – refrigerated warehouses are vital, because even brief exposure to intense heat or sunlight can cut the shelf life of fish, flowers or fruits by days. Lack of surface infrastructure can also be a big restriction when attempting to deliver relief supplies or famine relief. However, there are aircraft designed to operate in these conditions, which may be chartered for the occasion. Efficient air freight logistics depends on quick cargo handling and onward surface transport. Where there is no viable road network, relief goods may have to be dropped from the air. An airport which is dedicated to maximizing its cargo needs a multimodal strategy.

Conclusion

World trade is in a constantly evolving and volatile state. The current economic fragility is having a globally negative impact on buying patterns and hence manufacturing and supply. The air freight sector is the servant of this trade and has withstood several decades of economic cycles, downturns, wars and severe regulatory restrictions. Operating costs, especially for freighter operators, are now as high as they have ever been, putting huge pressure on all parts of the transport industries. Air freight's resilience and ability to overcome these obstacles is a shining beacon within the general gloom, which pervades world trade in the first decades of the twenty-first century. Thanks to some very innovative leaders, many of whom are contributing to this book, there will always be a growing need for air transportation.

3   A brief history of the air freight industry

Ninety-four years ago things looked rather different. In theory aircraft were fast: in practice they were irregular, prone to frequent accidents and expensive. They also had another disadvantage: no night flights. Compared with such inadequacies, the railways only showed advantages, as noted by postes, télégraphes et telephones, the French public administration of postal services and telecommunications in 1919:

> No doubt they are slower on paper but they are regular, safe and inexpensive. Above all, they travel through the night, this enchanted period beloved of postmen, which allows them to sort mail while their customers sleep.

The birth of air cargo

Apart from some often unsuccessful experiments with hot air balloons, it is generally agreed that true air freight was first employed to carry postal shipments in the US. The initial US airmail service was conducted during an aviation meeting at Nassau Boulevard, Long Island, New York the week beginning 23 September 1911. During this period Earle L. Ovington, with his 'Queen' monoplane, was appointed as an airmail carrier flying the route between the temporary post office established at a flying field on Long Island and the post office at Mineola. Some 37,000 pieces were delivered by the service.

In November 1910 an American businessman came up with the idea of flying ten bales of silk from Dayton, Ohio to Columbus, Ohio. He reached an agreement with the pioneers of American aviation, the Wright Brothers, who took on the job for $5,000 – a huge amount of money at the time given that the flight distance was only 100 km. On arrival at the destination, the businessman set about cutting the silk into small pieces and gluing them onto postcards as souvenirs. It was an astute investment as the items became instantly saleable and subsequently have become much sought-after as a collector's item.

Nine months later in August 1911, the first chapter in German air freight history began when the *Berliner Morgenpost* newspaper hired a biplane to fly from the Berlin-Johannisthal airfield to Frankfurt an der Oder. Its cargo consisted of a few bundles of newspapers, the latest edition of the *Berliner Morgenpost*. When pilot Siegfried Hoffmann landed, he also made media history: the newspapers fresh off the press arrived a whole hour earlier than was possible by rail. There was definitely no way at the time of being more up-to-date with the news of the day.

A few other similar experiments were made during the remainder of 1911, and the US Post Office Department recognized the possibility of developing the aircraft into a practicable means of freight transportation. It made a recommendation to the US Congress early in 1912 for an appropriation of $50,000 with which to start an experimental service. Congress refused to grant the appropriation.

After the First World War

After the end of the First World War all necessary factors for the development of commercial aviation were in place – available aircraft, capital investment and enthusiastic participants from within the former warring nations who had gained an enormous amount of flying expertise during the conflict. Although there were many aircraft available, most of them were unsuitable for civilian use and, in addition, a large pool of ex-military pilots was also seeking employment in the emerging new industry. However, several significant factors became evident during the first years of commercial aviation. First and foremost, military aircraft, although very cheap to acquire, suffered from very high operating and maintenance costs, especially the engines. Whereas in wartime, unlimited servicing, maintenance and repairs were taken for granted, such facilities were unaffordable for commercial operations. These machines, therefore, needed considerable modification and often newer engines, or even new designs.

Second, in order to operate regular and reliable services, some basic but essential supporting infrastructure was vital. This included landing strips within airports, connecting roads, handling facilities, as well as weather and flight controls. In most cases, these did not exist and many years of investment and construction would be needed to provide them for both freight and passenger services.

Third, sufficient paid traffic was needed, as well as subsidies, to get the new air freight services to commercial viability. Mail delivery, domestic and international, provided around 50 per cent of the income during the period 1919–1939. In addition, commercial aviation was not a profitable activity on its own and needed financial support from subsidies and high postal fees. Finally, it was impossible to operate legally across international boundaries without a framework of rules and legislation being put in place.

Figure 3.1 The First flight after the First World War, Salmson N2A2

Source: Air France, reprinted with permission from Air France: Air France Collection. DR/Air France Museum Collection.

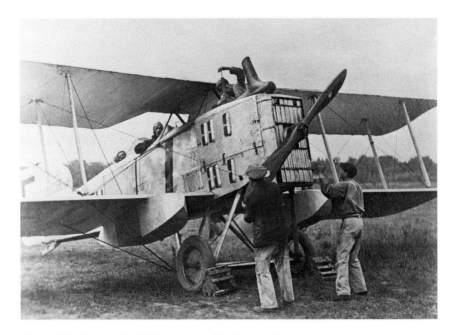

Figure 3.2 Breguet 14 1920 used on a South America route

Source: Air France, reprinted with permission from Air France: Air France Collection. DR/Air France Museum Collection.

Figure 3.3 Postal traffic, Paris

Source: Air France, reprinted with permission from Air France: Air France Collection. DR/Air France Museum Collection.

Figure 3.4 Latecore 300

Source: Air France, reprinted with permission from Air France: Air France Collection. DR/Air France Museum Collection.

Conventions

A number of conventions and agreements were introduced during the period between the two World Wars to cover the new aviation sector. The Paris International Air Convention, introduced in 1922, defined the sovereign control of national airspace. The principle of freedom to fly over a country's airspace was admitted. This treaty, containing nine separate chapters, also dealt with nationality of aircraft, certificates of airworthiness, patents and permissions for takeoff and landing. The International Commission of Air Navigation (ICAN), based in Paris, provided an umbrella of legal, technical and meteorological services. A conference was convened in Paris in October 1925, attended by representatives of 43 countries. Preliminary work was carried out in preparation for a second conference to be held in Warsaw in 1929. The resulting Warsaw Convention became the most important agreement of the aviation industry.

The Warsaw Convention was signed in 1929 by 152 different parties and came into force in 1933. It set out to regulate liability for international carriage of people, luggage or goods performed by aircraft for reward. It defined international carriage, the rules concerning documentation, the liability limitations of the carrier as well as rules governing jurisdiction. In 1955, following a review by the International Civil Aviation Organization (ICAO), the Hague Protocol was adopted by the ICAO council. In 1955 the two conventions were turned into one, known as the Warsaw Convention, as amended at the Hague in 1955.

Liabilities

While providing protection and compensation to passengers and freight operators, it was agreed that some of the risk should be borne by the users of air transport. This highly complex regulatory framework was open to considerable debate, but the convention remained the basis for settling litigation until recent times.

However, several important nations did not join, notably Germany, the Soviet Union, China and the US. These nations formed the Pan-American Convention on Commercial Aviation, which was signed by 22 countries in Havana in 1928.

Throughout the world, different regions developed their own air services with varying degrees of success. In Switzerland, a service was initiated in 1919 between Zürich and Berne. Although this was initially restricted to transporting mail and some goods, including newspapers, it was later opened to passengers. At this time the air consignment note (ACN) was introduced, a highly complex document covering the entire transport process, which was later simplified into the Air Waybill (AWB), still in use today.

In France, several airlines were formed, operating different routes within Europe, carrying passengers, goods and post. Compagnie des Messageries Aerienne (CMA) took over the Paris–Lille service from the postal administration, which was devoted only to mail and freight. This is generally regarded

Figure 3.5 Handley Page, Prince Henry

Source: Air France, reprinted with permission from Air France: Air France Collection. DR/Air France Museum Collection.

as the first genuine all-cargo service. The same company subsequently developed daily connections from Paris Le Bourget to London Croydon Airport. Aircraft Transport and Travel Ltd, which was launched in November 1919, offered regular airmail services between Paris and London. In April 1920, Handley Page Transport introduced a specially designed freighter aircraft with a tariff structure based on weight classification, still in use today. Many other companies emerged and vanished during the following era.

By contrast, in Germany, due to the social unrest, commercial aviation was somewhat chaotic with frequent fuel shortages playing a major role in restricting its development. However, an air postal network based in Hamburg operated successfully in the region consisting of the old Hanseatic League cities, to Scandinavia in the north and to Amsterdam and London in the south. It was the dirigible balloon that played a landmark role in increasing traffic. Between August and December 1919, the Bodensee model from the Zeppelin Company transported 2,250 passengers, 3,000 kg of mixed freight and 4,000 kg of mail between Berlin and Stockholm. Although many trials and experiments have been attempted over the intervening years to find a commercial use of air ships, no practicable formula has yet been developed.

Several initiatives of varying success were launched in Africa, Australia, China, Japan, Thailand, South America and Europe with a view of setting up commercially viable air services, but it was in the US that the main success can be seen.

Within a short period of time, air travel had established itself as a reliable means of transport. During 1926, the newly formed German Lufthansa company transported nearly 1,000 tonnes of air cargo and some 6,000 passengers. The new route network was soon followed by cooperation with the Deutsche Reichsbahn, the German National Railway System, in 1927. The over-the-counter market came into being during this period. While Lufthansa aircraft transported air cargo on its route network, the German railway took over the ground feeder services.

On 1 May 1926, Lufthansa established the first passenger night flight route in the world. Illuminated markings on the ground and on tall buildings and masts served as landmarks for pilots. Only the most experienced personnel were able to operate under these conditions.

The night flight service was organized by Hermann Kohl, who in 1928 would become famous because of his East to West crossing of the Atlantic. But the initial flights were often hazardous journeys into the unknown and the pioneers in the early days of aviation had to do without modern-day navigation standards, such as the artificial horizon on the instrument panel.

The worldwide air network was expanded continually during the 1930s. A huge milestone in the history of air cargo was the first trans-oceanic flight service on 3 February 1934, which inaugurated the airmail service between Germany and South America.

The impact of the Second World War

The Second World War brought about many major improvements in aviation technology. The aircraft played its biggest ever role, not only for wartime attack and defence in the shape of bombers and fighters, but also for the provision of heavy cargo transport. While most of these aircraft had no practical civil application, the capabilities of the manufacturers were honed during this period. Having put their machines through so much hardship and stress, the resulting generation of aircraft was ready for a new role in international transport. Consequently, the end of the war saw the start of a global network of flight connections. At first the large piston engines of the propeller aircraft shaped the industry. In the US, the sale of a great number of Douglas C-47 Skytrain or Dakota aircraft – a military transport developed from the Douglas DC-3 airline, belonging to the US Army – engendered a rush of airline start-ups. The reputation of this particular aircraft as an indestructible and reliable flying machine had become legendary. Very cheap prices for aircraft encouraged many former pilots to go into the aviation business for themselves. Small and even one-man airlines sprang up like mushrooms; initially it was the passenger business that attracted them, followed by the freight and mail business.

Because of falling air fares and low freight rates, some of the already established airlines came under pressure from these new competitors. Aviation as a means of travel and transporting goods experienced an unprecedented period of expansion. New types of aircraft were developed, starting with turbo propellers – and shortly afterwards came the jets. Again, it was the development of military aircraft that helped the civil sector to develop. Newly emerging quick-change or combi versions of aircraft allowed airlines to offer passengers and shippers the flexibility with which to operate at full capacity and profitably.

Fully automated processing of cargo, as it is today, is a far cry from the aviation practices of the post-war era, but many enthusiastic people dedicated their resources and energies to finding better ways of turning aviation into a vital part of the world economy.

Development of the industry in North America

Between 1920 and 1940, the transportation of mail was the main activity of the aviation business, while railways were considered fast, safe and comfortable for moving passengers. Furthermore, the lack of airports and facilities discouraged potential travellers. The enthusiasm of both a few individuals within the US Postal administration and the pilots themselves enabled the creation of a serious airmail service. It was the US Army that opened the Washington–New York service in 1918. After a moderately successful start, the military withdrew from the service. As a practical alternative to overnight on-time mail deliveries by train, the air service offered very little advantage. Initially, postage rates for airmail services were too high and then, with the eventual cuts in pricing to compete with ordinary mail charges, the service was commercially viable. Otto Praeger, originally a journalist by profession, persuaded his boss, the postmaster general Albert Burleson, to help develop long-distance flights to carry airmail. The De Havilland DH4, a wartime daylight bomber, was chosen to perform the task. After considerable modification, the aircraft came into service, but unfortunately required very high engine maintenance. With the addition of an exterior container under the fuselage, the aircraft could operate on the New York–San Francisco route via various intermediate stations, as well as the New York–Cleveland route. Conditions were hazardous due to bad weather, which resulted in a high death toll of pilots. In 1920, the service became truly established with a network of main and feeder routes like Chicago–Omaha–St. Louis and Minneapolis–Omaha–Sacramento.

The participation of rail was necessary as no night flights were yet possible. In 1922, when Paul Henderson was appointed as assistant postmaster general, his strategy was to prepare the routes of the US Postal Service for transfer to private hands. He was determined to improve safety and to investigate how night flights could be introduced. To achieve this, huge light beacons were installed at Chicago, Iowa, Omaha, North Platt and Cheyenne with supporting lights along the route. Now with a delivery time of around 33 hours, compared with the 91 hours by train, airmail charges were again introduced. The results were disappointing and the commercial users, mostly banks with cheques to clear, demanded a true overnight service. Finally, in 1925, following a major improvement in equipment and infrastructure, the overnight service between Chicago and New York was started, allowing next-morning deliveries.

The development of South American air connections relied very much upon a French–German–American strategy and the American network of Pan American Airways. After various disagreements and disputes, a well-organized air infrastructure was established in cooperation with various national airlines.

Growth in the USSR

The geography of the USSR – 13.7 million square miles – plus the harsh winters experienced in this vast country and the total lack of communication routes, cried out for some transport infrastructure. The Socialist government, with its five-year plans, while admitting that the USSR faced more transport problems than any other country in the world, considered developing the railways as a priority. Once again, it was the postal service which opened the air network, but the initial flights were often hazardous journeys into the unknown.

Unrealistically, big government plans demanded an aircraft manufacturing industry populated by people, like Andrei Tupolev, who designed several passenger- and freight-carrying aircraft, including the Tupolev ANT-9 and ANT-6, a civilian version of the Tupolev TB-3 heavy bomber. In the late 1920s, the coastline of the Arctic Circle from Archangel to the Bering Strait was designated as an official target for air exploitation under the country's latest five-year plan. The route was designed to serve isolated communities in mining areas, as well as scientific and weather stations. The flights had to endure appalling weather conditions with sub-zero temperatures, fog, snow and ice. To cope with these extreme condition, aircraft were equipped with skis or floats.

The global market

Overall freight traffic on long-haul international routes remained at a modest level up to the start of the Second World War. This was largely due to priority given to airmail and thus lack of capacity. KLM and Deutsche Lufthansa were the exception, carrying humanitarian cargo to Santiago de Chile in South America for victims of an earthquake in 1939. Daily newspapers also received priority on many routes operated by Air France, KLM and Lufthansa. Typical air freight traffic in the inter-war period included bank notes and gold bullion, perfume and fashion items, spare parts for machinery and live animals, including racing pigeons. KLM were the pioneers in the transport of large animals such as horses and cows, as well as fresh flowers. Most freighter aircraft used at this time were either converted passenger aircraft with the seats removed, or ex-military aircraft that had long proved to be unsuitable for the task, but remained in use. The German aircraft manufacturer Junkers had developed metallic structured passenger planes easily adaptable for freight. The Junkers G31 and Ju52 could carry 2,000 kg for 500 miles at a speed of 150 miles per hour.

The Berlin Airlift

After the Second World War, the former allied forces – France, Britain, the USSR and the US – controlled Germany in a delicate balance of power. Berlin, which was within the overall Soviet territory, was also split as a city between the four powers. In the summer of 1948, USSR leader Joseph Stalin, feeling threatened by the US presence in Berlin, decided to take control of the city and blockaded the western section, cutting off the inhabitants' access to food and supplies. In what would become the first major confrontation of the Cold War, US President Harry Truman made the historic decision to supply Berlin by air. In a heroic joint effort, the Americans and British delivered more than

Figure 3.6 Berlin Airlift
Source: American Veterans Museum.

two million tonnes of supplies to the beleaguered city over the next ten months, eventually forcing Stalin to give up his blockade.

When Stalin began the blockade of Berlin on 24 June 1948 he was hoping the Americans, French and British would not want to spend time and energy preserving their presence. He did this by cutting off all surface transport links between Berlin, i.e. the Russian sector, and the western sectors. However, Truman and his colleagues realized the importance of Berlin as a symbol of Western resistance to the growing threat of Communism. The decision to break the blockade was made, but the sheer technical and physical difficulties involved were immense.

In order to supply the two million citizens of Berlin with almost everything necessary for their daily life, American and British pilots flew day and night to land urgently required supplies of food, coal, medicines and other essential necessities.

The runways available in West Berlin, especially at the Templehof airfield in the American sector, were not sufficient to land large cargo aircraft safely, so plans were made to build a new airfield in the French sector. All of the equipment and materials for the new runways had to be flown in. The US provided a fleet of around 35 C-54 aircraft, the military version of the DC-4, with two squadrons of Sunderland flying boats based at Lake Havel in Berlin. When in full swing, around 260 American and British aircraft were ferrying the targeted 4,500 tonnes of supplies daily. This eventually rose to some 8,000

Figure 3.7 Ju52 – a successful military and civil plane
Source: Lufthansa.

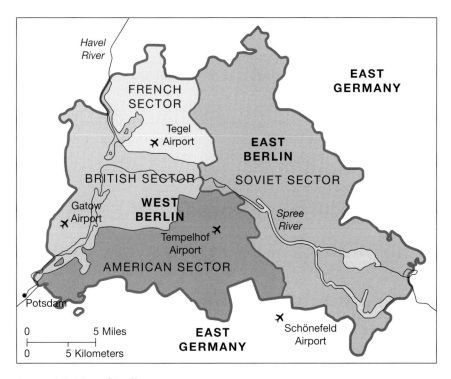

Figure 3.8 Map of Berlin
Source: American Veterans Museum.

tonnes per day. The aircraft flew so frequently, and were so densely scheduled that they often became stacked above the city in a dangerous waiting pattern. The Airlift moved a total of 2,325,000 tonnes of essential supplies during the 15-month period it was in operation. It is estimated that 621 aircraft took part in the Airlift, operating over 270,000 flights, with a total distance of over 124.5 million miles flown. The blockade of Berlin was finally lifted by the Soviets on 12 May 1949. Berlin became a symbol of the resolve to stand up to the Soviet threat without being forced into a direct conflict, although some 65 pilots lost their lives in this endeavour.

In the case of the Berlin Airlift, cost was not a factor. The priority was the need to overcome the logistical and political challenges. However, it is estimated that up to $3 million were expended, plus unknown maintenance costs incurred by both the American and British governments. These conflicting pressures of keeping costs down while fulfilling customers' needs are still present in the ever-changing challenge of successful air cargo operations in today's fluctuating world economy.

One of the most popular memories of the Berlin Airlift was 'Operation Little Vittles', which was started by Lieutenant Gail Halvorson. After meeting children in Berlin and being impressed by their resilience and fortitude in the light of the lack of everyday necessities, he began dropping candy suspended from mini-parachutes as he flew over Berlin. Soon many pilots were following suit and providing the children of Berlin with treats.

The main aircraft used during the Airlift were the Douglas C-54, with a 9–10 tonne capacity; the DC C-47 (three tonnes); Fairchild Packet C-82 (5.5 tonnes); Avro York (nine tonnes); the Handley Page Hastings (8.5 tonnes); the Halton (six tonnes); Avro Lancastrian (3.6 tonnes); and Short Sunderland hydroplanes (nine tonnes). Other larger aircraft were brought in at the end of the lift. It is generally agreed that the Berlin Airlift was the first occasion when air freight was employed to maximum effect. Aircraft, ground handlers and crews were forced to breaking point and many lessons were learned that were carried through into the next decades of commercial air freight operations.

The post-war years

The US was by far the most active in the use of domestic and later international air freight transport in the years immediately following the end of the Second World War. The explosion of industry and rising standard of living generated the appetite for industrial goods, as well as fresh produce. The period saw a flurry of activity in many countries, especially in the US. The availability of pilots and an array of aircraft encouraged the launch of dozens of start-up airlines. Most of these disappeared rapidly due to commercial viability issues. The Flying Tiger Line became a scheduled carrier in 1949, operating between Los Angeles and New York. But then, on 25 June 1950, North Korea invaded South Korea and within a few days Flying Tiger Line's C-46 aircraft were disembarking the first military reinforcements in Korea, establishing the airline's future.

In the commercial world, cargoes of flowers, fruits, vegetables, fish and fashion items were being flown from California and Florida to markets in Chicago, Boston and New York. Newspaper publishers also used carriers, such as Delta Air Lines, to deliver daily newspapers to US destinations, followed by Latin America and Europe. In Europe, emerging airlines like Alitalia began operating, while pre-war eastern European airlines like Polish airline LOT and Czech carrier CSA were absorbed into the Soviet Union. Air France, KLM, Swissair and Sabena, the Scandinavian group SAS and the British BOAC and BEA carriers took a lion's share of the cargo traffic. Many small charter operators emerged, frequently offering very low cargo rates to the market – and this remains a commercial bugbear to the major freight-carrying airlines right up to the present day.

One-way viability

It can be assumed that a passenger taking a flight will sooner or later return, along with new passengers embarking at the destination airport; airlines can therefore rely on balanced two-way traffic when carrying passengers. The problem with the one-way nature of cargo traffic has always made viability an issue for all-cargo operators. Over the years the cultivation of fruits and flowers in the Southern Hemisphere became the return freight for aircraft exporting Western goods. In this era, ground facilities were few and far between. Few airports were willing to invest in freight terminals and handling equipment. In addition, the problem of trade barriers and uncooperative Customs slowed the whole process down.

These difficulties were largely overcome with initiatives, such as the introduction of worldwide electronic Customs documents and standardized containers and pallets. Furthermore, both airlines and airports grew to recognize the added value and potential profits that cargo operations brought them, which in turn forced them into investing in the necessary facilities (see Chapter 4).

The difficulty of operating freight profitably was further aggravated by the lack of purpose-built freighter aircraft. Most of the aircraft in use were converted passenger or military aircraft, which were not suitable for the task. The high costs of operating them, and high maintenance, made viability almost impossible. A number of aircraft types were in use during the 1950s and 1960s, but what was needed was a custom-built aircraft suitable for the task. The aircraft would require a strong floor with roller beds for sliding heavy pallets, a lifting front nose cone or retractable back ramp, and a high interior cabin ceiling, which allows fast and efficient loading and unloading (see Chapter 11)

The jet age

The air freight industry as we know it today was revolutionized by the arrival of jet aircraft, which offered a much higher speed and greater payloads. Cruising speeds of around 550 miles per hour with a payload of 4–5 tonnes enabled new passenger aircraft, such as the DC-8 and Boeing 707, to carry freight shipments over long distances. Pan American Airways led the way in 1955 by acquiring a fleet of 23 B707s and 21 DC-8s.

The rapid adoption of these new jets meant there was a surplus of the old piston-engine aircraft. Many of these were used for cargo, but the ability of passenger jet aircraft to carry several tonnes in the bellyhold space made the process faster and cheaper, thus rendering the older aircraft partially redundant. Turbo prop aircraft such as the Canadair CL-44, with a swing tail and equipped for pallets, and the Armstrong Whitworth Argosy 100, which required a 95 per cent load factor to break even, are examples of the equipment in use at the time.

The two jet aircraft, the Boeing 707-320C and the Douglas DC-8F were designed as dual-use aircraft with a reinforced deck for cargo and a forward loading door. With windows added, this equipment could be quickly converted between freight and passenger configurations. Also, the use of the unit load

Figure 3.9 B707: jets transformed air cargo
Source: SASI.

device (ULD) air cargo container brought in faster and more controllable loading, and a more efficient use of available space.

The combi-aircraft was also introduced, which could carry both passengers and freight on the main deck. The combi allowed part of the main deck to be loaded with freight, which was divided from the other part for passengers. This method was very popular with a few airlines such as KLM, which enjoyed the flexibility to change the configuration depending on cargo loads. The DC-8-60, a stretch version of the basic aircraft, could carry some 45 tonnes of cargo over 3,000 miles (4,828 km). The smaller B727 and B737 that followed, along with the DC-9 cargo version, were later fitted with quick-change facilities which increased their flying hours. Later, such aircraft were used to lift freight at night and carry passengers during the day.

Unit load device (ULD)

The adoption of standard-sized containers was essential in the modern-day use of intermodal transport. Constructed of aluminium, the ULD is very light and fragile, but ideal for packing and carrying cargo. Other types of containers have evolved for specific purposes: for example, cool boxes for perishable cargo and special horse stalls that enable easy equine movements (see Chapter 5). The 1970s also witnessed the growth of the air cargo charter market, which took over 30 per cent of the lucrative transatlantic traffic (see Chapter 9).

The 1970s was a decade of change, starting with regional recessions in 1972; strong growth in 1973; the first oil crisis and more recession in 1975; rapid growth in world trade in 1976–1977; steady growth again in 1979; followed by another period of recession in 1981, caused by a second oil crisis, and a combination of high instability in oil and currencies.

The advent of the widebody aircraft

The Boeing 747-100 – the first jumbo jet – designed by Joe Sutter and his team at the Boeing production facility in Seattle took off on its maiden flight on 9 February 1969.

The B747 was first designed for the US Air Force, but as Lockheed won the contract for what became the C5-Galaxy, Boeing went on to concentrate on developing the B747 as a commercial aircraft with variants, which have endured for 44 years to date. A special model of the 100 series – the Boeing 747SP – was built with a shorter fuselage and taller tail fin to give a longer range, but with fewer seats. A freighter version with a larger side door and a nose-loading capability came in with the B747-200 series and the first freighter was delivered to Lufthansa in March 1972. Luxembourg-based Cargolux, one of the most successful of the all-cargo airlines, was one of the first customers and went on to operate a fleet of up to 14 B747 freighters, to become a launch customer for the aircraft's latest variant – the B747-48F.

Figure 3.10 Ulds in Air France warehouse Paris CDG
Source: General Press Photo.

Figure 3.11 B747-100: the first of the 747 family
Source: Air France archives.

Due to its large dimensions, the B747 freighter could accommodate 8 ft by 8 ft pallets, side by side on the main deck. After much debate, Lufthansa was the first to operate the B747F transatlantic on 19 April 1972 with its payload of 114 tonnes. Apart from the main deck, a large number of smaller units were accommodated.

The aircraft was the first freighter capable of carrying heavier, bulky shipments hitherto impossible for any aircraft (see Chapter 11). Sea–air was a multimodal concept whereby goods could be sent by sea and then loaded onto freighter aircraft to be flown on the next and last leg for delivery. It was cheaper than a 100 per cent cargo flight but faster than an all-sea voyage. The ports of Seattle, Sharjah and Dubai were the early leaders in this trade and the B747 freighter the workhorse of the business.

Between 1970 and 1991, Boeing built 476 aircraft, including the improved B747-200 and B747-300 versions. A wide variety of engines and configurations were adopted during this period. Many of the passenger aircraft were subsequently converted to freighter configurations. While passenger jumbo jets could carry 2.5 times more containerized cargo – between 14 and 18 tonnes – time was a vital element in loading and unloading. This massively capital-intensive investment needed its aircraft to be in the air to make money. Due to the hitherto unknown amount of capacity available on passenger flights, special daytime tariffs were introduced, but this move was not accepted by the air freight forwarders and was dropped.

The year 1970 saw the foundation of European aircraft manufacturer Airbus Industries, and in October 1972 came the maiden flight of its first aircraft – the A300. This was a challenge to the previous dominance of the US aircraft industry. The A300 also used the ULD system, but it was not until 1991 when FedEx acquired a fleet of 25 A300-600F cargo aircraft with a payload of 50 tonnes that it became a force in the industry. Several carriers, such as Martinair, adopted the freighter version of the aircraft.

Emerging new markets

New patterns in world trade have changed the air freight industry. As already mentioned, transportation is the servant of trade, and air freight closely follows the flow of international commerce. After the enormous domination of the US following the war, other economic power bases started to emerge around the world. Europe re-established its manufacturing and export strength, while the Far East was entering a new era of prosperity. At the sametime, the Middle East consolidated its strategic position, thanks largely to oil prosperity, taking advantage of its traditional trading position between the Indian subcontinent and Europe. The spectacular progress of the small Gulf Emirate of Dubai is still based on this historic tradition.

The express operators, known as integrators, emerged in this era (see Chapter 13). The modern methods they introduced would later force the traditional air cargo industry to change its methods and adopt many of the same techniques and technologies. Techniques including tracking and tracing made the integrators faster, more reliable and more transparent to the commercial user. The 1980s saw the progress of many international carriers, some operating large fleets of both passenger and freighter aircraft (Lufthansa, Korean Airlines, Singapore Airlines, Air France, Cathay Pacific) and others carrying bellyhold cargo only (American Airlines, Continental Airlines and British Airways). The all-cargo carriers, including Cargolux and Nippon Cargo Airline and many others, were also developing traffic.

Electronic systems

In order to offer competitive service and to avoid costly delays and losses, the airlines began to invest in computer-based systems with a view to communicating accurately and controlling the cargo processes. IATA led the way in promoting these solutions. The introduction of the cargo community system (CCS) was the first stage to be adopted in this process and the advent of electronic data interchange (EDI) successfully standardized methods of sending cargo messages. With the integrators' system of total freight control, the freight forwarders had to respond and offer a very similar level of service to their customers, such as door-to-door pick-up and delivery, with online tracking and tracing to back it up. To achieve this, the airlines were obliged to supply the data and an interface for the forwarder to access the network. Acceptance of this new technology was very slow and even today many companies are reluctant to adopt these e-freight systems.

Four airlines – Air France, Cathay Pacific, Japan Airlines and Lufthansa – through their mutual company, Traxon, were able to set up a network on a neutral platform. Over the next two decades some 84 airlines joined with Traxon, which was in turn connected to the offices of around 5,000 freight forwarders. Other systems have entered this market (see Chapter 14).

Humanitarian and relief flights

Over the last 30 years the air freight industry has stepped in on numerous occasions to supply vital food, medicines and survival equipment to victims of disasters, both natural and man-made. These flights can be commercial enterprises for the carriers, but are also often supplied free-of-charge as part of the total charitable effort – for example, the Haiti earthquake, the tsunamis in the Indian Ocean and the Far East and the victims of African tribal conflicts. These actions are mostly managed by official agencies such as UNICEF, the Red Cross, the World Food Programme (WFP), the World Health Organization (WHO) and Les Médecins sans Frontières. Bearing in mind that such emergencies frequently occur in areas with poor or severely damaged airport infrastructure, the use of conventional aircraft may not always be appropriate. However, specialized aircraft, many of which were initially designed for military operations, are able to cope with more primitive conditions: for example, the C130 Hercules, the Antonov AN-124 or AN-12 and AN-26 aircraft, the IL-76 and the C-17 Globemaster. In some emergency relief situations, military resources are used, especially helicopters of 'last mile' delivery in disaster zones.

The air freight market today

Several major factors are helping to set the pace of the air freight business in the second decade of the twenty-first century. The biggest influence has been global economic recessions, which have affected most world economies and cut purchasing power. This has led to fewer goods being made, bought and shipped.

The continuous rise in the price of fuel has brought with it much higher transport costs, making many older aircraft uneconomical to operate and only fit for the scrap heap. Also, the acquisition by major airlines of more fuel-efficient, widebody aircraft like the B777, B747-8 and A340, which can all carry large amounts of cargo in their bellyhold, has changed the face of the way air cargo moves. Freighter operators are finding it very tough to combat the level of competition in the rates that this extra space beneath the feet of fare-paying airline passengers has brought to the market.

Poorer countries in the developing world, needing capacity to export their valuable foreign-currency-earning produce, are unable to afford new aircraft costing $200 million. The converted older aircraft they are forced to use cost a fortune to operate, and in most cases are banned from European or American skies on safety issues or because of their noise and gas emissions.

Despite these difficulties, the air freight business manages to remain robust and is working harder to find better and more cost-effective ways of overcoming these obstacles – which it must do if it wants to survive.

I would like to thank the author of *The History of Air Cargo and Air Mail*, Camille Allaz, and the publisher Chris Foyle for permitting me to quote from this superb in-depth history of the air freight industry. The encyclopaedic knowledge and impeccable research contained has been an inspiration to myself and colleagues.

Further reading

Allaz, Camille (2004), *The History of Air Cargo and Air Mail*. London: Christopher Foyle Publishing.

Donovan, Frank (1968) *Bridge in the Sky*. New York: David McKay Inc.

Man, John (1973) *Berlin Blockade*. New York: Ballantine Books Inc.

Nelson, Daniel J. (1978) *Wartime Origins of the Berlin Dilemma*. Alabama: University of Alabama Press.

Tusa, Ann and Tusa, John (1988) *The Berlin Airlift*. New York: Athenaeum.

4 Airports
The vital connection

This chapter gives an insight into the function of airports as the link between the flights and the markets and looks at the varied range of airports around the world with a few detailed examples. There are 8,707 ICAO-designated airports throughout the world. Most of these are very small regional airports that support local and regional traffic, but little or no cargo except for some mail. It is difficult to qualify what is a significant airport in terms of cargo, as in some instances, like a sub-tropical country exporting seasonal fruit, cargo might well be the main traffic. Most airports handle some postal traffic in addition to passengers.

No two airports are the same, but all have one basic purpose, they connect air cargo traffic with the market. They may be the very large hubs, such as Frankfurt, New York's John F. Kennedy or Hong Kong, but at the other end of the scale small airports such as Ostend in Belgium, northern Spain's Vitoria, Hannover in Germany or Châteauroux, south of Paris, perform their own specialist functions.

Some airports also act as logistics centres, handling road traffic and distribution as well as assembly and repairs, often within duty-free zones. Globalization has introduced the concept of multi-source manufacturing with products, such as cars, becoming reliant on air cargo transportation keeping the assembly lines fed on a just-in-time (JIT) basis with components from different sources. For example, following the damage caused by the 2011 earthquake and tsunami in Japan, some companies in the country were unable to supply their customers and subsidiaries based in other countries, such as Toyota in the UK. After the natural disaster had affected the supply chain this factory was unable to continue working due to a lack of essential parts. This particular supply chain recovered within weeks, but the example illustrates that airports play an important role in securing the supply chain – and if the air gateways do not work, commerce is at risk.

Historically, as you would expect, the provision of airports and ground services were developed in parallel with the expansion of the airline industry. Before the 1920s, the lack of suitable ground facilities was one of the factors that severely limited the progress of this industry. Airlines cannot carry passengers, mail or freight unless there is safe navigation with landing beacons and lighting, as well as a base for loading, unloading, fuelling and onward transportation. At present, around 80 per cent of all air cargo in Europe is trucked, and in the US the percentage is even higher. The connection between flight and destination is the essential function of any airport. In today's aviation world, airports have become the economic drivers of business and industry and the service on the ground for both passengers and freight has become very competitive, especially when customers have alternative choices.

For air cargo, it is the minimum time spent on the ground before and after the flight that can make a particular airport attractive and will play a role in the ultimate selection by the forwarders and consolidators, who will mostly determine how much cargo is directed to and from a particular airport.

Cargo requires warehouses with access to the aircraft, plus a good road network nearby. Within the buildings there will be cool rooms, an animal hotel, a phytosanitary office, Customs and security, as well as skilled handling staff. Their job is to build and break down pallets as efficiently and quickly as possible. Truck-loading bays integrated into the warehouse aid both speed and security (see Chapter 5).

The provision of modern and well-equipped handling warehousing facilities is essential, as is easy access to an efficient surface transport infrastructure. Despite the congestion on the roads, especially in Europe, most road feeder services (RFSs) move during the night, thus having a reduced impact on traffic congestion. In less developed countries, airports are more basic and the provision of facilities such as cool storage is top priority when the main exports are perishable goods. In many cases, retail chains may operate their own farms and handling facilities within a specific country to ensure the integrity of their produce. The retail chain Marks and Spencer, for example, works with farmers in Kenya to ensure an unbroken supply chain. There is also a significant difference in handling containerized freight from passenger aircraft and main deck freighters. Handling companies are equipped for both (see Chapter 5).

Airports fall into several broad categories which often overlap: large-scale international hubs, where many different carriers operate for both passengers and cargo. These tend to be capital city or major regional hubs such as Beijing, Dubai, Paris, Frankfurt, London, Amsterdam, Hong Kong, Singapore, Sydney, Toronto, Tokyo, Atlanta, Chicago, New York, Los Angeles, Miami and many more. In each case, these are located in major catchment areas – conurbations with large concentrations of industrial and commercial activities.

Other airports also have substantial passenger and cargo businesses, like Athens, Guangzhou, Manchester, Milan, Munich, Düsseldorf, Barcelona, Geneva, St. Petersburg, Seattle, Montreal, Caracas or Houston. These also play their part in the air cargo supply chain by feeding local businesses with the raw material they need and taking the finished products to the marketplace.

Cargo-friendly airports, where the air freight business is likely to outperform passenger activity, include Huntsville and Kansas City in the US, Paris-Vatry in France, Vitoria in Spain and Hannover and Frankfurt-Hahn in Germany.

Figure 4.1 Antonov A-124 operating at Athens
Source: AIA Cargo.

For a comprehensive list of world airports, the A–Z Worldwide Airfreight Directory (www.azfreight.com) is a good source.

Whatever the size or location, all airports must operate with runways of over 3 km in length, plus suitable electronic navigation equipment, radar, beacons and perimeter fence security. Various international organizations, as well as national ones, such as the Federal Aviation Administration (FAA) in the US or the Civil Aviation Authority (CAA) in the UK, govern these basic requirements.

Round-the-clock access

All-night, 24-hour access is ideal for freighter and express traffic, but this is becoming more difficult due to political and environmental pressures. For example, Cologne (the European hub for UPS), Vitoria (the Spanish hub for DHL) and Hong Kong (with over 50 international cargo operators), are all able to operate 24-hour schedules to accommodate freighter flights. But today most airports enforce night curfews around which the airlines have to plan their schedules very carefully.

An airport is deemed to be a hub when airlines operate an interchange of flights on a hub-and-spoke system with a high proportion of both passengers and cargo being in transit. This is a highly efficient way of maximizing the energy and investment of the airlines and the airports. A perfect example of this would be Dallas/Fort Worth (DFW) in Texas, the main hub for American Airlines, a gateway with a network that covers the whole of the Americas and the rest of the world. A passenger or consignment of cargo flying from

London to Mexico using American Airlines, for example, would stop at DFW and change planes.

Examples of different airport types

Here are examples of how a few different airports around the world treat their cargo business.

Hong Kong International Airport has a very big airport cargo operation. It is the busiest air gateway in the world measured in terms of the amount of cargo it handles every year and provides all the facilities and services needed by exporters, importers, airlines, handlers and forwarders. Opened in 1998, it is a new state-of-the-art airport that has been able to design its operations not only for today's traffic, but also to accommodate the future development of its business. The airport also benefits from a location far from the city centre, thus decreasing its noise and emissions footprint.

Hong Kong is now the busiest international cargo hub airport in the world, handling around four million tonnes of freight annually. It is one of the leading gateways for the Chinese mainland and incorporates the highest standards in security. Its success is due to its strategic geographical position and the first-class connectivity it offers to the rest of the world. In cooperation with the various industry bodies, it has provided large-scale warehousing and facilities. The streamlined Customs operation has integrated electronic data interchange (EDI) links with the seven major ground operators. In addition, there are authorized cross-boundary bonded truck services with mainland China, linking up with manufacturing regions such as the Pearl River Delta.

The airport offers a choice of air cargo handling facilities, providing a complete range of services to airlines. Hong Kong Air Cargo Terminals (HACTL) is currently the majority cargo handler at the airport, with a capacity to process up to 2.6 million tonnes each year. It is equipped with an automated cargo handling system. The HACTL building also has special facilities for perishables, livestock, valuables, and refrigerated and dangerous goods.

Occupying around 17 hectares of on-airport space with 330,000 square metres of floor space in its terminal, the company offers multiple logistics services, including its SuperLink China Direct.

Asia Airfreight Terminal (AAT) has a 170,000 square metre complex of terminals with a capacity of 1.5 million tonnes each year. An automated handling system is backed up by special facilities, including strong and cold rooms, freezers, a dangerous goods room and a secure space for radioactive material. AAT offers Chinalink – a one-stop cargo service to and from major commercial and manufacturing centres in the Pearl River Delta.

The DHL Central Asia Hub, a dedicated express terminal at Hong Kong International Airport, can handle over 35,000 parcels and 40,000 documents an hour through its fully automated cargo handling system.

A new cargo terminal is under construction with a capacity of 2.6 million tonnes per year for home-based carrier Cathay Pacific; this facility is scheduled to open for business in 2013.

The airport also contains: an Airmail Centre, which provides the Hong Kong postal service with a state-of-the-art sorting system, handling 700,000 items every day; the Marine Cargo Terminal, operated by Chu Kong Air-Sea Union Transportation, which offers one-stop multimodal service links to ports in the Pearl River Delta; the 139,000 square metre Airport Freight Forwarding Centre, which offers cargo warehousing to freight forwarders for consolidation distribution; and the 31,000 square metre Tradeport Logistics Centre, providing a wide range of value-added services such as inventory management and order processing.

Gateway between two continents – and the world

Miami International Airport in southern Florida, which is currently ranked tenth in the world in the amount of cargo handled annually, is a fine example of a hub that treats its passengers and cargo with equal enthusiasm. Miami is unique in the Americas as it links North and South America, the Caribbean and the rest of the world, and the airport continues to invest in new facilities and develop new ideas for increasing world trade.

Thanks to its unique geographical and historical situation, Miami is often referred to as the *capital of Latin America*, with the airport connecting to the whole of the US and beyond. The airport and its support infrastructure dominate the flow of trade between North and South America, Central America and the Caribbean, handling over 82 per cent of air imports and 81 per cent of the air exports from the whole region. Goods traded through Miami include perishable produce, high-tech and telecoms, textiles, pharmaceuticals and machinery.

Further afield, Miami connects to markets in Europe, the Middle East and Asia, as well as Australasia. Sophisticated packaging and marketing techniques, such as labelling flowers and fruits directly at the grower for specific retailers, speed up the process and increase the shelf life of these delicate items. A total of some two million tonnes of air cargo, worth around $61.5 million, of which around 88 per cent is international, passes through Miami, much of it being in transit. Within this figure, around 650,000 tonnes of perishable goods are imported into the US each year, some 70 per cent of which goes via Miami. Of all the fruits and vegetables imported to North America, 72 per cent pass though Miami; for flowers this is 89 per cent, and for fresh fish, 54 per cent. This is also the only airport in the US which houses veterinary services, import and export operations, an inspection station and an air cargo unit all in one complex.

A corridor has been built which links the cargo area to the warehouse district and to the interstate highway system. An estimated 200,000 separate truck journeys are made annually to and from the airport.

Around 90 air carriers, including charter operators and 38 all-cargo carriers, are in business at the airport, serving around 150 cities on five continents, with freighter flights connecting to 94 global destinations. Cargo facilities comprise

17 warehouses, providing 2.7 million square feet of space with 64 parking positions for cargo aircraft, most of which offer airside to landside access. Construction is underway for a new 895,000 square feet of cargo warehouse/office/storage.

Miami's cargo route development programme is aimed at stimulating overall cargo traffic between the airport and new global markets. This includes further development of European and Asian routes and the establishment of new trade routes to Africa and the Middle East. Miami International Airport also conducts business expansion and promotion throughout its stronghold markets in Latin America and the Caribbean.

Munich: the southern European gateway

Bavaria's Munich Airport in southern Germany reflects a strong regional operation for both passengers and cargo. Again, being built only 20 years ago this is a comparatively new project and its air freight services concentrate on the regional strengths of modern Germany.

Bavaria is home to several famous brands of automobile and a fast-growing electronics industry, as well as being a major tourist centre. The fact that the airport is in a vibrant manufacturing zone also helps combat one of the major challenges facing operators of freighter aircraft – the need for return loads, as the aircraft is likely to run at a loss unless this is possible.

The growth of its freight segment is a major priority and the airport is planning a great deal of expansion. The national airline, Lufthansa, is developing Munich into an intercontinental hub in tandem with Frankfurt, as well as a central node of its European trucking network. A new freight forwarders' building opened in September 2012. The 16,000 square metre building has the annual capacity to handle 160,000 tonnes of cargo. A second phase is planned that will be 240 metres long, 65 metres deep, with an interior height of 12 metres. It will be linked to the air cargo centre via a covered track for forklifts and dolly ULD trains direct from the tarmac.

Following the opening of the new Border Inspection Office and Small Animal Station in 2007, the airport is examining the options for expanding this facility. There are plans at Munich for an increase in its temperature-controlled facilities and studies on its perishables and pharmaceuticals capabilities are in hand. The airport will need these extra facilities to remain competitive in the future.

Medium-sized airports

Apart from the capital city hubs, there are many regional and medium to small airports serving their local catchment areas for both passengers and cargo. In most cases cargo plays a minor role but is still important to the airport's bottom line. For example, Düsseldorf International Airport is situated in the North Rhine Westphalia region, the traditional home of Germany's industries.

In recent years it has been chosen by Chinese and Japanese companies as a base for their European offices. Thanks to its central position, it is an ideal base for distribution for the whole of northern Europe. Furthermore, the regional universities are graduating large numbers of scientifically trained young people needed by these companies, as well as the high-tech and environmental industries that are springing up in the region.

The airport is the third-busiest passenger gateway in Germany, with 70 airlines serving over 180 destinations worldwide. It serves as a secondary hub for Air Berlin and Lufthansa, as well as benefiting from multiple daily flights to and from the Middle East. Main-deck freighter traffic is relatively small, but bellyhold cargo represents over 100,000 tonnes of air cargo capacity per year.

The airport has become a busy hub connected to a growing number of intercontinental destinations, making it increasingly important for the big forwarders and logistics companies. Its ready access to a wide range of lower-deck capacity, together with an independent trucking network based in a high potential catchment area, is stimulating Düsseldorf's further cargo growth.

Cargo-friendly airports

There are a number of smaller airports around the world where cargo plays a more important role than passenger traffic. There may be a number of reasons for it. The airport may have space for large-scale seasonal charter operations – for example, the New Beaujolais traffic at Chateauroux in France, seasonal produce imports at Ostend (Belgium) or fresh fish imports at Vitoria (Spain). Each one of these airports has marginal low-cost airline traffic and they are all situated some distance from major passenger destinations. They are mostly open at night and can all handle large freighter aircraft such as an Antonov AN-124 or a B747F. Thanks to an absence of congestion they are capable of achieving a fast turnaround.

An example of this kind of operation is Vatry International Airport, 150 km east of Paris, which has dedicated cargo and ground handling facilities. The airport has the total annual capacity to handle 120,000 tonnes of cargo in two terminals. It has a border inspection post open 24 hours per day, with 2,500 square metres of temperature-controlled warehouses and five cold rooms for temperature-sensitive and perishable goods. Vatry is ideal for freighter traffic and is more economical and flexible than Paris' Charles de Gaulle Airport (CDG). It has a comparatively short road connection to CDG, as well as the fresh produce market at Rungis in southern Paris.

Located in northern Spain, and connected by motorway to major cities on the Iberian Peninsula and in southern France, its long runway and 24-hour operations have made Vitoria a useful cargo centre. Over the last two decades it has specialized in fresh fish and seafood from southern Africa and Canada.

But due to the high cost of fuel and the effects of recession, the market for fresh fish in major Spanish cities, especially Madrid and Barcelona, could not sustain the prices. A large number of fish shipments, however, pass through London, Paris, Frankfurt and other major European gateways, and Vitoria is still useful as a trucking hub and distribution centre.

DHL has expanded its hub at the airport dealing with traffic from north Africa and the Iberian markets. Here, the ability to operate a large number of feeder aircraft at night makes Vitoria a good site for integrators.

In summary, modern airports around the world have become an essential factor in a county's economy. Passenger traffic combines with freight, express and mail, plus the expansion of aviation-related businesses around the airport perimeter to create a vital industrial component of the local, regional and national economy. In the world of the global supply chain, these airports are the key performance engines of the business world.

International Customs in air freight

The task of Customs has become very complex in today's global lifestyle. Not all countries have identical rules and methods, but the World Customs Organization (WCO) is the coordinating international body. The work of Customs includes ensuring that the correct duty is paid on goods crossing a country's borders. Information held on file helps identify legitimate and illegitimate cross-border transactions such as counterfeit goods.

Thanks to the global marketplace and the practice of purchasing goods via the internet, there has been a huge increase in the variety and successful selling of counterfeit goods, including high-priced fashions, medicines and branded toys, some of which are highly dangerous. Customs officers have powers to stop, inspect and arrest where necessary. After the 9/11 attacks, a much higher level of airport security was introduced, with Customs playing a major role.

In 2005, the WCO introduced the SAFE framework of standards to secure and facilitate global trade, and strengthen cooperation, networking and data sharing between Customs authorities. The initiative was especially concerned with risk analysis and export control, based on advance cargo data. The WCO has strong links with other international organizations such as ICAO and IATA, and together they promote synergies to take advantage of their combined resources.

The Customs authorities in many countries around the world now require advance submission of electronic cargo information for risk assessment purposes. Unfortunately, not all the requirements and systems are aligned with international standards. With a harmonized approach, the movement of cargo will be facilitated for both airlines and forwarders and unnecessary delay and fines will be avoided at points controlled by Customs authorities.

To develop a more proactive relationship in Customs administrations, the IATA Cargo Committee has established a senior Customs Advisory Group (CUSAG). In order to have forwarders and airlines benefit from a common approach, CUSAG will also coordinate this effort with the IATA/FIATA Customs Working Group (IFCWG) to identify standard recommendations.

Airports case study

From theory into reality: the new Athens International Airport "Eleftherios Venizelos" – the concept

The move from the old to the new airport

In a record construction time of 51 months, one of the largest greenfield infrastructure development projects in Europe during recent periods was successfully completed, well ahead of its scheduled date. Fully integrated and stand-alone simulation trials confirmed the attainment of operational readiness and state-of-the-art technological standards.

Through detailed planning and careful organization, a timely and seamless transition from the 'old' Hellinikon Airport to the new site in Spata was achieved. This highly complex logistical endeavour translated into an un-precedented moving exercise in modern Greek history. Shortly thereafter, all remaining teething problems were overcome, thus achieving full func-tionality. It has been widely acknowledged that the whole endeavour led to the most successful international airport opening of the decade.

In less than a month after the opening on 28 March 2001 and during the April Easter week, the whole project was put under a close-to-capacity stress test under real operational conditions, and proved capable of seamlessly accommodating approximately 50,000 passengers daily.

An innovative public–private partnership

It is essential to underline that such performance attainments were pursued in the context of a fundamental business policy orientation transcending Athens International Airport's (AIA) overall corporate philosophy. This orientation was founded on the successful implementation of a strategic public–private partnership scheme, which takes advantage of mutually supportive contributions of each party. Such an innovative partnership represented at the time a test case for the use of structural support funds from the European Community budget to help materialize priority integration projects. Furthermore, the implementation of this joint venture activated large-scale, long-term develop-ment funding of close to €1 billion from the European Investment Bank.

Furthermore, this project represents a real showcase for successfully implementing a key policy decision taken by the Greek government in its own economic development strategy. It gives priority to attracting top managerial, technological and investment partners from the international markets to join local productive forces in major business undertakings.

Two founding principles set the stage upon which all initiatives would be conditioned. First, it was decided that the entire cost for the development of the airport of approximately €2.2 billion would be provided on competitive terms and covered over a long period of time by its users, hence not burdening the tax payer. Second, a modern approach to airport management was followed, focusing, in line with EU regulations, on competitive outsourcing of a wide range of inputs instead of burdening the company's operating performance with a heavy overhead load. The chosen option adds significant degrees of business flexibility. At the same time, though, total coordination and supervision of the airport's commercial and operational performance are maintained under the control of AIA's core corporate functions.

It turned out that AIA commenced operating just before the beginning of the most turbulent five-year period in the history of the air transport industry, including the 9/11 attacks in New York, the wars in Afghanistan and Iraq, the SARS epidemic and the dramatic increase in fuel prices. Despite these enormous and unforeseen external challenges, in the course of the past ten years AIA has performed exceptionally well, the most outstanding achievements including:

- the flawless handling of an enormous increase in passenger and cargo traffic during the Olympic and Paralympic Games of 2004;
- development of an airport staff and workforce of very high quality, with an expressed demand for providing quality services on airport operations to a number of other international airports;
- a steady growth in traffic even during interim periods of worldwide recession in air travel (e.g. 2001–2005);
- the winning of a number of 'Best Airport' awards in international competitions and expert evaluations both in the passenger and the cargo sector; and
- an impressive record of strong financial results in the context of a sound mix between aeronautical and non-aeronautical activities gradually turning AIA from a greenfield investment project into a sustainable, successful going concern

AIA's contribution to the national economy

Eleven years since the launch of its operations in March 2001, AIA celebrates a very active decade marked by operational excellence, strong entrepreneurship and numerous distinctions and awards for accomplishments in diverse areas. The robust and diversified business model of the Airport Company coupled with its dynamic aviation development strategy have resulted in outstanding performance – not only in years of economic growth but also through the recent international and Greek economic crisis – with significant positive impacts on employment, entrepreneurship and tourism at local, regional and national levels. Today, AIA has evolved into a major asset for the Greek economy based on a multifaceted business community comprising 300 entities and more than 15,000 employees, with an annual added value corresponding to 2.14 per cent of the national GDP, creating 63,000 jobs in Greece both within and out-side the airport's perimeter. On top of this, the Airport Company has directly contributed to the Greek state in the form of income tax, dividends and Airport Development Funds for the period of 2002–2010 a total of €755 million, which corresponds to 75 per cent of the company's net distributions to its shareholders.

AIA's cargo strategy

The strategic location of AIA, its highly functional environment, the competitive operational framework and high standards of services offered, as well as its close cooperation with all airport users and members of the local cargo community contribute greatly towards the airport's vision to develop into a major cargo gateway of southeastern Europe, aiming to provide connecting/feeder traffic from the eastern Mediterranean region, the Middle East and Africa to Europe and overseas destinations.

Setting up a new cargo environment

The move to the new airport brought along a breakthrough with regard to the cargo business when compared to the facility and operational set up of the old environment at Hellinikon Airport.

- For the first time in Greek aviation history, a privately managed company, AIA SA, was to replace the Hellenic Civil Aviation Authority (HCAA), the managing body of the former Hellinikon Airport and operator of all other Greek airports even today.
- The handling monopoly of the national flag carrier at the time, Olympic Airways, came to an end. In the context of the new European and Greek ground handling at the time of legislation (Directive 96/67 on Ground-Handling), the cargo (and ramp handling) market was opened up to multiple players.
- Hellenic Customs – as opposed to the former airport, at which it would carry out its own handling operations in a separate terminal regarding all non-EU cargo(!) – was accommodated in a second-line (off-apron) administration building. From now onwards it was agreed that it would concentrate on its main function – the clearance of goods handled by specialized handling companies.

During a European benchmark trip prior to the airport opening, when the head of Customs at Frankfurt Airport was informed of the different role that Hellenic Customs were to play at the new airport and that this shift was to be introduced overnight, he said: 'This is going to be no evolution, this is going to be a revolution!' As the following chapters will reveal, this 'revolution' has born fruits to quite a large extent.

AIA SA itself decided not to enter the handling business, and hence take up, according to legislation, the role of the tender manager and consequently administrator of the concessions.

Furthermore, acknowledging the strategic importance of the ownership of front-line facilities, AIA SA invested in and developed the cargo infrastructure, renting it out to the different cargo operators and state authorities (cargo handlers, Customs, Customs brokers, forwarders, veterinary and phytosanitary inspectors).

AIA's involvement: moving from tender management to a stand-alone 'Cargo Development Department'

The local market situation in the late 1990s, the vision of creating a regional gateway into southeastern Europe for both passengers and cargo, and the dynamic involvement of the local and international cargo industry in participating in the freight and mail handling tender which was launched in 2000 all resulted in the adjustment of AIA SA's organizational structure. While cargo matters were originally pursued under the umbrella of a wider ground handling concessions department, in time for airport opening a new stand-alone department was set up, the Cargo Development Department (CRD), with the aim of carrying responsibility for cargo operations and furthermore the development of the business through the airport.

Cargo development at AIA: the principles

AIA's cargo development strategy is based on the following principles:

- The introduction of a competitive cargo environment was decided, in line with the European and Greek Ground-Handling Directive and the Airport Development Agreement.
- Limited access is guaranteed through the award of multiple airport rights, i.e. three third-party handling rights, two self-handling rights (one currently idle). The aforementioned rights are the outcome of an international tender, which is carried out every seven years (the current term is from March 2008 to March 2015).

As explained in the previous section, the majority of the cargo facilities were developed by the Airport Company, including:

- three out of four bonded airside cargo terminals (a further cargo terminal was constructed by Olympic Airways) with a total operational area of 30,000 square metres;
- a total mezzanine office area of 7,000 square metres;
- a total annual handling potential of about 275,000 tonnes;
- one airmail centre (airside);
- one control station for veterinary and phytosanitary purposes (airside);
- one cargo community administration building for Customs, forwarders and Customs brokers (landside).

AIA SA's enactment through CRD ranged from the role of the guarantor of quality, safety and security and competition to the benefit of the users, i.e. the shippers and consignees on the landside and the airlines on the airside, to the developer of new projects.

The operational concept

The operational concept was developed by AIA following extensive consultation and close cooperation with all members of the cargo community, and can be summarized as follows:

- Full responsibility by the four freight and mail handlers for the operation of their respective cargo terminals. Handlers are responsible for the physical handling, storage and delivery, as well as for the safety and security of the shipments within the cargo terminals.
- Operation of the cargo terminals as bonded storage areas. Monitoring of cargo flows by Customs authorities through spot checks.
- Cargo terminal operation is 24 hours per day, 7 days per week.
- All four cargo terminals, the airmail centre and the station for veterinary and phytosanitary control have direct access to the airside.
- Provision of office space for airline representatives in the mezzanine areas of the respective cargo terminal.
- The cargo community administration building located in the cargo area houses the Customs authority, the General Chemistry of the State, a branch of the Bank of Greece, a branch of a commercial bank and Customs brokers and forwarders.

The development of the cargo terminals

As noted above, AIA SA made the decision to develop the bulk of the cargo infrastructure of the airport, including three cargo terminals. As construction took place prior to the appointment of the cargo handlers, it was crucial to develop terminals that were as flexible as possible to fit any kind of operations (e.g. standard operations of low to high automation, courier operations, etc.). Hence it was decided to merely build the shell and core of the facilities, allowing the future tenants to fit out the terminal as they wished. Furthermore, emphasis was laid on the dimensions of the terminals, the wide-span construction and the operational height of 15 metres allowing for the fitting in of any kind of cargo handling equipment at the time.

Notwithstanding the above, following the conclusion of the freight and mail handling tender in autumn 2000, the selected handlers – Olympic Airways, Swissport Hellas Cargo, Goldair Handling and European Air Transport, and the aviation leg of DHL (now part of Deutsche Post) – were prompted to offer the following range of services:

- bonded storage
- refrigerated and deep-freeze storage
- radioactive storage and handling
- dangerous goods storage and handling
- valuables storage and handling
- special cargo handling
- express/courier services
- 100 per cent screening of outbound cargo (X-ray equipment)
- 'regulated agent' status of all four cargo handlers and the airmail centre.

AIA's CRD in the role of the facilitator and marketer of new projects

The business approach: 'We communicate, facilitate, integrate'

Aiming to bring all stakeholders under one 'roof', AIA has introduced an innovative business approach: it has established a 'living supply chain' by connecting the members of the local cargo community through an efficient communication platform, the Airport Cargo Community Committee (ACCC).

The members include senior members of all airport cargo stakeholders:

- the four freight and mail handlers
- the airlines and the integrators
- the forwarders and Customs brokers
- Customs
- the Greek Postal Authority
- the veterinary and phytosanitary inspectors.

The ACCC, which was established in 2003 and is chaired by the CRD's manager, has an advisory role. Its meetings are held on a monthly basis, the aim being to enhance communication among the various members and generate synergies inside and outside the airport fence, leading to joint decision-making regarding new projects and developments.

In the context of the above, promoting AIA's cargo community internationally has been of utmost importance. While AIA has hosted a global cargo event itself, namely the Freighter Conference in 2006, the airport's cargo community has exhibited under one 'roof' at Air Cargo Europe in Munich four times in a row (in 2005, 2007, 2009 and 2011).

The unique approach mentioned above has been a key reason for which AIA has earned various awards in the cargo sector in previous years, including 'Cargo Airport of the Year 2006' by *Air Cargo News* and 'Air Cargo Award of Excellence' by *Air Cargo World* from 2008 until 2011.

Striving for operational excellence

From the outset of airport operations, the CRD has taken up the role of the catalyst and guarantor of change among the airport's cargo community members with regard to the ongoing adjustment and/or modification of cargo procedures. This approach has led and is continuously leading to the enhancement of physical and document flows of cargo, the latter being an important prerequisite for the attraction of additional traffic through the airport.

Enhancing cargo handling quality

Aiming to set objective standards in regards to the quality of cargo handling at AIA, the CRD and the ACCC have set up a flow-monitoring scheme which addresses the velocity of physical and document flows for each individual freight and mail handler. The resulting minimum service delivery standards (MSDS) are the forerunner of the cargo key performance indicator (C-KPI), which was introduced later and attempts to evaluate, in addition to the speed, the overall handling activity.

Setting minimum service delivery standards

The initial question to be answered was 'How swiftly is cargo handling performed at AIA?'. This gave rise to agreement on the establishment of certain service categories, such as the transport of cargo or the relevant shipping documents from the aircraft to the cargo terminal. Following intensive time monitoring by AIA, the processed results were once again presented and discussed with the parties and consequently MSDS were set and agreed upon.

In the event that certain service category results fall below required levels, corrective actions are discussed between the relevant cargo handler and AIA and are then implemented.

The MSDS for inbound cargo have been incorporated into the freight and mail handling agreements signed with the cargo handlers during 2008. This sets AIA as one of the few airports that actively enforce and monitor delivery standards in cargo handling, thereby showing its commitment to air cargo operations and its development.

Applying an overall performance index

Following the implementation of the MSDS, the question became 'How efficient and qualitative is the overall cargo handling performance?'. Further consultation with the cargo handlers and the local cargo community led to the development of the C-KPI.

The C-KPI is a single index composed of the MSDS as well as the handlers' performance in the following fields: operations, housekeeping and access monitoring; safety management; environmental management; and business development and synergies. Furthermore, the feedback of third parties (airlines and forwarders) is sought. The C-KPI results are discussed in detail and the methods for further operational improvements are discussed.

Obviously, the C-KPI is an objective tool in the overall measurement of cargo handling performance and its trend over time. This overall approach to cargo quality ensures continuous contact with the cargo handlers, operational efficiency, and sets the basis for further growth.

Simplifying Customs procedures

The cargo community regards the continuous simplification of Customs clearance procedures as a very important endeavour.

In the course of the first decade since the airport opening, procedures have been enhanced significantly and so has the attitude of the airport Customs Authority. The approach followed is a bottom-up one, whereby all issues raised by the cargo community members are initially raised at the Customs airport level, at which a solution is sought. Only in the case of disagreement or if local Customs lack the authority to adjust a specific procedure is the request forwarded to Customs headquarters for further negotiation. While agreeing on a joint way forward following consultations or even agreeing on a disagreement and hence seeking consultation at a higher level has raised immensely the level of appreciation and respect, the 'hard on the issue, soft on the people' approach continuously followed has significantly strengthened the bonding of the various cargo community members with Customs.

Enhancing and expanding the business

AIA's efforts are focused on developing and expanding to new markets, as well as increasing frequencies on existing routes and developing incentive strategies to support new and current customers.

AIA places a strong emphasis on preserving and further developing the existing traffic; therefore, it mainly focuses on the full exploitation of the Greek origin–destination market, aiming at minimizing eventual losses to alternative means of transport (e.g. sea transport to the Greek islands and/or road transport to the Balkans and central/Western Europe).

Moreover, it focuses its activities towards creating new, mainly transit, flows through the airport via the development of multimodal traffic, i.e. combined sea–air and air–road traffic RFSs.

Sea–air cargo

AIA is the first European airport to launch multimodal flows in the form of the combination of maritime, road and air traffic. The project provides an attractive alternative to pure air transport and enables shippers to forward their cargo from the eastern Mediterranean region via Piraeus seaport and AIA to final destinations in northern Europe and North America.

THE THEORETICAL BACKGROUND

A study conducted on behalf of AIA by the University of Piraeus (Department of Marine Studies) in 2004 concluded that in the case of Greece and Athens there are two prerequisites for a sea–air link to be successful:

- The air transportation leg must be the longest leg in the whole transportation chain. Hence, in the case of Athens, the target markets include:
  - origin markets in the wider eastern Mediterranean region;
  - destination airports at a distance of at least 2,800 km from Athens;
- commodity types should range from perishables and garments to electronics and machinery.

THE MEMORANDUMS OF UNDERSTANDING

AIA SA signed memorandums of understanding (MoUs) in regards to a link between Piraeus port and the airport with both port operators – the state-owned Piraeus Port Authority (PPA/ΟΛΠ) in 2006 and the new entrant, privately held Piraeus Container Terminal (PCT) affiliate of the Chinese shipping giant Cosco – in 2010.

Both agreements relate to the acceleration of on-seaport flows to the seamless link (through a shuttle service) between the two ports, the acceleration of on-airport flows and the same-day onward connection to the final destination.

THE PROGRESS TO DATE

The project gradually took off in 2007 when a series of successful shipments were carried out:

- average shipment: 15 tonnes
- main commodity: garments and perishables
- main origin port: Haifa, Israel
- final destination: US and Canada.

It is worthwhile to note that the same-day link between Piraeus and AIA has been achieved at all times to date, while the total transit time never exceeded the five-day time window.

Unfortunately, following the overly promising start to the project, the government's absolutely appropriate decision to open up the market in 2008 and award access to a second operator, PCT, led to extended strikes at the port, which brought the project to a halt. Nevertheless, the new player has meanwhile established itself and offers additional capacity; there is widespread hope that this type of transit business will gradually rise to higher levels.

The project's logo reads 'seanairgy', and has a dual sense: it addresses the *joint undertaking* and the *dual mode* of transport, i.e. the sea and the air. Furthermore, the flying fish stands for an accelerated flow in the air and sea.

Road feeder services

In order to meet the requirements of various international lead carriers, the cargo community is currently designing an RFS connecting international markets via AIA with Salonika and the Balkan States in one and two days, respectively. Encouraging such traffic will gradually render Athens a regional hub and gateway of southeastern Europe. The Athens RFS project is expected to be launched during 2013.

Promotional material

AIA's development activities and the 'community' spirit have been the main message of AIA's promotional campaign.

Offering financial incentives

Aiming to promote the development of cargo traffic through Athens, AIA offers a special incentive programme for airlines planning to operate international or domestic cargo flights. In particular, by offering discounts on airport charges, AIA invites airlines to introduce new or additional international cargo services by taking advantage of the resulting reduced operating costs and mitigating the risk involved during the first years of operation.

The supportive scheme is valid for a period of three years and offers a 50 per cent, 37.5 per cent and 25 per cent reduction of the published landing and parking charges during years one, two and three of operation, respectively.

Why Athens? Cargo in a nutshell

There are several good reasons for flying cargo through Athens.

- Strategic position:

    - southeastern gateway to Europe
    - proximity to a major seaport (Port of Piraeus)
    - fast access to the Balkans.

- Functional environment:

    - 24-hour airport operation with no slot or night constraints
    - two independent runways
    - a new flexible infrastructure, modern technology and equipment

Figure 4.2 View of the new Athens International Airport
Source: AIA Cargo.

- – high standards of safety and security
- – an EU Border Inspection Post for Veterinary and Phytosanitary Control.

- Dedicated people:

  - – AIA acts as a guarantor of airport users' interests
  - – the ACCC acts as a communication and development platform
  - – the AIA acts as a coordinator of the cargo community and developer of new cargo-relevant projects.

- Attractive incentives:

  - – competitive handling environment
  - – incentive scheme for new or additional cargo flights.

AIA amidst the crisis

Air freight has always been a good indicator of global economic performance. The European debt crisis and the slowing growth rates of major economies, together with declining business confidence and consumer spending, had an immediate negative effect on trade volumes in 2011 and the first half of 2012. In 2011, world cargo traffic declined by 0.7 per cent compared to the previous year.

The Greek economy itself has been tumbling for a fourth consecutive year and in mid-2012 there were definitely no signs of recovery ahead. The financial turmoil has led to reduced consumer spending and a significantly lower consumption of goods, which is evident especially in the development of international inbound traffic, on one hand, and outbound domestic volumes, on the other. The impact on the total traffic volume through AIA has been severe. Throughput that had gradually risen from 105,000 tonnes in the opening year to 122,000 tonnes in 2008 suffered a loss of almost one-third in only three years, reaching 86,000 tonnes in 2011.

In addition to the financial turmoil, another factor that negatively affected freight traffic was the continuous decline of the freight rates from competing transportation modes (mainly shipping). Air freight performance from AIA to the islands has been almost completely substituted by the upswing in sea transport.

What next?

A Greek saying reads: 'The blessed man proves himself in tough times.' It is evident that AIA and the local cargo community need to join forces even more now in order to stay afloat. While AIA has made its strongest attempt to meet the challenge by adjusting airport charges and providing additional financial incentives to the airport community, it is a common belief that only through additional extroversion and synergies will there be a chance to steer the boat away from the ongoing storm. Having said that, a set-up of four cargo handlers to serve a cargo market of 80,000 annual tonnes or less is anything but sustainable.

Along these lines, the local community has decided to promote the advantages of air transport and the airport's qualities shown in this chapter at the national level, and more especially vis-à-vis various industries and chambers of commerce, as well as producers of different commodities in order to generate rising export traffic that has to date been transported using other means. While rendering AIA as a regional gateway of southeastern Europe still remains the airport's overall goal, the attraction of domestic production to the airport in the shorter run is considered more tangible. In the parallel anticipation of interest in its sea–air cargo product and the imminent launch of RFS traffic, there are good chances AIA will reach the end of the tunnel.

5 Ground handling and IT systems for cargo processing

It has always been the curse of air freight that however fast and efficient the flight itself, it is on the ground where the delays accumulate. Today, there are many techniques and systems available for handlers to streamline their operations, but at the same time new security and dangerous goods regulations, cargo screening and Customs rules must be factored into the handling process.

Ground or shed handling involves accepting cargo into the warehouse from the shipper. It may also include trucking cargo from the shipper or another airport. The handler must prepare cargo for shipment by building it into pallets or loading into containers (ULDs). All the necessary documentation and Customs clearances must be obtained before handing it over to the ramp handler. Inbound cargo is treated in reverse, by breaking down the pallets and containers and preparing the cargo for the consignee. High standards are vital in order to keep the airlines under contract. At the same time, the handlers are under pressure to keep prices down. Continuous staff training is necessary in order to fulfil these different demands. In some airports there may be a quality standards programme in place where key performance indicators (KPIs) are measured against actual performance. Within the handler's buildings, some special facilities would be required – cool storage rooms, a border inspection office, animal hotel and strong room (see Chapter 4). Handlers work very closely with airlines, general sales agents (GSAs) and forwarders in combining and maximizing their efforts to achieve the best possible results.

The ramp handler's job is to take the palletized cargo from the ground handler, load it into the aircraft and to deliver inbound cargo to the ground handler. In some cases it may be the same company doing both tasks, as well as passenger handling. In Figures 5.1–5.2, the exact process at Düsseldorf Airport can be seen in detail.

It is perhaps surprising, given the technological sophistication of the aircraft, handling equipment and warehouse inventory control systems, that the air cargo industry was until very recently dependent on the filling in and exchange of paper documents. According to IATA, each air cargo shipment carried with it as many as 30 paper documents as it made its way from shipper to consignee, via the forwarder, haulier, terminal operator, airline, ground and ramp handlers and Customs authorities. The organization calculated that the

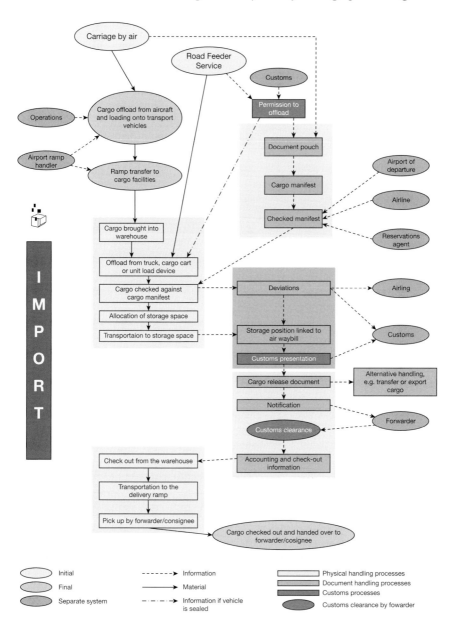

Figure 5.1 Diagram of the handling process
Source: Düsseldorf Cargo Logistics.

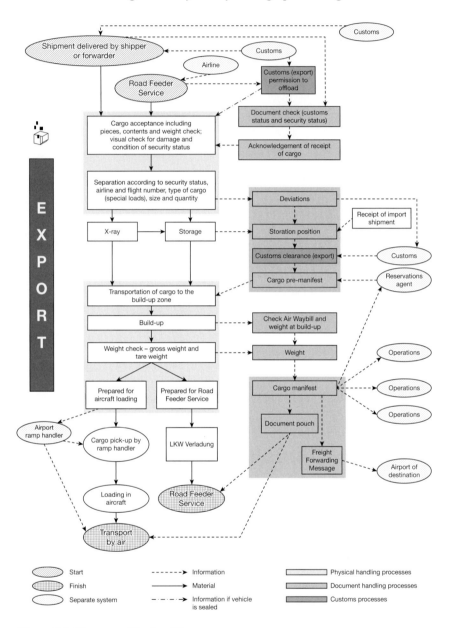

Figure 5.2 Diagram of the handling process
Source: Düsseldorf Cargo Logistics.

industry generated 7,800 tonnes of documents annually, equivalent to the carrying capacity of 80 B747 freighters.

Even where there was a growing use of computer-based message systems, most of these were developed independently and often in-house by the major airlines, with the result that ground handlers were forced to use a plethora of old, cumbersome legacy systems to communicate with their airline customers. The arrival of IATA-led initiatives, such as Cargo 2000 (C2K) and e-freight, coupled with the development of the internet into a universally used business tool has done much to remove the pen-pushing drudgery from the offices of ground handlers.

Electronic air waybills (e-AWBs) are now commonplace, as are status updates and information on special cargo, such as dangerous goods or express shipments. Evermore stringent security controls mean that more pre-arrival, or pre-shipment, data must now be sent to the airlines and on to Customs and other authorities in the country of destination.

Customs authorities are now requiring entries, as well as security information, in electronic format. In Europe, the most recent Customs development is the Import Control System (ICS). Although the airlines are responsible for submitting ICS data to Customs, most have appointed handlers as their agents and it is now down to these ground handlers to ensure that the correct information is obtained in time to make a submission to Customs.

The computer systems can now alert handlers if ICS data has not arrived; if there are problems with the data, such as errors or inconsistencies; or if Customs has rejected an entry for any reason. The EU's Export Control System (ECS) tends to be more straightforward as it deals with master air waybills (MAWBs), while ICS deals with house air waybills (HAWBs). The EU is now considering changing the cut-off time at which ICS data must be submitted before a flight from two hours to five hours so the Customs authorities can return a 'do not load' message if required.

IATA e-freight

IATA launched its e-freight project with the aim of taking the paper out of air cargo and replacing it with cheaper, more accurate and more reliable electronic messaging.

Benefits of e-freight include:

- lower costs, with an average annual saving of between $3.1 and $4.9 billion for the industry, depending on the level of adoption;
- faster supply chain transit times – the ability to send shipment documentation before the cargo itself can reduce the end-to-end transport cycle time by an average of 24 hours;
- greater accuracy – electronic documents allow auto-population, allowing one-time electronic data entry at the point of origin, which reduces delays to shipments due to inaccurate or inconsistent data entry. Electronic

documents also have a lower risk of being misplaced, so shipments will no longer be delayed because of missing documentation;

- regulatory compliance – where it is implemented, e-freight meets all international and local regulations relating to the provision of electronic documents and data required by Customs, civil aviation and other regulatory authorities.

By the end of 2011, e-freight was live with 48 airlines in 42 countries, representing over 80 per cent of international tonnage, while 430 airports worldwide offered e-freight. The plan is to have 100 per cent e-freight coverage by 2015.

Cargo 2000

Cargo 2000 (C2K) defines quality standards for the supply chain, improving the efficiency of the air cargo industry, improving customer service and reducing costs for all participants through implementation of a programme of agreed business and automation standards which are measurable and promote quality competitive performance.

The C2K Master Operating Plan (MOP) has been developed based on detailed customer research and with the assistance of leading IT companies. It sits at the heart of an air cargo industry-wide process control and reporting system that in turn drives data management and corrective action systems.

By reducing the number of individual processes in the air cargo supply chain from 40 to just 19, C2K is less labour-intensive and improves the processes for managing shipments in a paperless environment. It substantially reduces time spent managing irregularities, such as service failures, cuts the time required for manual track-and-trace procedures and leads to a reduction in service recovery costs.

Since 2010, C2K has been offering open access to its standard processes as part of its continuous initiative to improve quality management for customers and service providers across the air cargo supply chain.

C2K's quality management system is being implemented in three distinct phases. The key to the MOP is the creation of a unique 'route map' for individual shipments that is monitored and measured throughout the delivery cycle of each shipment.

Phase 1 manages airport-to-airport movements – shipment planning and tracking at the MAWB level. Once a booking is made, a plan is automatically created with a series of checkpoints against which the transportation of every air cargo shipment is managed and measured. This enables the system to alert C2K members to any exceptions to the plan, allowing them to respond proactively to fulfil their customers' expectations.

Phase 2 is responsible for shipment planning and tracking at the HAWB level and provides interactive monitoring of the door-to-door movement.

The third and final phase of C2K manages shipment planning and tracking at the individual piece level, plus document tracking. This provides for real-time management of the transportation channel at the piece level. It will also control the flow of information, which will be vital for current and future security requirements. In Phase 3, the control of information is most important as the need for paper will be limited to the bare minimum required by law. In the attempt to operate in a paperless environment, the IATA e-freight initiative and C2K complement each other.

Unit load devices

Handling the load – in neat little boxes

The unit load device (ULD) is the small silver container you see rattling furiously across the tarmac of an airport in trains towed by a tractor. It is a container or pallet used to package freight and mail for carriage on all types of aircraft, including freighters.

The introduction of the ULD helped airlines to maximize the use of their capacity and also to save time when loading and unloading aircraft. The containers are made of aluminium and various composite materials in order to be as light as possible, but tough enough for everyday handling and flight duties. If treated carefully, these containers can last for 10–15 years, but this is rarely the case as they are in constant use every day all around the world by people whose very job title states that speed is always of the essence.

The pallets and containers are built up (a term generally meaning they are carefully packed as tightly as possible with revenue-earning freight) by cargo handlers, whose skill is vital in order to achieve the maximum density possible. Pallets are covered with plastic sheets and nets before being loaded onto an aircraft. On arrival at the destination the reverse process is followed. This is termed 'break-bulk' by the industry – a much better revenue-earning ploy than just unpacking the ULD or pallet.

The cargo is then either handed over to the consignee when a representative calls at the airport, consolidated into truck loads for delivery or repacked into another ULD for onward carriage by air to its final destination.

The basic types of container are:

- LD1 (covers half the width of the aircraft), with a capacity of 4.59 cubic metres;
- LD2 (half-width), 3.4 cubic metres;
- LD3 (half-width), 4.5 cubic metres;
- LD6 (covers the full width of the aircraft), 8.9 cubic metres;
- LD8 (full-width), 6.88 cubic metres;
- LD11 (full width, rectangular), 7.16 cubic metres.

LD3, LD6 and LD11 are designed for B787, B777, B747, MD-11, IL-86, IL-96 and L-1011 aircraft, as well as all Airbus widebody aircraft.

Figure 5.3 Pallets ready for loading
Source: AIA Cargo.

The LD2 and LD8 fit the B767, while the LD3 will fit the A320 series. In some cases ULDs can be transferred to another aircraft type. The capacity of an aircraft is expressed in ULD and pallet positions and normally the half-width containers, such as the LD1, LD2 and LD3 (which have chamfered sides designed to fit neatly in the fuselage of the aircraft bellyhold space), each occupy one position while a full-width LD6, LD8 and LD11 will occupy two positions.

All ULDs are identifiable by a three-letter prefix followed by a four- or five-digit number; for example, LD3s will have AKE plus the number. Some ULDs are shaped to fit the interior shape of the aircraft hull. Main-deck pallets are built to fit the specific aircraft.

Each individual aircraft type has a weight-limit factor, governed, in the case of the passenger-carrying aircraft, by the number of people on the flight. This is organized on the ground by the loadmaster, taking into consideration freight loads, passenger numbers and the distance of the flight. Clearly it is vital that the loaded aircraft conforms to the maximum weight allowed and the weight is carefully balanced for safety and efficiency.

Large freighter aircraft such as the AN-124, B747F, MD-11F and IL-76F are frequently used to transport outsized items, including vehicles, helicopters, locomotives, bridge sections and oilfield equipment. Such items are loaded

Figure 5.4 Loading a heavy steel structure
Source: VIA.

onto the aircraft main deck with an internal winch system, external cranes, retractable loading ramps built into the aircraft and by hand, depending on the load and aircraft type being used. They are then securely fixed to the main floor with heavy-duty ties. Diagrams of the most frequently used ULDs are displayed later, in Figures 5.5–5.7.

The ULD pool

ULDs are rated as being an integral part of the aircraft's structure when loaded and must therefore be properly maintained. An aviation authority will certify a ULD only when it is satisfied that the ULD has been designed, tested and manufactured to the approved standards. An airline may not fit any item to its aircraft, including ULDs, unless the manufacturer of that item can provide acceptable certification. They may be loaned to shippers and agents for loading purposes, provided these parties can prove that they are equipped and capable of handling ULDs in accordance with the aircraft load and balance manuals.

While ULDs are as light as possible to save weight on the aircraft, they are often handled very roughly in the cargo terminals and at forwarder warehouses. Repatriating containers for maintenance is expensive and there is always a problem of having the right amount of containers in the right place at the right time. These issues have given rise to the ULD pool – a method by which dedicated companies have sprung up that provide multiple solutions to the problems facing an airline.

Two leading companies in the ULD pooling business are Germany's Jettainer, a wholly owned subsidiary of Lufthansa Cargo, and CHEP Aerospace Solutions, which integrates the aviation industry experience of leading ULD pooling provider Unitpool with Driessen Services, a specialist in the outsourced repair and maintenance of ULD equipment. These companies will usually agree to purchase the existing ULD stock of a carrier joining its pool and add the equipment to its dedicated fleet. This outsourcing move creates an immediate cash flow for the airline and removes its need to add more capital cost for purchase and maintenance of its ULD fleet. The airline then leases back exactly the amount of ULDs it needs to meet actual demand. This reduces the cost caused by unproductive ULD overstock at any station and the hassle caused by understock situations, and removes the maintenance headache from the airline.

The pooling provider will look after repair and maintenance costs, capital expenditure, extra costs driven by new technologies or changes to the aircraft fleet, directly and indirectly associated with lost and unreported ULDs, and any problems associated with managing peaks and troughs in demand at any of the airline's network stations.

Loose cargo

Large freighter aircraft such as the AN-124, B747F and MD-11 are frequently used to transport outsized items including vehicles, helicopters, locomotives, bridge sections and oilfield equipment. Such items are loaded by cranes, ramps and by hand, depending on the load and aircraft. They are then fixed to the main floor with heavy duty ties. Diagrams of ULDs are displayed in Figures 5.5–5.7.

Dangerous goods

Ensuring that undeclared dangerous goods do not get on board an aircraft is one of many key objectives of the dangerous goods programme implemented by IATA.

UNIT LOAD DEVICES

Aircraft Unit Load Device

"A standard-sized aircraft container unit used to facilitate rapid loading and unloading of aircraft having compatible handling and restraint systems."

Figures in the illustrations reflect internal measurements in unit cm.

PALLET   Base Size: 243 × 605 cm (96 × 238.5 in)

IATA ID Code (New)	PGE
IATA ID Code (Old)	P7E
IATA ID Code	M-2
Tare Weight	500 kg/1 102 lbs
BUC Type	1 (96H)
Weight Limitation	
Max. Gross Weight	*11 340KG/25 000 lbs
Limitation per Square	3 905 m²/800 ft²
Loadable Comp't	M/D

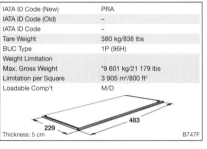

229   600
Thickness: 5 cm   B747F

PALLET   Base Size: 243 × 498 cm (96 × 196 in)

IATA ID Code (New)	PRA
IATA ID Code (Old)	–
IATA ID Code	–
Tare Weight	380 kg/838 lbs
BUC Type	1P (96H)
Weight Limitation	
Max. Gross Weight	*9 601 kg/21 179 lbs
Limitation per Square	3 905 m²/800 ft²
Loadable Comp't	M/D

229   483
Thickness: 5 cm   B747F

PALLET   Base Size: 243 × 317 cm (96 × 125 in)

IATA ID Code (New)	PMP/PMC	
IATA ID Code (Old)	P6P	
IATA ID Code	–	
Tare Weight	115 kg/254 lbs	
BUC Type	2H(118H) 2(96H)	2W(64H)
Weight Limitation		
Max. Gross Weight	*6 803 kg/15 000 lbs	
Limitation per Square	1 952 m²/400 ft²	
Loadable Comp't	M/D L/D	

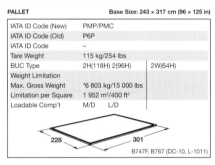

228   301
B747F, B767 (DC-10, L-1011)

CONTAINER Base Size: 243 × 317 cm (96 × 125 in) Height: 299 cm (118 in)

IATA ID Code (New)	AMD
IATA ID Code (Old)	AQ7
IATA ID Code	–
Tare Weight	270 kg/595 lbs
BUC Type	2H
Weight Limitation	
Max. Gross Weight	6 803 kg/15 000 lbs
Limitation per Square	1 952 m²/400 ft²
Internal Volume	19.9 m³/701 ft³

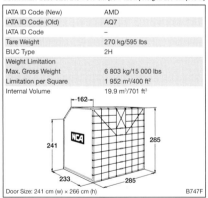

162
241   285
233   285
Door Size: 241 cm (w) × 266 cm (h)   B747F

CONTAINER Base Size: 243 × 317 cm (96 × 125 in) Height: 243 cm (96 in)

IATA ID Code (New)	AMA
IATA ID Code (Old)	AQ6
IATA ID Code	M-1
Tare Weight	335 kg/7395 lbs
BUC Type	2
Weight Limitation	
Max. Gross Weight	6 803 kg/15 000 lbs
Limitation per Square	1 952 m²/400 ft²
Internal Volume	17.7 m³/625 ft³

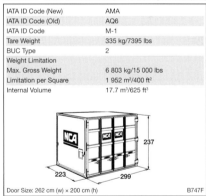

237
223   299
Door Size: 262 cm (w) × 200 cm (h)   B747F

Figure 5.5

Figures 5.5, 5.6, 5.7 ULDs past and present

Source: A–Z Directory, reprinted with permission from A–Z Group.

UNIT LOAD DEVICES

CONTAINER   Base Size: 223 × 317 cm (88 × 125 in) Height: 162 cm (64 in)

IATA ID Code (New)	AAF
IATA ID Code (Old)	–
IATA ID Code	–
Tare Weight	260 kg/573 lbs
BUC Type	5W
Weight Limitation	
Max. Gross Weight	4 626 kg/10 200 lbs
Limitation per Square	1 952 m²/400 ft²
Internal Volume	9.91 m³/349 ft³

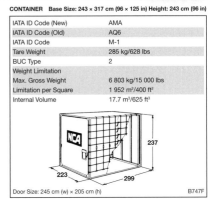

Door Size: 289 cm (w) × 145 cm (h)	B747F, A300 (DC-10, L-1011)

CONTAINER   Base Size: 243 × 317 cm (96 × 125 in) Height: 243 cm (96 in)

IATA ID Code (New)	AMA
IATA ID Code (Old)	AQ6
IATA ID Code	M-1
Tare Weight	285 kg/628 lbs
BUC Type	2
Weight Limitation	
Max. Gross Weight	6 803 kg/15 000 lbs
Limitation per Square	1 952 m²/400 ft²
Internal Volume	17.7 m³/625 ft³

Door Size: 245 cm (w) × 205 cm (h)	B747F

PALLET   Base Size: 223 × 317 cm (88 × 125 in)

IATA ID Code (New)	PAP/PAG	
IATA ID Code (Old)	P1P	
IATA ID Code	–	
Tare Weight	110 kg/243 lbs	
BUC Type	2A(96H) 5(64H)	
Weight Limitation		
Max. Gross Weight	6 803 kg/15 000 lbs	4 262 kg/10 200 lbs
Limitation per Square	1 952 m²/400 ft²	
Loadable Comp't	M/D	L/D

	B747F, B767, DC-8F, B707F (DC-10, L1011)

PALLET   Base Size: 153 × 317 cm (60.4 × 125 in)

IATA ID Code (New)	PLB
IATA ID Code (Old)	–
IATA ID Code	–
Tare Weight	90 kg/198 lbs
BUC Type	–
Weight Limitation	
Max. Gross Weight	3 175 kg/7 000 lbs
Limitation per Square	976 m²/200 ft²

	B747F

CONTAINER   Base Size: 243 × 317 cm (96 × 125 in) Height: 243 cm (96 in)

IATA ID Code (New)	MMA
IATA ID Code (Old)	MQ6
IATA ID Code	–
Tare Weight	1 000 kg/2 205 lbs
BUC Type	–
Weight Limitation	
Max. Gross Weight	6 803 kg/15 000 lbs
Limitation per Square	1 952 m²/400 ft²
Internal Volume	13.7 m³/483 ft³

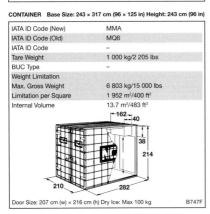

Door Size: 207 cm (w) × 216 cm (h) Dry Ice: Max 100 kg	B747F

REFCON   Base Size: 223 × 317 cm (88 × 125 in) Height: 162 cm (64 in)

IATA ID Code (New)	MAP
IATA ID Code (Old)	MA2
IATA ID Code	–
Tare Weight	840 kg/1 852 lbs
BUC Type	–
Weight Limitation	
Max. Gross Weight	4 626 kg/10 200 lbs
Limitation per Square	1 952 m²/400 ft²
Internal Volume	9.0 m³/318 ft³

Door Size: 188 cm (w) × 129 cm (h) Dry Ice: Max 80 kg	B747F, B767, A300 (DC-10), L-1011)

Worldwide Airfreight Directory   *Without Local Tie Down   83

Figure 5.6

UNIT LOAD DEVICES

CONTAINER Base Size: 153 × 156cm (60.4 × 61.5in) Height: 162cm (64in)

IATA ID Code (New)	AKE
IATA ID Code (Old)	AVE
IATA ID Code	LD-3
Tare Weight	95 kg/209 lbs 90 kg/198 lbs without shelf
BUC Type	8
Weight Limitation	
Max. Gross Weight	1 587 kg/3 500 lbs
Limitation per Square	976 m²/200 ft²
Internal Volume	4.3 m³/152 ft³

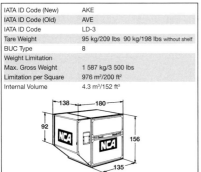

Door Size: 116 cm (w) × 140 cm (h)   B747F, B767, A300 (DC-10, L-1011)

REFCON Base Size: 153 × 156 cm (60.4 × 61.5 in) Height: 162 cm (64 in)

IATA ID Code (New)	MKN
IATA ID Code (Old)	AVE
IATA ID Code	LD-3
Tare Weight	320 kg/705 lbs
BUC Type	8
Weight Limitation	
Max. Gross Weight	1 587 kg/3 500 lbs
Limitation per Square	976 m²/200 ft²
Internal Volume	3.4 m³/120 ft³

Door Size: 133 cm (w) × 130 cm (h)
Dry Ice: Max 40 kg   B747F, B767, A300 (DC-10, L-1011)

GARMENT Base Size: 243 × 317 cm (96 × 125 in) Height: 243 cm (96 in)

IATA ID Code (New)	UMB
IATA ID Code (Old)	–
IATA ID Code	M-1
Tare Weight	655 kg/1 443 lbs
BUC Type	2
Weight Limitation	
Max. Gross Weight	6 803 kg/15 000 lbs
Limitation per Square	1 952 m²/400 ft²
Internal Volume	14.7 m³/521 ft³

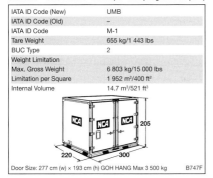

Door Size: 277 cm (w) × 193 cm (h) GOH HANG Max 3 500 kg   B747F

HORSE STALL Base Size: 243 × 317cm (96 × 125in) Height: 162cm (96in)

IATA ID Code (New)	HMA
IATA ID Code (Old)	–
IATA ID Code	–
Tare Weight	920 kg/2 208 lbs
BUC Type	–
Weight Limitation	
Max. Gross Weight	6 803 kg/15 000 lbs
Limitation per Square	1 952 m²/400 ft²
Internal Volume	14.7 m³/519 ft³

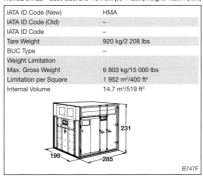

B747F

GARMENT Base Size: 223 × 317 cm (83 × 125 in) Height: 162 cm (64 in)

IATA ID Code (New)	AAP
IATA ID Code (Old)	AA2
IATA ID Code	–
Tare Weight	225 kg/496 lbs
BUC Type	5
Weight Limitation	
Max. Gross Weight	4 626 kg/10 200 lbs
Limitation per Square	1 500 m²/3 307 ft²
Internal Volume	10.4 m³/367 ft³

Door Size: 303 cm (w) × 153 cm (h)   B747F, B767, A300 (DC-10, L-1011)

CATTLE PEN Base Size: 223 × 317 cm (88 × 125 in) Height: 122 cm (88 in)

IATA ID Code (New)	KAP
IATA ID Code (Old)	–
IATA ID Code	–
Tare Weight	225 kg/495 lbs
BUC Type	–
Weight Limitation	
Max. Gross Weight	6 033 kg/13 300 lbs
Limitation per Square	1 952 m²/400 ft²
Internal Volume	7.9 m³/278 ft³

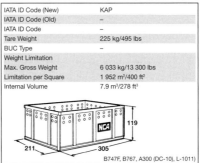

B747F, B767, A300 (DC-10, L-1011)

Figure 5.7

Figure 5.8 Dangerous goods sign

By defining standards for documentation, handling and training in its dangerous goods regulations (DGRs), and by actively promoting the adoption and use of those standards by the air cargo industry, a very high degree of safety has been achieved in the transportation of dangerous goods by air.

Working closely with governments in the development of the regulations, including ICAO and other national authorities, IATA ensures that the rules and regulations governing dangerous goods transport are effective and efficient. The goal is to make it just as easy to ship dangerous goods by air as any other product, so it removes any incentive to bypass the regulations.

Dangerous goods are articles or substances that are capable of posing a risk to health, safety, property or the environment, and which are shown on the list of dangerous goods in the IATA DGRs or which are classified according to those regulations.

Dangerous goods and their maximum quantities, packaging, handling, marking and documentation requirements are specified in detail in the DGRs published annually by IATA. These regulations are based on those laid down by ICAO, which in turn are derived from United Nations recommendations concerning the transportation of dangerous goods for all modes of transport.

When a shipment contains one or more of the dangerous substances from the DGR list, the carrier requires the shipper to complete and sign a Shipper's Declaration for Dangerous Goods. This is a legal document declaring that the shipper has complied with all relevant regulations and instructions. It must be completed in duplicate and strictly follow the detailed instructions given in IATA DGR 8.1.6.

In practice, the shipper may use a specialist freight forwarder to handle the goods, but it remains the shipper's responsibility to provide the right information at the origin of the shipment. Completing a dangerous goods note is an effective way to do this for international shipments.

Examples of dangerous goods are:

• Dry ice (also carbon dioxide, solid carbon dioxide, solid (dry ice)). This is produced by expanding liquid carbon dioxide to vapour and 'snow' in presses that compact the product into blocks. It is used primarily for cooling and due to its very low temperature (about $-79°C$) can cause severe burns to skin upon direct contact. When solid carbon dioxide (dry ice) converts (sublimates) directly to gaseous carbon dioxide it takes in heat from its surroundings. The resulting gas is heavier than air and can cause suffocation in confined areas as it displaces air. Packages containing solid carbon dioxide must be designed and constructed so as to prevent build-up of pressure due to the release of carbon dioxide gas.

- Flammable liquid. This category comprises liquids, mixtures of liquids or liquids containing solids in solution or in suspension (for example, paints, varnishes, lacquers, etc.), but not substances otherwise classified on account of their dangerous characteristics, which give off a flammable vapour at temperatures of not more than $60°C$ ($140°F$) in a closed-cup test or not more than $65.6°C$ ($150°F$) in an open-cup test, normally referred to as the flash point.

- Blood samples. This relates to infectious substances which are known or are reasonably expected to contain pathogens. Pathogens are defined as microorganisms (including bacteria, viruses, rickettsiae, parasites, fungi and other agents such as prions), which can cause disease in humans or animals.

- Corrosive substances. These are substances which by chemical action can cause severe damage when in contact with living tissue or, in the case of leakage, will materially damage or even destroy other goods or the means of transport – i.e. the aircraft itself!

- Gas. Definition 3.2.1.1: a gas is a substance which: (a) at $50°C$ ($122°F$) has a vapour pressure greater than 300 kPa (3.0 bar, 43.5 lb/in^2); or (b) is completely gaseous at $20°C$ ($68°F$) at a standard pressure of 101.3 kPa (1.01 bar, 14.7 lb/in^2). Definition 3.21.2: the transport condition of a gas is described according to its physical state as: (a) compressed gas, which is a gas which, when packaged under pressure for transport, is entirely gaseous at $-50°C$ ($-58°F$); this category includes all gases with a critical temperature less than or equal to $-50°C$ ($-58°F$); (b) liquefied gas, which is a gas which, when packaged under pressure for transport, is partially liquid at temperature above $-50°C$ ($-58°F$). A distinction is made between high-pressure liquefied gas (a gas with a critical temperature between $-50°C$ ($-58°F$) and $+65°C$ ($+149°F$)) and low-pressure liquefied gas (a gas with a critical temperature above $+65°C$ ($149°F$)); (c) refrigerated liquefied gas, which is a gas which, when packaged for transport, is made partially liquid because of its low temperature.

- Flammable gas. Gases which at $20°C$ ($68°F$) and a standard pressure of 101.3 kPa (1.01 bar, 14.7 lb/in^2) (a) are ignitable when in a mixture of 13 per cent or less by volume with air, or (b) have a flammable range with air of at least 12 percentage points regardless of the lower flammable limit. Flammability must be determined by tests or by calculation in accordance with methods adopted by ISO (see ISO Standard 10156:1996). Where insufficient data are available to use these methods, tests by a comparable method recognized by the appropriate national authority must be used.

- Non-flammable, non-toxic gas. Gases which (a) are asphyxiates (those which dilute or replace the oxygen normally in the atmosphere) or (b) are oxidizing (those which may, generally by providing oxygen, cause or contribute to the combustion of other material more than air does. The oxidizing ability must be determined by tests or by calculation in accordance with methods adopted by ISO (see ISO Standard 10156:2010).
- Toxic gas. Gases which (a) are known to be so toxic or corrosive to humans as to pose a hazard to health or (b) are presumed to be toxic or corrosive to humans because they have an LC50 value equal to or less than 5,000 ml/m^3 (ppm) when tested in accordance with subsection 3.6.1.5.3 of the DGR.
- Matches. Also known as safety matches, book, card, or strike-on-box, are matches intended to be struck on a prepared surface. Strike-anywhere matches usually contain phosphorus sesquisulfide, potassium chlorate and other ingredients. The strike-anywhere matches are readily ignited by friction on almost any dry surface. When a closed package of strike-anywhere matches is ignited by impact or friction the head composition burs off the matches and the fire then usually goes out unless the package is broken. If the package is broken, allowing access of air, the fire will continue. Packages of these matches that have been wetted for any reason and subsequently dried should be handled with extreme caution.

Reducing flight risks

Having the correct information easily to hand is key to any safety programme, no less for dangerous goods in air transport. Through its DGRs and a comprehensive and effective training programme, IATA ensures that shippers, forwarders and carriers have the tools and resources to ship dangerous goods safely.

It is a requirement in law that comprehensive and approved training must be given to all staff involved in the packaging, documentation or handling of dangerous goods destined for transportation by air, whether in the bellyhold space of passenger aircraft or on full-freighter aircraft.

Through a network of IATA-accredited training schools, the association provides training worldwide through local partners. These warrant that the high IATA training standards are maintained and that local regulations are fully complied with. There are many independent training schools around the world.

DGR print manuals

The 2013 IATA DGR manuals are available in five languages: English, French, Spanish, German and Russian, as well as a spiral English version for frequent usage. For information on the Chinese or Japanese versions of the DGR, contact cutserv@iata.org.

Dangerous Goods Regulations (DGR) Regular Bound Manual –
2013 (54th edition)

The global reference for shipping dangerous goods by air and the only reference recognized by the world's airlines in regular bound format. Each copy includes a quick-reference card.

Compliance with regulations-specific training

The successful application of regulations concerning the transport of dangerous goods greatly depends on the appreciation by all individuals concerned of the risks involved and on a detailed understanding of the regulations. This can only be achieved by properly planned initial and recurrent training programmes.

The regulations covering the transportation of dangerous goods by air are issued by ICAO.

IATA course

The UK Civil Aviation Authority (CAA) requires that staff responsible for the shipment and packing of consignments of dangerous goods for air transport be successfully trained on a course approved by them, and be retrained every two years thereafter. IATA publishes an annual *Dangerous Goods Manual* which is recognized as the industry standard and is used on the course. All students who pass the examinations are registered as internationally approved to sign for dangerous goods consignments. It is also a requirement of law that revalidation training be carried out every 24 months.

Cargo Training International trainers are approved by Civil Aviation authorities. The full three-day course will enable students to:

* apply the information given in the ICAO and IATA regulations to dangerous goods shipments;
* check that packing, marking and labelling meet ICAO/IATA standards;
* interpret dangerous goods lists;
* recognize prohibited items;
* recognize marking and labelling;
* understand the shipper's and carrier's responsibilities;
* complete dangerous goods documentation.

On completion of this course – which includes a written examination – candidates will receive a certificate. All certificate holders are registered with the Approval Authority.

Revalidation

The two-day revalidation course will enable students to:

* check knowledge of the regulations;
* update on amendments and new rules.

Depending on the respective responsibilities of the person, the training must be in line with the scope of the applicable staff category. Download or view Sub-Section 1.5 of the *IATA Dangerous Goods Regulations* for further information.

Cameon Ltd

Cameon Ltd is a UK-based specialist provider of DGSA (Dangerous Goods Safety Adviser) and dangerous goods training courses. The company's clients include major chemical manufacturers, distributors and shipping lines, as well as government agencies. Cameon offers both public and in-company dangerous goods training covering UK and international transport regulations. For further information visit www.cameon.com, email danger@cameon.com or phone +44 (0) 131 334 1929.

DGR training books

IATA's training programmes are designed to be used in conjunction with the DGRs to familiarize students with various sections of the *Dangerous Goods Manual* and how and when to apply them. The training workbooks are based on practical application of the IATA DGRs, which includes all ICAO requirements.

Dangerous goods incidents

In a cargo hangar, a container that had been stuffed in a container loading area some miles away was sitting on the loading dock prior to being loaded onto a passenger aircraft. The cargo burst into flames. Airport emergency services were called to control a fierce blaze. One item of cargo in the container was, it was later learned, an oxygen generator – undeclared as dangerous goods. These devices produce oxygen by a chemical reaction which creates significant heat. The fire services made several attempts to extinguish the fire but it kept on erupting and burned almost the entire contents of the container. It was fortunate that it did not erupt four or five hours later over the Pacific Ocean, as in spite of the fire-fighting facilities in the aircraft cargo hold, this fire would have fed upon the oxygen it was creating.

It is easy to draw some parallels here with an aircraft that crashed into the Indian Ocean some years ago as a result of what is strongly suspected to be undeclared bottles of nitric acid. They broke and caused a severe fire by igniting other organic material in the vicinity. Another recent accident which also involved these oxygen generators highlights the need for declaration and proper packaging of all dangerous goods.

In another incident, undeclared dangerous goods described as 'laundry products' loaded about two hours earlier almost caused the loss of a passenger aircraft. By the time the aircraft landed, the floor had started to sag from the heat generated by a fire caused by a mixture of a hydrogen peroxide solution, an oxidizer and about 12 kg of a sodium-based orthosilicate-based mixture (a corrosive solid). Because the consignment was not declared as dangerous goods, no labels or orientation markings were on the package. It was loaded on its side in the cargo compartment and the liquid leaked onto the solid, causing a very hot fire. It was estimated by aircraft accident investigators that this aircraft could have broken in two within another 10–15 minutes.

In another case an aircraft crashed due, it is thought, to a leakage of flammable liquid, probably contained in a passenger's stowed baggage. An ignition source ignited the liquid, causing the explosion which caused the aircraft to crash, resulting in the deaths of all on board.

The following list indicates known incidents from dangerous goods:

- leaking/spillage of acid from wet cell batteries – three incidents;
- spillage from fuel tanks on motor mowers, chainsaws and other internal combustion engines – at least four incidents;
- explosives (1.4S – Article or substance so packed that any hazardous effects arising from accidental functioning are confined within the package unless the package has been degraded by fire) – two incidents;
- aerosol pressure packs – at least four incidents;
- flammable paint/thinners – at least four incidents.

Investigation

It is interesting that in a number of these incidents, investigation has revealed that not only was the shipper at fault for not declaring the dangerous goods, there was a sufficient number of tell-tale signs that should have alerted the cargo acceptance staff that there may be something wrong. For example, in one case the shipper described the consignment as 'paint' on the consignment note – yet it got through. It is difficult to understand how a chainsaw or a motor mower with fuel in the tank can be accepted without question.

6　Perishable supply chain

Bringing fresh food to the table

In the wealthy consumer societies of the world, eating fresh food at the table every day of the year has become a standard part of life – so much so that no one questions its availability or even bothers to enquire how it got there in the first place. It just comes from the supermarket. But behind the scenes, the air cargo industry is a vital link in the process of feeding the world.

Mention the transportation of perishable foodstuff by air and the first topics to be voraciously talked about will be carbon emissions, food 'air miles' and preservation of the environment. Over a laden dinner table this can very quickly become a heated topic leading to raised voices, the pointing of asparagus spears, accusations of environmental vandalism and the violent spitting of pomegranate pips.

But just think a little more about it and there are some other socially important areas surrounding this subject that deserve mention. In a massively capital-intensive industry, no one has worked harder than – or indeed has invested as much money as – the aviation industry in its effort to 'clean up its act' and provide cheaper transportation costs while improving its impact on the environment.

Likewise, little mention is made of the benefits that accrue to the growers and their employees in some very poor parts of the developing world from their ability to air freight valuable consignments of foreign currency-earning perishables to eager consumer markets in more wealthy countries around the globe.

The flower-growing industry in Kenya is a good example. It is one of the country's leading sources of foreign revenue, gainfully employing some 50,000 workers who are growing, picking, grading and packing cut flowers in a country with high rates of unemployment and a few well-paid jobs. This industry is now positioned alongside tea growing and tourism as one of Kenya's leading foreign exchange earners. In a similar way, asparagus is a major revenue earner for Peru, with the country having become the world's largest single exporter of the luxury comestible, bringing in more than $480 million to the national exchequer in 2011.

On the ground in these countries the undeniable fact is that housing, schools, modern medical facilities – let alone the ability to earn a decent living wage on a regular basis – have all been provided by a perishables industry that relies almost entirely on the transportation of its goods by air to the world's consumer markets, where they have become an everyday commodity on the supermarket shelves.

Fresh food now flies every day from countries all around the world to the consumer societies that regard luxury goods as a normal commodity of life. In many countries there is now no seasonal period in which exotic fresh fruits and vegetables are available in the shops – they are there for sale 365 days a year, although in most parts of the world there are still short seasons that can be seen for locally grown and sourced produce. It has led to a situation where the end-consumers often have no idea at all where the food on their table comes from. Ask them the question and the answer will usually be: 'From the supermarket.'

Well, yes, that is true, more often than not it does – but how does that food get to the supermarket in the first place? Most importantly, the question is how did it get there in a fresh enough state to be attractive to the buyer and saleable as an edible commodity? The answer is that the modern air freight industry can now provide all the expertise and facilities required and the consumer has responded eagerly to the year-round availability of fresh produce – in the UK alone the importing of perishables has trebled in the last ten years.

According to IATA, perishable goods were among the first commercial commodities to be carried regularly by air, and over the years the airlines have developed very effective and cost-effective handling techniques to look after chilled and frozen products in transport.

As you read in Chapter 3, the ability of air transport to move huge amounts of food to feed a needy population became front page news during the days of the Berlin Airlift, when two million people were left without access to food and fuel by conventional modes of road and rail transport. A total of 2.3 million tonnes of food and fuel were airlifted into the city on 277,569 flights during the period and the whole operation became a high-profile illustration of the way the delivery of food and other perishable commodities could work in the future.

The cool chain

American Airlines Cargo describes perishables as being shipments that, due to their nature, will spoil without proper care and handling. This includes, but is not limited to, fresh produce, seafood, floral products, fruits, berries and live tropical fish. Swiss WorldCargo points out that drugs, cosmetics and electronic elements require just as much speed in transportation, careful handling and controlled temperature conditions as do shipments of fresh fish, freshly cut flowers or dairy products; the air cargo industry's ability to handle the movement of vital pharmaceutical products to where they are urgently needed is dealt with in more detail later in this chapter.

A vitally important factor for the air cargo industry is that food will not move off the retailer's shelves if it is unattractive to the purchaser, and in many parts of the world stringent and rigorously enforced health and safety legislation prohibit its sale in the first place if it does not conform to mandatory guidelines. Therefore, the way perishables travel successfully from their point of origin to the consumer requires the use of specialized equipment, the application of a lot of knowledge and expertise, and the implementation of a quality management system that allows the cool chain of any shipment to be analysed, measured, controlled, documented and validated.

Maintaining a constant and unbroken temperature-controlled supply chain is, therefore, of major importance in ensuring that goods in the supply chain stay fresh. Most importantly, right from the moment they are harvested at source by the grower to their arrival with the end-consumer, the temperature of the goods consigned to the air cargo supply chain must not fluctuate beyond set parameters. Refrigerated trucks (reefers), airport warehouses with cool rooms, insulated temperature-controlled ULD containers and various other specialized equipment, like 'cool dollies', are used to move shipments between the cargo warehouse and the aircraft. In the extremely hot temperatures experienced on the airport tarmac in some of the growing or transit countries, this sort of procedure is now regarded as normal practice. To help protect perishable shipments from temperature extremes, special packaging requirements are put in place to ensure the freshness of shipments, as well as to protect the aircraft from damage caused by leaking boxes or shipping containers.

Temperature-controlled containers

One of the biggest advances in recent years has been the introduction of the temperature-controlled air freight container; different versions of these are now available from suppliers such as Sweden-based Envirotainer or C-Safe, a joint venture between AmSafe and AcuTemp of the US.

Active temperature-controlled containers allow the carriage of commodities at a constant temperature, both in the air and on the ground, boosting the life of temperature-sensitive commodities by preserving the cool chain throughout the complete life cycle of the end-to-end transportation process. They work by an active temperature-control system based on compressor cooling and electric heating equipment, or have an active temperature control system based on dry ice refrigeration. The standard size containers can be carried on board most common widebody aircraft types.

For the general transportation of perishable foodstuffs, containers maintaining a constant +2°C to +8°C (+36°F to +46°F) temperature are those most often utilized, although there are versions available that support a +15°C to +25°C (+59°F to +77°F) and > –20°C (–4°F) temperature range that can be deployed for specialized shipping requirements.

The containers enable precise end-to-end temperature control throughout every stage of the cold chain transportation cycle to ensure that the cargo inside

Figure 6.1 Temperature-controlled container
Source: www.envirotainer.com.

is never affected by variable conditions encountered during their journey. This can be vital when cargo such as roses grown in the Ethiopian highlands transit the 45°C (113°F) heat in Dubai. It also prevents shellfish from cold Atlantic waters being exposed for long periods of the 30°C (86°F) summertime temperatures on the tarmac at London Heathrow Airport. Roses will quickly wilt if subject to such temperature extremes, severely reducing their saleable shelf life and enjoyable vase life, while bacteria can develop in shellfish that will subject the end-consumer to the risk of food poisoning.

The key features for consistent temperature control contained in the most commonly available standard temperature-sensitive containers are:

- insulated container shell built in an all-composite material for superior insulation properties;
- full electric heating and compressor cooling system;
- rechargeable batteries that can be charged at standard AC power connection points;
- enhanced air circulation system inside the container ensuring a low temperature gradient within the entire cargo space;
- air circulated by the heating and cooling unit is close to the set temperature;
- an easy-to-use control unit allows simple operation of the container;

- fully validated recording solutions for temperature and battery information;
- they can be accessed from all sides by forklifts, even when fully loaded, eliminating the need for roller beds to move the containers in the warehouse and to and from trucking docks.

Temperature-controlled containers come in different sizes and technical specifications. They are suitable for all types of perishable shipments like meat, seafood, fruits, vegetables and dairy products. In addition, because each temperature-controlled container has its own mechanism by which the parameters can be preset, airlines can transport a wide range of products on the same flight.

Responding to cold chain complexities

DHL Global Forwarding, the air and ocean freight specialist within Deutsche Post DHL, is one air freight provider that has expanded its services to deal with temperature-controlled shipments. The company has entered into a master lease agreement with CSafe, LLC, a leading heat-and-cool container provider for the temperature-sensitive air freight market, located in Ohio. DHL customers can now choose from a wider range of special air freight containers.

Since its launch in 2008, thousands of successful shipments have been made with CSafe's heat-and-cool container. During flight, the temperature is maintained within the range +4°C to +25°C by means of rechargeable batteries – whether ambient temperatures are normal or extreme, i.e. ranging from –30°C to +49°C.

The use of temperature-controlled ULD equipment is advantageous, but the companies involved in their production usually rent the equipment to freight forwarders and airlines on a time-specific basis and they are therefore considered too expensive for some of the lower-cost perishable items transported by air.

This results in shipments being packed in ice or covered with a reusable protective cover designed to shield temperature-sensitive cargo from solar heat. Being water resistant, yet breathable, the protective covering is considered ideal for the transportation of 'living' food and flower products as well as offering additional protection for packaged pharmaceutical shipments.

Time and temperature management

The transportation of time- and temperature-sensitive goods is a core service offered by IATA airlines and affiliated freight forwarders or logistics service providers. The IATA perishable cargo regulations (PCRs) have become an essential reference guide for all parties involved in the packaging and handling of perishables for air transportation. It has been developed based on the experience of a number of major airlines and the scientific data supplied by research institutions.

The 12th edition of the PCRs introduces new mandatory requirements for the transportation logistics of healthcare products, such as the mandatory use of the time- and temperature-sensitive labelling system as of 1 July 2012. These changes are the result of the collaboration by carriers with pharmaceutical companies and associations, as well as other stakeholders in the supply chain, including but not limited to shippers, freight forwarders, terminal operators, ULD manufacturers, packaging providers and track-and-trace companies.

The new requirements emphasize the importance of the initial booking that triggers the process and that the label is only intended to support the booking. Thus, shipments requiring a temperature-controlled service, and booked as such, must carry IATA's new time and temperature label.

Case study

Emirates SkyCargo, the air freight division of Dubai-based Emirates Airlines, pays particular attention to the air transportation of pharmaceuticals and perishables. It has developed its Cool Chain solution, which ensures that highly temperature-sensitive consignments, from pharmaceuticals to flowers, are protected at each stage of their journey.

The airline's Cargo Mega Terminal in Dubai is equipped with a dedicated perishables handling area of 4,623 square metres that can handle an annual capacity of 175,000 tonnes of fresh produce.

The facility forms the hub of the airline's perishables operations and houses independently controlled storage zones to maintain the critical requirements of temperature-sensitive pharmaceuticals, healthcare products and perishable goods.

The facility is divided into two main zones: Perishable 1, which maintains an average temperature of 5°C and Perishable 2, which maintains an average temperature of 12°C. In addition, the pallet and container handling system (PCHS) used during cool storage is capable of maintaining temperature settings between 5°C and 18°C.

Moreover, the terminal houses a freezer section of 400 cubic metres and maintains a temperature of −18°C, accommodating 20 AKE containers. There are 12 dedicated perishable docks, a screening facility for intact ULDs and power sockets to serve heating and cooling containers. There is also storage space for 218 perishable cargo ULDs covering over 3,927 square metres. There are 14 workstations allocated for break-down and build-up of perishable cargo, as well as dedicated customer counters and truck docks for acceptance and deliveries.

Pharma: a healthy business

The global pharmaceutical industry is generally referred to in the air cargo world as the pharma business. It is expected to increase at a 5–8 per cent compound annual growth rate, to be worth some $1.1 trillion in 2014. During this period many leading products will lose their patent protection in developed markets, which will lead to a rush to ship in generic versions. This commercial bonanza for the air freight industry, as well as the strong overall growth forecast in the world's emerging countries, will drive expansion in the pharma cool chain business.

The pharmaceuticals industry markets drugs licensed for use as medications. It is a fast-growing and valuable market that relies heavily on the availability of air freight transportation modes to source its raw materials and bring its products to the consumer. Americans alone now spend over $200 billion each year on prescription drugs – a figure that is increasing at a rate of about 12 per cent per year – and they are the fastest-growing part of the nation's healthcare bill. This makes a company's involvement in any part of the pharmaceutical supply chain cycle a very lucrative proposition.

As people lead longer and healthier lives than ever before, the wellbeing of many depends on access to vaccines, insulin, blood plasma and other temperature-sensitive healthcare products. This has given rise to a vibrant and image-conscious business sector where companies notoriously spend more on marketing than they do on research, so there is an increasingly urgent need to get goods to the marketplace on time, at an attractive price and ahead of the competition.

The increase in the use of lower-cost generic medications – for example, the UK National Health Service has already implemented mandatory generic drug substitutions – has given rise to a variety of laws and regulations regarding the patenting and testing, and ensuring the safety, efficacy and marketing of drugs, including the ways in which they are transported.

But the physical process of lifting the goods by air is only part of the equation in this heavily regulated sector. Pharmaceutical products need to maintain an absolutely constant temperature throughout their complete supply chain cycle and they are transported in specially developed containers with a constant temperature that can be individually set between –20°C and +20°C. The ability to maintain a constant preset level of temperature control is called the cool chain, and it is especially valuable when it comes to delivering large consignments of extremely sensitive, high-value goods such as vaccines.

The production and distribution of temperature-sensitive pharmaceuticals, clinical trials, biotechnology products, high-tech materials and reagents has significantly expanded in recent years. The US Food & Drug Administration (FDA) estimates that 70 per cent of drugs in clinical trials today are temperature-sensitive and the air cargo industry has had to learn how to cope with an increasing raft of rules and regulations regarding their transportation.

The vital cool chain

Handling and quality standards that are uniform throughout the world at all stages of the supply chain cycle are necessary to take pharmaceutical products to their destination in impeccable condition through an unbroken cool chain

– and a proper system of monitoring the goods in transit must be in place so that an unbroken cool chain can be proven to the customer and to the appropriate authorities when required.

One of the most effective ways to maintain the cool chain of goods in transit by air is to use the active temperature-controlled ULDs, air cargo containers now widely available. Healthcare companies and regulatory authorities increasingly demand extremely high standards from their forwarders to properly handle their products, so when they reach the patient they are just as medically effective and safe to use as when they left the production line. The active temperature-controlled containers are generally available for a rental period, thereby keeping costs down as they need only be obtained when required and returned to the supplier when the lease period is finished. The containers are then maintained, cleaned and prepared in ideal conditions, ready for the next customer

The healthcare cold chain market is growing by 10 per cent every year, and being able to offer specially tailored services ensures that the freight forwarders and their partner airlines can secure a very profitable and sustainable business.

Swedish cool-chain logistics specialist Envirotainer is one company playing an important role in the transportation of pharmaceuticals with its range of active temperature-controlled air cargo containers, which it rents to users when they are required. Maintaining the active shipping containers provides

Figure 6.2 Cool container
Source: www.envirotainer.com.

the needed shipping consistency, regardless of most challenges. As long as the refrigerants are maintained, usually dry ice, and the batteries are powered, the temperature can be maintained as needed – no matter how long the journey, or whether cooling or heating is the key requirement.

Peak condition

When blood plasma, insulin, vaccines or other biological pharmaceuticals are being produced, the transportation modes must be chosen carefully to ensure that products will always arrive in peak condition. Envirotainer estimates that some 20 per cent of temperature-sensitive healthcare products are wasted during transportation due to an improperly maintained and/or broken cool chain.

A large percentage of any air cargo transportation cycle is actually spent on the ground, so that is where the most common risks occur, usually due to wide variations in ambient temperature ranges on intercontinental supply chain movements as shipments transit hot and cold weather conditions in different parts of the world. Active sensors in the containers monitor the temperature in order to maintain the required conditions and data monitoring and documentation ensure that a shipper can follow up and verify the exact status of the shipment.

While most temperature-controlled supply chain systems rely on passive technology – cool packs or polystyrene insulation – to keep temperatures down during transportation, Envirotainer's active temperature-control technology consists of a ULD container manufactured using high-performance insulation material, with an internal fan and sensor. Warm air drawn into the sealed container by the fan passes over dry ice in a separate compartment and is cooled before being guided back out to the loading area. This convection process promotes a constant, regulated environment providing a stable pre-set temperature for up to 72 hours. The internal sensor helps keep the temperature within the required limits, which can range from –20°C to +20°C, depending on the product.

US-based CSafe is a similar company to Envirotainer, formed to address the demand for a cold chain air transport container that meets the temperature and regulatory requirements for pharmaceutical cold chain management. CSafe says its RKN thermal pallet shipper was designed to lower the operating costs involved with cold chain air transport while offering optimum temperature reliability and ease of use.

With handling and quality standards that are uniform throughout the world, shippers, freight forwarders and the cargo-carrying airlines need specially trained and certified staff to handle pharmaceutical products during the supply chain and get them to their destination in impeccable condition. Here, Envirotainer offers its Qualified Envirotainer Provider (QEP) programme at the request of shippers of pharmaceutical products and in response to industry guidance. The programme acknowledges service providers capable of properly managing shipments using Envirotainer containers. Switzerland-headquartered freight forwarder and logistics services provider Panalpina has many of its stations worldwide accredited to QEP status. Panalpina gained the accreditation after meeting the strict requirements of Envirotainer's Training and Quality Program for Good Distribution Practices guidance documents, including the requirements of the Parenteral Drug Association (PDA) and IATA.

On-the-ground handling

The teams at dnata Cargo – which provide their freight ground handling services to over 120 airlines flying into Dubai all year round – are sometimes required to work in temperatures near to 50°C (122°F). The need to protect the pharmaceutical cool chain during ULD transit from the aircraft and while in the warehouse awaiting transhipment or collection is absolutely imperative.

To protect sensitive products from temperature fluctuations during off-loading and transportation to the warehouse, staff use specially designed 'cool dollies' to combat the extreme weather conditions. Equipped with advanced communication and tracking equipment linked real-time to the computer systems of both dnata Cargo and Dubai International Airport, the ground handling teams operate a fleet of high-speed tow tractors and rapid delivery vehicles to ensure a smooth and speedy link between the aircraft on the ground and the storage facility.

Cool rooms in airport warehouses are also operated under the same stringent guidelines. Loading and unloading procedures involving the aircraft or air cargo trucks are identified as points in the supply chain where the integrity of the cool chain is most at risk. Equally, the air cargo warehouse is another area where the application of expertise and knowledge is required. The conditions for pharmaceutical products should always be maintained within acceptable limits during the time the cargo spends in the warehouse.

Working to the premise in the air cargo business that urgent freight is not for storage, it is for transhipment as quickly as possible, pharmaceutical shipments always move quickly through the airport warehouse – but even a small delay can be harmful to the maintenance of an unbroken cool chain if a watchful eye is not kept on the process.

Dangerous or hazardous goods

Many goods used in biotechnology and pharmaceuticals are potentially hazardous, so the shipper, forwarder, trucker, warehouse operator, cargo ground handler and air carriage provider must all ensure they are properly identified, packaged and handled, and that the special documentation required is correct and in good order.

Some types of goods are subject to particular rules, such as pesticides and biocides, where higher risks are associated with transportation, for example, flying chloroform by air rather than moving it by road where the container can be ventilated in an open atmosphere.

Key requirements generally include ensuring that goods are appropriately classified, packaged and labelled before they are loaded onto an aircraft. It is also important that everyone involved understands how to minimize the risks involved. Special training may be required for employees in all parts of the supply chain dealing with dangerous goods.

The regulations surrounding the carriage of dangerous goods by air are defined by IATA, which publishes comprehensive guidance and offers specialized training courses for all those involved. More detailed information is contained in this book in Chapter 5.

Case study

The air freight wing of Dubai-based Emirates Airline is Emirates SkyCargo, which offers its branded Cool Chain solution, which is especially designed for the movement of highly temperature-sensitive goods, including pharmaceuticals, healthcare products and perishables. Using protective measures such as temperature-controlled air cargo containers, cool dollies during transit and temperature-controlled warehouses, the quality of the product is preserved and the integrity of cool chain processes right from pick-up to delivery is ensured.

In line with IATA requirements, Cool Chain is also geared to handle transportation of perishable goods requiring basic preservation of freshness from heat and frost.

The successful transportation of perishables takes a high degree of skill, careful handling, meticulous organization and sophisticated systems, facilities and equipment. The widebody aircraft in the Emirates passenger fleet offers cargo capacities varying from 8,000 kg to 23,000 kg, and hold volumes from 60 cubic metres to 210 cubic metres.

The airline also offers its own freighter fleet, consisting of the Boeing 747-400F and the Boeing 777F aircraft, offering a payload capacity up to 117 tonnes and 103 tonnes, respectively.

The B747-400F has independently controlled air-conditioned zones, enabling Emirates SkyCargo to carry items requiring different temperatures on the same flight. Each zone may be maintained at different temperature levels. On other Emirates aircraft, special temperature-controlled containers are also available to ensure that your temperature-critical goods are stored in ideal conditions.

The cool dolly can accommodate either containers or pallets while regulating the temperature inside the dolly within a specific temperature range to enable safe ramp transport and warehouse storage of perishable shipments in hot climates.

The equipment consists of a steel trailer and an insulated aluminium container built on top, the latter equipped with a compressor-driven cooling system.

The cooling system is installed on the front side of the dolly. Power required for cooling or heating can be arranged via a diesel engine when working rampside or via a 380 V power supply when operating inside the warehouse.

7 Animals by air

When dealing with live animals a wide variety of conditions, regulations and considerations are brought to bear. These apply to the animals themselves, for their health and wellbeing, but equally to the grooms and attendants looking after the animals in transit. The airlines transporting the animals must not only provide the right facilities – stalls, cages and safety levels – but they must also, in their own interests, ensure the integrity and safety of the aircraft. While horses, breeding stock and large zoo animals will usually be transported on board a freighter aircraft, large numbers of smaller animals – cats, dogs, monkeys and fish – are most likely to travel in the bellyhold compartments of passenger aircraft. The new widebody aircraft such as the Boeing 777 or 747-8 have considerable bellyhold cargo capacity and can easily accommodate the cages of fully grown lions, tigers or cheetahs in their bellyhold space. The transportation by air of famous animals such as the Chinese pandas and killer whales often make the front pages of newspapers, but for the majority of animals, travelling is routine business.

In dealing with live animals and products, airports are governed by strict regulations for quarantine and phytosanitary supervision. Although restrictions on the global movement of animals have been greatly eased in recent years, border inspection controls are in place in all countries to ensure that legal procedures are followed. In addition, it is equally important to guarantee the provision of a calm, humane environment while the animals are in the care of handlers and airlines.

Most animals suffer stress in these circumstances, and it is vital that they be treated as gently as possible. Although some airlines decline to carry animals, it is a significant part of regular air freight commerce, and sometimes may impact on the profitability of a particular airline route or airport. For example, a busy airport that refuses to handle animals due to lack of appropriate facilities may lose passengers who need to transport their pets. Most large animals, such as horses, are transported in chartered freighters together with their grooms and attendants and may well be delivered to an airport with specialist facilities. In the case of racehorses, for example, they will usually be landed as close as possible to the racecourse to avoid additional long road links.

Regulations governing the transport of animals are applied from a variety of sources – each national department of agriculture and health, which will vary from country to country, has its own regulations, while international rules may also come into play. Thus, the company shipping the animals will need to ensure that the appropriate documentation, licences and any other documents required are obtained well in advance of the flight. Apart from domestic pets, animals usually travel in special freighter aircraft with stalls and cages arranged by the shipper. IATA lists various regulations that are applied globally. The Animal Transport Association (ATA) based in the US has developed rules and advisory conditions, and is largely dedicated to promoting the wellbeing of animals in transport. Despite the combined efforts of the global regulatory bodies, however, many of the regulations are flouted in countries where illegal trade continues. Regulations are set by IATA, and the protection of endangered species is governed by CITES (Convention on International Trade in Endangered Species) regulations.

Animal diseases and regulations

IATA publishes its *Live Animals Regulations* (LAR) that demonstrates how to transport animals safely, legally, efficiently and cost effectively. For more information see www.iata.org/lar.

One of the factors to have had the effect of decreasing the transport of farm animals has been the outbreak of several virulent and destructive diseases. These occur around the world, and strong efforts are made to contain and restrict their spread. Many animals are transported for breeding purposes, with the aim of improving conditions and stock quality in developing countries. The main diseases are rabies, foot and mouth disease, bluetongue, bovine spongiform encephalopathy, equine influenza, equine infectious anaemia, equine piroplasmosis, equine rhinopneumonitis, glanders, equine viral arteritis, classical swine fever and avian influenza. The impact of regulations, disease and extremism impact constantly on the successful transport of animals by both surface and air transport. The regulated companies and organizations involved in this business are dedicated to the humane and safe movement of this precious cargo. Stress is a very important negative factor, as it can damage or even kill an animal in transport.

Animals are broadly classified as follows, although there is a cross-over between the various groups:

- pets, which may include some laboratory animals;
- agricultural, covering the full range of cattle, pigs, sheep, goats, poultry;
- horses and other equine species, which includes racehorses, show horses, polo ponies and breeding stock;
- zoo animals, including dolphins, sharks and whales. As most zoo animals cannot tolerate a long journey time, air transport is often the best or only solution.

- exotics, which includes monkeys, lemurs, tropical birds, snakes and reptiles, insects and a number of rare breeds. This is a highly controversial subject as in the past many rare breeds have been smuggled into Western countries illegally, often resulting in a mass death of the creatures in the consignment. This category will often overlap with zoo animals and pets such as mice and ostriches.

Moving domestic pets

Since the changes in international controls, it is now comparatively straight-forward to either accompany pets on flights or send them separately. This has greatly increased the traffic of pets.

Sally Smith is President of IPATA (International Pet and Animal Trans-portation Association) and also proprietor of Airborne Animals. She has been active in the pet business for her entire working career. She has been a licensed veterinary technician, pet groomer and boarding kennel operator. Her company, Airborne Animals, established in 1987 in New Jersey in the US, moves pets across the US and around the world. She has been a board member of IPATA for several years and comments about today's situation.

* * *

It is important to clarify what a pet is. Normally airlines consider dogs, cats, ferrets, rabbits and hamsters as pets. However, some companies move snakes, turtles, reptiles and amphibians, as well as mice, rats and guinea pigs. Most of the traffic, however, is for families taking conventional pets to new locations for work, retirement and so on. Many people, of course, make their own arrangements and are therefore responsible for organizing their own documentation and dealing directly with the airlines.

Regulations vary from country to country according to the national agricultural and health administration, which sets controls for vaccinations against rabies, etc. In the US, for example, the Department of Agriculture (USDA) sets the requirements of the Animal Welfare Act. This covers not only air and road transport, but also pet shops and boarding kennels. In the UK, DEFRA (the Department for Environment, Food and Rural Affairs) does much the same thing. Each country has its own equivalent controlling body, but the rules are very similar. There is no accurate figure of the number of pets moving by air as no formal records are required, but a general estimate of two million pets are shipped worldwide in any given year. Some animals will be shipped independently of their owners, while many will accompany them on the same aircraft. The business of pet transportation tends to coincide with school vacations, particularly in the summer, as companies prefer to relocate personnel during this season to lessen the disruption. The busiest markets for pet transport are North America, Australia and Europe, but the rest of the world is still active.

The pet transportation business has grown tremendously in the past few years, largely due to the mobility of society in the twenty-first century. Now that companies are including pet shipping as part of a good relocation package, the number of speciality pet shippers has increased, along with IPATA's membership. Approximately 50 per cent of families have one or more pets, which means that this aspect of the transportation business will grow accordingly. Airport authorities have a big responsibility to providing inspection and border controls if international transport is involved. Both airports and the airlines risk losing passenger traffic if no facilities exist, thus forcing passengers to choose a suitable alternative airport. Following the rules on health, documentation is essential for individuals shipping their pets. The problems occur only when these are not respected.

Horse transport: and they're off!

Due to the increasing costs of air transport, only high-value animals are likely to warrant air transfer. Such value can be commercial, as with racehorses and equine competition horses moving to show events. There are also horses moving between champion breeders, or the flight can be part of a programme to preserve rare breeds.

Although the traffic is less than it was a few years ago, and there are no official statistics for these movements, it is estimated that some 20,000 horses are flying annually. The numbers of those that travel for racing careers would be a couple of thousand, those for sport and polo several thousand, and those for breeding (of all types) a few thousand. The process of transporting a typical group of racehorses, including the documentation and physical requirements in Europe, is as follows.

Typically a horse going for a racing career would require a number of veterinary tests and possibly quarantine or isolation; this process may take 2–3 weeks. The horse is then taken to the chosen airport. Then, depending on the protocol in the country of destination, it may be stabled for the night beforehand and then loaded into a specially designed horse or jetstall and typically loaded into a B747 freighter or combi, an MD-11, B777 or Airbus freighter aircraft. The animal will have been Customs cleared at its port of departure, will be accompanied by its passport and health certificate, food, water and some equipment and escorted by a competent trained attendant throughout the flight. Some smaller aircraft are used which carry only a few horses. On board the aircraft, the ideal temperature should be around the mid-60°F mark (18°C). That way horses can stand without rugs and their own body heat means the ambient temperature in the jetstall is often higher. There are still open-stall charter systems in use on some DC-8, B737 and Airbus freighters, but the vast majority travel now in enclosed stalls, which makes life simpler for ground handling. A competent groom always accompanies horses. Nowadays these members of staff have to be security cleared by the airline in order to travel on a freighter. Medical facilities are limited. Even

Figure 7.1 Horses arriving at Athens International Airport
Source: AIA.

when the airline will permit a veterinary surgeon on board, there is little that can be done within the confines of a stall or an aircraft. The journey recovery time for a horse will vary considerably depending on the length of the flight. For example, horses could fly into England from Ireland and race the same day then fly back. From Turkey or the Middle East, the horse would fly on Wednesday for a Saturday race. To and from further afield requires at least a week and in the case of Japan, ten days are needed, while Australia has a two-week arrival quarantine, so a much longer period of rest is required.

On the ground, horses require very special attention to avoid stress and panic. Events such as the Olympic Games, when around 140 competing horses must be moved within 2–3 days and again afterwards, require enormous skill and planning, but during the last decade there have been real problems encountered with this specialized type of air freight movement.

Pioneering days

Dutch airline KLM is considered one of the pioneers of animal transport, putting in place specialized procedures that many other carriers have since followed. Gerton Hulsman, a leading cargo innovator with the airline, comments on this brief history.

*   *   *

The airline had always been involved in animal transport right from the early days, but it was in the mid-1980s that KLM Cargo, with the purchase of the B747 combi, saw tremendous opportunities for transporting live horses by air.

Of course, before this time, horses had already been transported by air. These were mainly over shorter distances, for example UK–Europe, or in some rare cases, further overseas with chartered aircraft. In the 1960s this was carried out by means of CL-44 swing tail aircraft, DC-6, DC-7 converted from passenger aircraft into freighters and B707 and DC-8 freighters. The real boost came with the introduction of the B747 combi aircraft, enabling airlines to uplift complete jumping-team horses, grooms, staff and equipment to overseas destinations.

The big question was how to transport these valuable animals without stress while keeping them in perfect condition? This was a question that could not be solved so easily. Again, as in the case of tropical fish, airline staff were entering new territory in which any form of new technique or experience had to be invented and developed by the hands-on cargo people. In the past, with the chartered aircraft, horses were put in pens or horse stalls. Roel Wigman and his team tried to develop, with van Riemsdijk in Rotterdam, a horse stall to be mounted on a pallet, suitable to transport two horses at a time. The container looked very much like a road horse trailer. The issue was that the horses needed to enter the container walking forward but were obliged to leave the container backwards. This was stressful for the animals, especially when they were being unloaded on noisy airfields after a long trip.

Also, there was the issue of who should accompany the animals. Should it be the owner, who did not have any flight experience, or did KLM Cargo have to train staff especially to accompany these animals on their trips, enabling safe transportation not only for the animals but also for the passengers?

In cooperation with van Riemsdijk a better stall was developed, now containing three adult horses. They could enter walking forward and could also exit by walking forward by means of a ramp. In front of the area where the horses were accommodated in their stalls, there was a place for the animal attendant, as he or she was now called. The grooms could stand during taxiing, takeoff and landings. Also, these animal attendants checked the horses while in flight and gave them food, water and any necessary medicines. This was a great development of the new product – Live Animals, as it was later to become known. The Royal Mounted Canadian Police, equestrian jumping teams from all over the world and, last but not least, horse traders made use of this excellent product from KLM. The destinations of New York, Miami and Los Angeles were famous cities and regions to where these horses flew. Not to forget the various Olympics Games, where many horses travelled by air. Of course, KLM was not the only airline to transport horses.

Figure 7.2 Animal hotel
Source: Vitoria Airport.

Lufthansa, Martinair, Cargolux and later even FedEx started to earn money with this kind of traffic.

The service that KLM Cargo rendered to its customers was much wider than just the provision of transportation. The shipping of the blood samples to be examined in the US and Canada for the so-called equine piroplasmosis test, required before the animals were shipped, was carried out by KLM. The shipper brought the blood sample to KLM and they arranged for the sample to be sent to a laboratory in Miami, New York or Los Angeles, where it was examined. On the basis of this result the licence was given to import the horses into the US or Canada.

Eventually the North Atlantic routes were extended to include Far Eastern destinations and the Middle East. Nowadays horses fly to and from any continent in the world. The KLM Cargo horse stalls were not collapsible (Martinair had collapsible ones). On the return flights, if the stalls were empty, they were filled with mail bags and some were even shipped back by sea! It speaks for itself that this was not a cheap operation, so the yield per container had to be high. KLM Cargo invested heavily in horse stalls, the training of the airline's animal attendants and even in an animal hotel at the Amsterdam Airport, Schiphol, where these horses were temporarily housed before they were accepted by the importers. This animal hotel was, of course, also available for other animals, pets, birds, reptiles and rodents.

Global business

The immense number of horses moving around the world has become part of a major entertainment industry, providing employment for thousands of people. Air transport of animals, especially horses, has become almost routine and is carried out by special brokers with the correct equipment and training. In some countries such as the United Arab Emirates, where summer temperatures can reach over 40°C (104°F), special facilities have been developed. Horse and camel racing is a passion in the Gulf states and especially in Dubai. Thanks to the global nature and status of this sport, horses are shipped all year round, although movements are a bit quieter in the very hot months of late June to early September. Air-conditioned horseboxes are used most of the time as there is a ministry requirement for transporting horses in air-conditioned horseboxes during the summer months. At the racing club all quarantine boxes are air-conditioned.

Regulations state that any horse that travels more than six hours must have 48 hours of hand walking only in order to allow recovery from the journey. If the horse travels less than six hours stable to stable, only 12 hours need be allowed for recovery. Other types of horses are regularly flown, for example the Icelandic breed that has become very popular in Europe and the US. Large numbers of polo ponies also travel long distances, again managed by specially trained grooms.

Zoo and exotic animals

The traditional role of the zoo as a menagerie has, in modern times, progressed to become that of a refuge for threatened wildlife, as well as being centres for education, conservation, biodiversity and the preservation of endangered species. The combined effects of human activity, loss of habitat, weather patterns, climate change and poaching have all had a drastic impact on the world's wildlife. The transport of these animals is a vital part of these efforts.

Why would zoo animals need to be moved? This could be for a number of reasons, such as:

- a gift from one country or zoo to another;
- better breeding conditions;
- facilities could be inadequate in an existing zoo but better in another;
- a particular zoo could be facing closure. During the second Gulf War a mission was organized to rescue all the animals from the Baghdad Zoo, which were in extreme danger during some of the hostilities.

The World Association of Zoos and Aquariums (WAZA) provides guidance, support and leadership for zoos and organizations involved in animal care, welfare, conservation of biodiversity, environmental education and global sustainability. The transfer of some species is considered vital in order to

Figure 7.3 Elephant in the room
Source: Lufthansa Cargo.

undertake cooperative breeding programmes for conserving wildlife with the help of WAZA studbooks. CITES was established in 1975 to control inter- national trade in endangered species, in some cases facing extinction. Today, over 150 countries are involved. Resources include a database managed by the World Conservation Monitoring Centre (WCMC), part of the UN Environ- ment Programme. This contains data on over 70,000 animals and 89,000 plants.

To move an animal such as a rhinoceros requires certain processes, probably several months in advance of the journey. The exception would be in an emerg- ency requiring life-saving measures. The animal would need to be measured for a cage or container that would allow it sufficient room, but at the same time restrict its ability to break free, as these animals can weigh several tonnes. Ideally they would be cage-trained so that when the moment arrives for the final transportation they are relaxed within the container. Circumstances permitting, the crate should be placed in a position where the animal can become familiar with it, and where possible some animals might use it as a sleeping area. Great care is needed to load the cage into its vehicle and eventually the aircraft – the animal would probably have been sedated for the safety of all concerned. This is in the case of a zoo animal already in captivity being moved to another zoo. The same process in reverse would apply on arrival at the final destination, where the animal is released into its new environment. During the flight, adequate ventilation, food, water and, if necessary, appropriate medication should be on hand. There is a different approach for animals caught in the wild, which require a totally different handling process.

In order to deal with the increasing movement of animals around the world, border inspection posts and animal reception centres have been built at strategic airports. Some will handle all kinds of animals, while others may specialize in horses or farm stock. Large zoo animals, such as elephants, hippos or rhinos, would normally be transferred directly from the airport to the zoo.

Animal Reception Centre

The Animal Reception Centre at London Heathrow Airport is the main southern border control post and is part of the City of London Council. It was built in 1976 and was the first secure purpose-built animal portal in the world. During the early 1990s it was designated a border inspection post, applying health rules for animals arriving at the airport. It has stayed at the same site to this day. Its primary task has always been to enforce animal health regulations that apply to pets, livestock, horses, fish, reptiles, invertebrates and coral, as well as eggs, pupae and animal products. With a qualified staff of 30, the centre is open 24 hours per day, 365 days per year. Robert Quest, who manages the centre, explains that due to the easing of international restrictions the traffic has increased dramatically. It is now possible to move pets anywhere in the world, providing the documentation and vaccination requirements are met. Similar posts are in place at most major European airports – Frankfurt and Amsterdam being the biggest. Such centres may be run by airports themselves or, in some cases, by airlines.

Following the 9/11 terrorist attacks in 2001, airport security has been greatly intensified, which in turn has eliminated most of the smuggling of small animals by airline passengers. The biggest single challenge now faced by the reception staff is incorrect documentation, which can lead to the confiscation or incarceration of the animal until the papers are correct. In order to avoid shipping costs, some dealers may send consignments of insects, for example, by courier package or even in the mail.

The daily tasks of the Animal Reception Centre staff at Heathrow are to check the documents, the identity of the animal as well as its health. The more exotic animals, such as big cats and large primates, are often moved or exchanged between zoos directly. While most horses in the UK pass through specially equipped airports such as London Stansted, the Heathrow centre is equipped to handle a number of polo ponies, as well as race and show horses.

During the 12-month period up to September 2012, the following quantities of live animals were handled by the centre in quarantine, transit and re-export:

- pets – 13,000
- primates – 62
- birds – 200
- fish – 162,000
- reptiles – 200,000

- mixed others – 1,021
- sea lions – 6
- cheetahs – 3
- white lions – 2

Figure 7.4 De Brazza's monkey zoo transit
Source: Heathrow Animal Reception Centre.

Figure 7.5 White lion cub in transit
Source: Heathrow Animal Reception Centre.

Figure 7.6 Cheetah being checked
Source: Heathrow Animal Reception Centre.

In addition, thousands of fish eggs, insects and live coral were handled. A small proportion of these were seized by Customs and in some cases the confiscated animals were sent for re-homing. The centre's own vehicles are often sent to collect animals directly from an arriving aircraft; otherwise a specialist broker carries out the task.

Cattle and farm animals

This business is mostly concerned with breeding stock required by countries wishing to improve domestic quality. In China, for example, now that the population has acquired the taste for meat on a regular basis, significant numbers of beef cattle are being imported in order to increase local herds. Over the years, pigs and sheep have been shipped from countries such as Ireland to Korea. In 2012 a consignment of 180 cattle of the French Limousine and Montbelliard breeds was flown in a B747 freighter from France to Mongolia. These animals were for breeding and herd development in the country.

The international traffic of farm animals is controlled and monitored by a set of regulations within the IATA LAR. It covers the basic conditions under which animals may be transported on an aircraft. It is the responsibility of the local competent authority to ensure that the rules are followed. Journey times, including transport by road to and from the airport, must be carefully planned and sufficient food, water and medication must be available at all times. Containers, pens or stalls must comply with IATA specifications, including the amount of space for each animal. Bad weather conditions or delays must be taken into account. Air quality is very important as some animals such as cows produce moisture and gas. The correct level of lighting will vary between different types of livestock. Some will be better in darkness, whereas others will need some low-level lighting.

On freighter aircraft with access to the animals, close attention can be maintained, but in the bellyhold space of passenger aircraft access is not possible so the animals must be carefully packed in safe containers. The correct use of a recommended space for each animal avoids dangerous overcrowding. The staff involved must be trained and able to deal with emergencies including, in some extreme cases, the slaughtering of sick or badly injured animals.

The entire animal transport process, which is routine for those in this trade, is carried out safely all over the world with few problems.

8   Security

Keeping cargo safe

David Brooks, who headed the air cargo division at American Airlines for many years, and steered it through the security strictures that followed the terrorist atrocities of 9/11, reviews the current state of air cargo security measures and how they will affect the industry.

* * *

'It was a bomb.' Those words came from a TV news reporter in 1996 covering the crash of TWA 800 in the Atlantic Ocean off the coast of Long Island, New York. The TV footage showed rings of fire burning on the surface of the ocean with debris and body parts floating among the rescue vessels. For weeks the broadcast networks aired simulations of the B747 blowing up in mid-air and then spiralling down in pieces into the ocean.

These images engraved awe and fear of the potential catastrophe of an air disaster in the minds of the general public, even when the statistics portrayed air travel as being safer than any other mode of transport.

The TWA 800 investigation later concluded that the aeroplane had exploded due to a fuel tank defect, not a bomb. But the tragedy propelled introspection about aviation safety at the political level. US Vice President Al Gore commissioned a panel of experts to make recommendations to improve aviation security:

> The federal government should consider aviation security as a national security issue, and provide substantial funding for capital improvements. The Commission believes that terrorist attacks on civil aviation are directed at the United States, and that there should be an ongoing federal commitment to reducing the threats that they pose.
> (White House Commission on Aviation Safety and
> Security, Final Report to President Clinton,
> 12 February 1997)

Today, such a narrative would not be controversial – but before the 9/11 terrorist attacks on the US the absence of a visible and present threat against aviation led politicians and the aviation interests that supported them to resist changing much in the way of anything on the aviation security front. The US Federal Aviation Administration did implement several new procedures for passenger airlines to affirm the identity of passengers and shippers, but the fundamental mission of the agency and the resources available to increase cargo security did not materially change.

So while 9/11 was widely believed to have been the watershed moment for air cargo security, it was really TWA 800 – an event that had nothing to do with terrorist threats or bombs – that was the canary in the coal mine for commercial aviation and for air cargo security in particular.

The 9/11 aftermath

Although the TWA 800 tragedy caused little security concern over the safety of cargo shipments, the 9/11 tragedies led to ten years of upheaval in air cargo security policy, even though the whole affair was exposed as being the result of sweeping failures in national threat intelligence and not someone sneaking a bomb onto an aeroplane.

As the shock of the disaster started to wear off, the nation became subject to congressional action that reflected more the need just to 'do something' rather than to do something smart. The federalization of the aviation inspection process, for example, led to the hiring of 45,000 federal employees to perform airport passenger screening, even though the 9/11 terrorists had been screened in accordance with the federal requirements at the time by the then-qualified screening companies.

Motivated by the belief that threats could be contained by superior technology, screening equipment manufacturers set up shop in Washington, DC to hawk the latest in emerging (but not yet proven) technology that could screen passengers for more than just 'pointy things' at the airport. Money started to flow into testing programmes to certify new technology – including such low-tech applications as the use of dogs – but the US Transportation Security Administration (TSA) – today an $8 billion per year agency – was less able to gain traction on the underlying intelligence threats that were the root cause of the 9/11 disaster.

Meanwhile, back at the airport, passengers were starting to fly again, but they encountered long security lines and inexperienced and either over- or understaffed security screens – collectively coining a new paradigm of flying, the 'hassle factor' as it has become known.

The tension of the new aviation security era, coupled with the growing majority of Democrats in the US Congress with a Republican President, bred conditions for populist activity on all fronts of the aviation security challenge. But none affected the cargo aviation community more directly than the call by Massachusetts Democrat Congressman Ed Markey to screen all bellyhold cargo being loaded to fly on passenger aircraft.

The political and regulatory evolution of air cargo security

As Congressman Markey was crafting legislation to require 100 per cent screening of cargo on passenger aircraft, it became apparent that many members of the US Congress had no idea that passenger aircraft – the very planes they flew on themselves – even carried air cargo, let alone the value of carrying air cargo to airlines and to the supply chain (and there was this new term to learn 'supply chain' – was it an automotive part?). And then there was the realization that little or none of this cargo was being screened, even though Grandma was being strip-searched when travelling as a passenger on the same aeroplane.

There was plenty of incentive for most congressmen to support Markey's position. What would be gained by not going along with the idea? Heaven forbid they vote 'no' and something like 9/11 happened again and that its origin would be found in an air freight shipment!

This is the right place to clarify that Congressman Markey and his colleagues did take a genuine interest in air cargo security and were not simply grandstanding to give President Bush a partisan snootful. But it was true that most air cargo was not screened and that a man from Mars could conclude that the al Qaeda terrorist organization might well take advantage of this potential vulnerability.

On the other hand, Congressman Markey's public statements, which often included alarmist language such as 'the gaping hole' of air cargo on passenger aircraft, coupled with a lack of meaningful non-public engagement with the air cargo industry itself, alienated air cargo constituencies and the regulatory community. Not to mention the risk that such public comments might in fact empower terrorists to target air cargo before reforms could be implemented.

With passenger airlines, air freight forwarders and large air cargo shippers on the defensive, significant energy went into resisting a 100 per cent screening mandate: (1) it was not possible due to the limitations of space at airport facilities; (2) it would render air cargo obsolete due to the extra time required to screen every piece of every shipment at every location every time; and (3) there was not enough approved screening technology to do the work.

Unfortunately, very little constructive dialogue occurred around the core objective of making air travel safer. Would 100 per cent screening of air cargo on passenger aircraft make Joe Public safer from terrorist activity? What about freighter aircraft? Would not terrorists find some other modal way of conveyance if the entire supply chain were not subject to the same level of screening as well? Are there enough resources to try to screen everything, as opposed to isolating where the greatest risks lie and concentrating resources appropriately? And who would pay for all this activity?

The legislative debate over a new law requiring 100 per cent screening consumed several years, with the opportunity lost of deferring the implementation to a consensus solution. In 2007, with the Republicans on the run, US Congress passed the 9/11 Act requiring the phasing-in of 100 per cent screening on passenger aircraft by the end of a three-year period.

While this outcome achieved the political objectives of Congress, regulators were left with the task of implementation. Fortunately, as a result of some very effective collaboration among industry constituents and congressional staffers, language was included in the 100 per cent screening requirement to allow the TSA to designate third-party entities (including shippers and forwarders) to screen air freight. This would avoid bottlenecks at the airline cargo docks as well as exposing packaging-sensitive cargo to airline handling.

Without this provision, enforcing the 100 per cent mandate by August 2010 would have been nearly impossible to achieve without compromising the whole efficiency of the international supply chain.

Total screening is achieved – but are we safer?

August 2010 arrived, and because of effective advocacy and industry–regulator collaboration during the formulation of the 100 per cent requirement legislation, qualified members of the supply chain were allowed to screen their own cargo, resulting in very few disruptions in the flow of air cargo. Packaging-critical commodities such as pharmaceuticals, medical shipments and museum collections all came to appreciate the value of engagement and thoughtful planning. The oft-scorned TSA proved it could implement an enormously challenging programme that met legislative requirements and was supported by industry. New business opportunities were created – independent or third-party security companies got into the business of screening air cargo as an alternative to shippers or carriers doing the work themselves.

Just when it appeared that the final chapter of air cargo security on passenger aircraft had been written, on 29 October 2012, an al Qaeda operative dropped off two shipments at FedEx and UPS offices in Yemen. The packages were screened by mechanical and canine means and flew out of the country on both cargo and passenger aircraft. The rest of the story was widely reported – each shipment, comprising a standard HP printer, contained just under 1 lb (0.45 kg) of PETN, a major ingredient of Semtex and a difficult explosive to detect. Most alarming to all constituencies of the supply chain, regulators and politicians, after all the effort that went into implementing 100 per cent screening of air cargo on passenger aircraft, here were two deadly devices that evaded detection even when screened with multiple applications. Even more worrisome was that the shipments were re-inspected during transhipment and only after the printers were disassembled were the explosives detected (Wikipedia has an excellent write up of the incident, for those interested in more details, in a feature entitled 'Cargo planes bomb plot').

Had the world not been overwhelmed by the simultaneous near-collapse of the global financial system, the Yemen incident would have – and should have – garnered significantly more public attention than it did. Why? Because the accepted protocol that supported not only safe air cargo security but also safe air passenger security had been undermined. Disaster had been averted only as a result of superior intelligence from Saudi Arabia, including the tracking numbers of the two shipments.

So now the elephant in the room could no longer be ignored. Screening a shipment (or a person, for that matter) only shows a limited picture of something or somebody. Safer security only comes when we know the full *story* behind the shipment or person. Why would someone spend $300 to ship a $150 printer from Yemen to a synagogue in Chicago? Yemen is not known for its printers.

The bullet dodged here put a bright and convincing light on the need for the second and third legs of the cargo security three-legged stool. Along with effective screening must come shipper/shipment intelligence and risk-based application of security resources. Global coordination of intelligence is a tall order to be sure, but the international community should be given sufficient incentive to share information as part of an effective global supply chain security standard. The idea that every shipment or person requires the same level of security vetting is no longer sustainable or affordable. Like any valuable resource, security resources are scarce and should be allocated to shipping scenarios based on a risk assessment.

While it is hard to refer to a near-disaster as any sort of blessing, the Yemen incident did activate a rapid reassessment of aviation security at all levels. In particular, the TSA and US Customs and Border Patrol Agency came to the conclusion that a joint strategy for aviation security could leverage their information sources and together more accurately target shipments that have elevated risk characteristics. Higher-risk shipments could then be subjected to more rigorous screening and inspection. At the time of writing, both agencies are working together (another remarkable and welcome milestone to many observers) to implement such a system.

9   The charter broker

The world of aircraft charter broking has changed enormously in the 50 years that I have been a part of it, writes Chris Chapman, one of the co-founders of global broker Chapman Freeborn.

*   *   *

When I started, the broker was very much the 'post office', literally taking the enquiry from the would-be charterer and asking the airline for a quote and passing the quote back to the client and retaining a commission for his pains. In those days the centre of the broking world was the Baltic Exchange; beyond that in cities like Hamburg and Rotterdam there were other brokers. There was a reason – a large part of the work of a broker was the movement of urgent ships spares for a vessel that had broken down. Of course, there were also passenger requests – some for ships crews and others for what was still a travel industry, although still in its infancy.

In the days of the Baltic Exchange's pre-eminence, the airlines had their broker representatives on the exchange – known as the 'carrier's broker' and a charterer would use another broker, the 'charterer's broker', who was obliged to negotiate the charter price through the carrier's broker. Obviously a time-consuming business, but early on the aircraft being chartered were piston engine machines and the need for speed was not as it is today. As the days of the jet came in this practice began to show its flaws. Today, the Baltic Exchange for the world of aircraft charter has become the Baltic Air Charter Association and has become a very worthy meeting place for the aircraft charter industry while still trying to maintain among its membership an honourable approach to the world of aircraft charter. The motto was and should still be 'My word is my bond.'

The brokers of the age on the Baltic Exchange were part of the Airbrokers Association, which was actually formed in 1949 and were in many cases by-products of the ship brokers and part of the shipping world – companies like Clarksons, Furness Withy, Lambert Brothers, E.A. Gibson, etc. On a further note, the brokers even developed their own aircraft charter contract for use with the airlines, although I can seldom remember it being used by the airlines.

Curiously enough, these companies are no longer involved in the charter broking world, although many of these early brokers subsequently formed their own broking companies.

We have moved on since those early days – we have a new language,

- just-in-time (JIT) inventory,
- logistics,
- globalization,

and many others. With JIT inventory we first started to see the auto manufacturers cut their factory stocks and rely on their suppliers to get their goods to the factory line just as they became needed – saving along the way a vast amount on both storage and premature capital outlays. Of course, suppliers could get 'stymied' by weather, strikes and their own internal problems. These events were a bonanza to the charter broker, who became the point of focus as usually speed was of the essence, the broker usually knew which aircraft was where and from the moment of enquiry to the moment of fixture was often less than one hour. Sometimes an aircraft would be chartered one way for one factory and in exactly the reverse direction for another – in the words of a well-known TV comic, 'a nice little earner'.

By this time, the world of shipping had been transformed and no longer were the vessels being used as the major form of passenger transport around the globe – this pleasure was being taken up by aircraft, and well-known shipping companies were involving themselves in aircraft charter, so we saw names like Cunard Eagle – with Cunard one of the best-known names in the surface transport world tying the knot with Harold Bamberg's Eagle Aviation. In 1971, Trafalgar House bought Cunard and they had 42 cargo ships (as well as passenger vessels), with 14 more under construction; by 1983 they were down to 18 and by 1989 they sold off their remaining fleet. In 1977, Trafalgar House bought 90 per cent of a major UK-based cargo charter airline, which regrettably is no longer part of the scene.

This charter airline in the 1970s was heavily involved, as were others in transport of heavy materials to the Far East, with aircraft frequently returning empty. How curious when we look at today's market, where the trade works in the reverse direction with aircraft frequently light loaded into the Orient and fully laden coming back.

So we have entered the world of logistics – and early on a vital part of a charter broker's armoury was knowledge of the return-load market. Very often this back load would be perishables, and as supermarkets grew so their need to extend the season for fresh produce also grew. Early on in the late 1960s this had been confined to things like tomatoes coming in from the Canary Islands and then as the weather warmed in mainland Europe the tomatoes would come from Holland or the Channel Islands. Tastes were growing and changing, and soon in the 1970s the business had moved onto grapes from Cyprus, an interesting short-season market because grapes could be transported by vessel much cheaper, but in order to 'get a jump' on the market, producers would fly in their 'Red Cardinal' (to name one variety) grapes as soon as they were ripe enough. However, price was an issue and so such a shipment could only work if it was to use an 'empty leg' – in other words, a one-way price. This particular producer tied himself very closely to an aircraft charter broker who effectively cornered this market. Another similar movement was the flying of green beans from Cairo, and again another broker neatly packaged this market. Other similar movements took place with peppers from Ethiopia – our tastes were getting more exotic, avocados from Israel, and so forth. I seem to recall flowers also coming from Israel, which in years to come would develop a new industry for countries such as Kenya or Columbia, which exists to this very day. In my view, all of these markets were aided by brokers seeking ways to get an edge and be able to offer the market ever cheaper ways to move their freight.

In the list above we also should look at the garment industry – in these early days of transport to the Far East, one of the products that became available for shipment was garments which could be produced at much lower cost in Hong Kong. These were frequently amassed by local freight forwarders in consolidations from a variety of small producers and moved cheaply from Hong Kong to markets around the world. They were often poorly packaged and voluminous, but it did not take the shippers long to realize that if the packaging was improved, costs would come down. Later in the development – as with fresh produce – packaging was developed so that products could travel directly from plane to store. More than ever, aircraft were becoming about gaining time – ships for many items of transport had been abandoned as time was becoming more critical.

Further along, cost and time were again playing their part – there was another development, sea–air, with products being moved from places like India by ship into the Middle East and then on by air. That meant we saw the start of a charter broking market in the Middle East, especially Dubai, which remains strong today.

Omitted from the story to date is the role played by catastrophes – from strikes to war on the man-made list, and from earthquakes to famine on the humanitarian side. Early on in 1967 the Suez Canal was blocked. This caused a massive interruption in trade as ships had to pass around the Cape instead of taking the shorter route through what was sometimes called the Highway to India, and although globalization was well short of its current levels the impact on trade was enormous. At the time there were no super freighters like the Boeing 747 or Antonov AN-124 in the sky, instead we were looking at Douglas DC-6s and the like, with maximum 12 tonnes of capacity. The Boeing 707-320C was still not a major part of the aircraft charter world and so it was then, as we have seen often since, a time of strain on the world's charter capacity. In 1969–1970, after the secession of the Eastern State of Nigeria – known as Biafra – there was first of all a large airlift of humanitarian goods which was flown or shipped via Sao Tome on aircraft like the Douglas

DC7CF, and then onwards by an American outfit operating into a crossroads named Uli. Much of it for relief organizations like Caritas and the ICRC, which was not handled through the broking world. However, after the war ended there was a large airlift handled by Baltic brokers with vehicles and other aid material. Other, similar events during this period included a National Dock Strike in the UK, starting at the end of July 1972, which virtually shut down the entire shipping industry with the exception of some ro-ro non-union ports. The strike ran on for several weeks and brokers worked 24-hour days locating aircraft wherever and whenever possible. It was not without its problems as airports became log jammed, and so a new art was to try and find airports that were less busy, as well as to find airports that were not picketed.

The 1970s was an age that saw larger aircraft becoming available for charter – one that comes to mind in Europe was the CL-44 or swing tail freighter, the first of which was put into service in the mid-1960s for a scheduled airline and subsequently on schedule for Flying Tigers and Seaboard, both of whom operated scheduled freighter operations. Later, as they developed into the jet-based scheduled freight market, they sold off their CL-44s to airlines in the UK like Transmeridian Air Cargo, Cargolux and Tradewinds. This was a step up in weight-carrying capability as they could manage 28–29 tonnes, and also had a long-range capability; in fact, the Yukon, which in effect was a CL-44 without the swing tail, held the world long-range flying record of almost 24 hours continuously airborne, a record that held until the introduction of the B747SP.

Globalization has transformed the broking industry – in the 1960s and 1970s it was very rare for a broker to contract a series of flights, but in today's world of product launches and hyped product, manufacturers of everything, be it the latest mobile phone or computer product, need to get their product to market with the minimum of delay. It does not have to be an existing product either; it can be a new item like a smokeless cigarette that a manufacturer wants to blast out there. Such launches, although handled by a freight forwarder, very often wind up being chartered through a broker who would know which aircraft were available and reliable.

Having reached the present day, the broker has been transformed, or should have been. The current world sees the broker taking on many extra responsibilities. Apart from having a duty of care to the client to ensure that the aircraft chartered is a machine worthy in every respect to be used by the would-be charterer, there are myriad other areas to be covered. But let's stay with the duty of care.

In today's global world a lot of effort has to be expended just to ensure the plane being chartered is insured. It's no good just asking the airline 'Are you covered?' The insurance certificate has to be checked, and it is not beyond a cowboy operator to produce a false certificate. The certificate of insurance also needs to be checked to ensure that it is not out of date and covers the registration of the plane being chartered. It is also necessary to verify that the airline has a certificate authorizing them not just to act as an airline, but also that the aircraft being used is authorized. The verification process doesn't always end there, but in itself it is time-consuming. Going beyond this, it is not unknown for aircraft to be offered for charter that are not authorized in any way to be used for 'hire and reward' i.e. for use on a charter. This latter use is more frequently the case with privately owned executive aircraft.

Twenty years or so ago, leading into the present day, we started to see the emergence of Russian aircraft which had been hidden behind the Iron Curtain – first the Ilyushin-76 (IL-76) and then the Antonov AN-124, and alongside these two larger freight-carrying machines were a range of smaller Antonovs. Because of the economics of Russian aviation, these aircraft could knock spots off the prices of the Western machines and so we witnessed the gradual demise of the previous standard machines in use in the charter market – mainly the Boeing 707F, which was no longer the cheapest transport plane out there. These ex-Soviet aircraft were springing up in all sorts of places that had never previously had a charter aircraft on their register. They were also sometimes operated by very shady characters.

The value of the IL-76, for example, was a relatively short runway requirement and a cargo fuselage that could accommodate larger freight and more containers. They also had a ramp loading capability, enormously useful for all types of freight. The first IL-76 flew in 1971, but with the collapse of the Berlin Wall, the break-up of the old Soviet Union and changes in Aeroflot, many of them became available on the charter market. I think at its peak there were probably 30 airlines offering over 100 such aircraft for charter. As a side note, this aircraft was developed as a freighter, whereas, apart from the Hercules, all other freighter aircraft in the charter market at that time had been built as passenger machines and subsequently converted into freighters.

The other massively influential cargo aircraft in the charter market is the Antonov AN-124 Ruslan, which was first commercially certified in 1992, with nearly 30 flying today. This is in effect the largest freighter aircraft (if you discount the one-off Antonov AN-225 and maybe the Boeing 747-8F).

The brokers were the first to realize the potential for these machines and started putting them to work on an almost global basis – although to start with some authorities resisted their lure, many others were quick to embrace them. To this day some of these older aircraft can be found in distant corners of the globe, but now many of the major authorities have introduced a list of banned operators and sometimes countries.

The brokers began to sell the services of these freighters – especially the large Antonov AN-124 – to governments who could see that using chartered aircraft like these would cut the cost of their military support operations. This is happening even today, although the age of the Ilyushin aircraft in many cases makes them less suitable and acceptable. So it is that brokers, and this is key to their usefulness in the market, are forever searching for ways of operating at ever lower costs. Much changes in the economics of operation with the cost of fuel; as this rises, more fuel-efficient aircraft have a greater value – aircraft such as the Boeing 747-400; but when fuel prices drop heavily then the older classic Boeing 747s can come into their own.

Figure 9.1 Antonov AN-124 loading heavy cargo
Source: VIA.

The broker of today has to be aware of market conditions – as demand drops and recession bites, available capacity increases, especially in the bellyhold space of passenger aircraft, which today are far larger than 30 years ago. But at the same time the traditional scheduled airline, which has been trying to build its own cargo fleet, starts to suffer a massive downturn in demand and starts to axe these scheduled freighters. This creates holes in the market that the broker is called upon to fill.

Today, the major brokers are global companies and are constantly being fed information from their worldwide offices and using the network to piece together an operation that keeps the costs down as well as having someone on hand to ensure the smooth transfer of freight from one service to another or ensure the speedy approval of traffic rights. More than ever the business is a 24/7 one and no broker worth his weight would not carry a mobile phone at all times.

In line with all air transport, the use of aircraft is heavily weighted towards passengers, and so it is in the broking world – there are far more specialist passenger charter brokers than air freight brokers. In turn, many of these passenger brokers specialize in particular niches in the market – be it sport (and even this breaks down), entertainment, executive and so on. In the air freight world this is less the case, although there are areas of specialization,

Figure 9.2 Special cargo: Madonna's tour equipment
Source: VIA.

such as livestock and automotive, but these are few and far between. There are freight brokers now around the globe, but the larger international ones tend to be Europe-based, particularly in the UK, which is fitting as that is pretty much where it all started. However, the same cannot be said for the airlines being used, as they are far more widely spread.

As we face the future, looking forward from 2013 the broker is looking at the IL-76s, where we have gone from a market of 30 operators with 100 machines to barely 10–12 air operator's certificates with 30-odd aircraft. Only four or five can now operate in EU airspace; two of these have Stage 4 noise-compliant aircraft only – a total of seven airframes – the rest have Stage 2 versions and it is much tougher for them to operate in the commercial market. If it carries on like this, and with no Afghan traffic, there are likely to be only four or five carriers by 2015 or 2016, with a total of 20–25 aircraft in service.

As for the Boeing 747s, the last big downturn in 2009 caused virtually all the classics to leave the major league, with almost no exceptions. There is now perhaps a crisis with the mortgaged, financed or lessor-owned Boeing 747-400Fs and converted BCFs.

It is just starting, but there could be terrible troubles ahead for airlines, especially charter ones, in the near future. The reasons are varied, but the crisis is both economic conditions on the one hand and the steep decline since the spring of US military flying on the other (affecting the US 74F majors that rely on AMC/MAC and ACMI/charter operations).

On top of that are two other factors. First, freighters ordered two or three years ago, such as the Boeing 777F and the delayed B747-8F – which came to the market nearly two years late – are coming online now in 2012. Fortunately, there are very few, if any, conversions left to be done to Boeing 747 passenger aircraft. Second, the huge number of large-capacity passenger widebody equipment coming online now, especially the 'freight-friendly' Boeing 777, with some of the Middle East airlines alone having around 80 of these aircraft to come still from the manufacturer. This will create a great volume of bellyhold space on global routes that will eat away at charter demand.

In early June, Airbus and Boeing had orders on their books for 2,240 widebody aircraft – A330s, A350s, A380s and Boeing's 777, 787 and 787-88 models – all of which can carry more than 15 tonnes of cargo in their bellyhold space. The B777 can lift as much as 40 tonnes, even with a full passenger load, which is as much as a DC-8 freighter, the very aircraft that was at the heart of some charter broker programmes less than ten years ago. Compared to the Boeing 767s and A330s, and at the top end of the range, the A350 and (above all) the Boeing 777, can load more freight than a B747-400. These aircraft will be flying frequent scheduled passenger services between many of the cities that did have such big birds in their skies a few years ago, and will mop up cargo that would have been the basis for a charter operation even five years ago.

What does this mean for the broker? Probably retrenchment, but as always, in 50 years it means looking for innovative answers in niche markets to meet sudden and unexpected demands. Many experts believe the day of the pure freighter aircraft is over and certainly some major airlines are pulling back from full-freighter service. This will create spot demand – an area where the broker can always be 'first to the post' with a ready solution.

10 Air freight to the rescue

Care by air when disaster strikes

When disaster strikes and human lives are at risk, a fast response to the emergency is essential and air transportation is the obvious way to speed supplies and services to the places they are needed governed by the principles of humanity, neutrality, impartiality and independence.

According to the International Federation of Red Cross and Red Crescent Societies (IFRC), in the immediate aftermath of a disaster, the primary aid items include food, water, temporary shelter and medicine, among other requirements. An effective and well-coordinated logistics operation becomes crucial in a humanitarian context – it means saving lives and diminishing the impact of communicable diseases, the IFRC adds.

In many areas where disaster strikes, the basic infrastructure of the area can be undeveloped in the first place. After a catastrophic event it can be non-existent, partially destroyed or in total disarray. Flying in urgently needed relief supplies by air is often the only solution.

The role of the IFRC's Global Logistics Service is to ensure that the IFRC has a robust, competent and efficient logistics capacity to effectively carry out its humanitarian assistance activities and achieve its goals. Its mission is to create a world-class service to support the core work of the IFRC network and to share resources with other humanitarian organizations.

The worldwide activities of the IFRC's global logistics service focus on three strategic objectives:

- support the enhancement of national society logistics capacity;
- increase the IFRC's logistics capacity to deliver logistics services for preparedness and operational activities;
- provide agreed logistics services to third parties in the humanitarian sector.

A team you can trust

The IFRC's global logistics activities are built on 90 years' experience of delivering humanitarian logistics services. Since 2005, and in recognition of its global logistics expertise, the IFRC has been accredited by the European Commission's Humanitarian Aid Office (ECHO) as a humanitarian procurement centre. In 2006, the IFRC's excellence in logistics was recognized once again when it was declared overall winner of the European Supply Chain Excellence Award, competing against strong candidates from the commercial sector. Humanitarian aid is material or logistical assistance provided for humanitarian purposes, typically in response to humanitarian crises, including natural disasters and man-made disasters. The primary objective of humanitarian aid is to save lives, alleviate suffering and maintain human dignity. It may therefore be distinguished from development aid, which seeks to address the underlying socioeconomic factors which may have led to a crisis or emergency.

According to the Overseas Development Institute (ODI), a London-based research establishment whose findings were released in April 2009 in the paper 'Providing aid in insecure environments: 2009 update', the most lethal year in the history of humanitarianism was 2008, in which 122 aid workers were murdered and 260 assaulted. Those countries deemed least safe were Somalia and Afghanistan.

Aid is funded by donations from individuals, corporations, governments and other organizations. The funding and delivery of humanitarian aid is increasingly international, making it much faster, more responsive and more effective in coping with major emergencies affecting large numbers of people (e.g. the Central Emergency Response Fund). The United Nations Office for the Coordination of Humanitarian Affairs (OCHA) coordinates the international humanitarian response to a crisis or emergency pursuant to Resolution 46/182 of the United Nations General Assembly.

A worldwide network with a global capacity

We have a permanent network of logistics hubs – strategically located in Panama, Dubai, Kuala Lumpur, Amman, Nairobi and Las Palmas – that are staffed by logistics specialists. By regionalizing our operational capacity, we have reduced the cost of providing a family kit by 85 per cent and the delivery time by 75 per cent.

Consolidated purchasing power. By consolidating orders and sourcing items strategically, we can use large purchase volumes to achieve the most competitive prices.

Flexibility. No request is too large or too complex. Thanks to our global structure, we can satisfy the majority of requests. We can offer standard service packages or we can consider requests for non-standard services that are customized to your requirements.

Quality assurance. Our emergency items catalogue provides the exact specification of over 2,000 relief items, which guarantees quality and equity for the people assisted. We also use framework agreements as an effective way of securing the required goods and services at a competitive price, while guaranteeing quality, quantity and delivery terms.

Ethical action. We always give strong consideration to the ethical and environmental impact of our work, and we expect the same from the people we do business with.

Defining humanitarian aid

Humanitarian aid is aid and action designed to save lives, alleviate suffering and maintain and protect human dignity during and in the aftermath of emergencies. Traditional responses to humanitarian crises, and the easiest to categorize as such, are those that fall under the aegis of 'emergency response':

- material relief assistance and services (shelter, water, medicines, etc.);
- emergency food aid (short-term distribution and supplementary feeding programmes);
- relief coordination, protection and support services (coordination, logistics and communications).

But humanitarian aid can also include reconstruction and rehabilitation (repairing pre-existing infrastructure as opposed to longer-term activities designed to improve the level of infrastructure), and disaster prevention and preparedness (disaster risk reduction (DRR), early warning systems, contingency stocks and planning). Under the Organization for Economic Cooperation and Development (OECD) Development Assistance Committee (DAC) reporting criteria, humanitarian aid has very clear cut-off points – for example, 'disaster preparedness' excludes longer-term work such as prevention of floods or conflicts. 'Reconstruction relief and rehabilitation' includes repairing pre-existing infrastructure but excludes longer-term activities designed to improve the level of infrastructure.

Humanitarian aid is given by governments, individuals, NGOs, multilateral organizations, domestic organizations and private companies. Some differentiate their humanitarian assistance from development or other foreign assistance, but they draw the line in different places and according to different criteria. We report what others themselves report as 'humanitarian' assistance but try to consistently label and source this.

A professional and thorough service

Founded in the UK in 1990, the Air Charter Service provides humanitarian aid relief charters for disasters assisting government, relief agency and NGO efforts around the globe.

Agents for the British government

Our extensive work has directly led to us being appointed the official air charter providers for the British government's Department for International Development (DFID).

Providing a rapid response for people in need

Over the last few years we have operated relief flights for many of the major humanitarian disasters and conflicts that have occurred across the world:

- relief aid charter programmes into regions including Rwanda, Kosovo, Afghanistan, Iraq and Haiti
- a massive charter programme for the tsunami-hit countries of southeast Asia.

Delivering life-saving supplies

We can ensure that the maximum help gets to the people that need it the most, quickly and with the minimum of cost, including:

- medicines and medical equipment
- food and water
- vital machinery
- shelter and clothing.

With our spread of offices we are able to respond to a crisis at any point on the globe, which makes us a valuable contact for all aid agencies.

Aid, relief and humanitarian services

Bringing together the logistics prowess of DHL and the passion of our staff, Aid & Relief Services is dedicated to providing professional logistics services to the international aid, humanitarian and development sector.

Working with a number of high-profile agencies, international humanitarian agencies, NGOs and suppliers to the humanitarian arena, DHL is recognized as a leading provider of professional logistics services to the sector.

According to Georges Fenton, Chairman of the Humanitarian Logistics Association (HLA), humanitarian logistics differ from commercial logistics and therefore promote the development of the profession among a wide range of aid organizations and donors. A humanitarian (or emergency) logistician, as distinct from a commercial logistics professional, must tackle a wide range of often complex issues in order to optimize operational efficiency and cope with the variety of bottlenecks that can hamper effective disaster response.

Not only must a humanitarian logistician implement demanding logistics and supply chain management tasks, but she/he will often have to do this within sensitive political and security situations. Humanitarian logisticians often have to act under their own initiative, taking responsibility, for example, for the provision of shelter to protect the wellbeing of hundreds or even thousands of people that might have been displaced by a natural disaster, conflict or even pandemic. They must be able to act decisively within the remit of international humanitarian law and international disaster response law, according to the Red Cross Code of Conduct and in full compliance with inter-agency 'Sphere' standards. To meet the needs of beneficiaries effectively, programme teams must also be supported, requiring the humanitarian logistician to set up operational bases and radio communications in remote locations. Challenges are compounded when large-scale complex emergencies involve multiple actors, frequently including the military, and so an understanding of civil–military cooperation is vital.

Do you have the right aptitude, strength of character, diplomatic skills – not to mention professional logistics skills – and are ready to meet such humanitarian logistics challenges? The HLA will help you to achieve this and more as part of a rewarding career.

The three Ps of transportation

- Pay: paying for transportation is the quickest and easiest form of shipping aid.
- Partner: partnering with another organization can help reduce the cost of the shipment. Keep in mind that America Relief Team helps NGOs find transportation for their humanitarian aid. We also bring our partners together for this purpose.
- Post: post your organization's needs in registers that will match your needs with donors that fit with your needs.

Making arrangements for sending humanitarian aid

- While receiving monetary donations to ship aid, allow room in the budget to cover the costs associated with transportation of commodities and distribution on the ground.
- Partnering with other organizations can help avoid a bottleneck effect. This will create less clogging in the delivery system.
- Take into consideration what items are being sent and who they are for. By doing research, you can avoid sending items that may be considered culturally insensitive or irrelevant.
- Try to send items that will help the recovery of the local economy.
- Make sure you have a consignee or partner on the ground that is able to receive and distribute aid. Often, materials go unclaimed due to lack of planning in this area. Don't allow your efforts to be in vain.

Almost all of the world's airlines have in some form responded to disaster scenarios in one way or another. Care by Air is a non-profit organization delivering at-cost transportation and logistics to help balance the needs of humanitarian organizations. The 'at cost' approach is a means of doing a good deed and good business simultaneously. By offering cargo space, fuel, warehousing, handling and haulage at cost to a humanitarian organization, costs proportionally go down. The bottom line is increased margins and probably the most rewarding operation your company can ever do.

Sheikh Hamdan was briefed by Buhazza on 'Care by Air: A helping hand from the UAE', a UAE non-profit humanitarian relief initiative, launched by Maximus Air Cargo in 2009 in partnership with Etihad Airways, Abu Dhabi Airports Company and Aramex, to deliver at-cost transportation and logistics services to help balance the needs of humanitarian organizations.

Sheikh Hamdan, who got a deep insight into the mission, vision and future plans of the initiative, voiced his unflinching support for the UAE world humanitarian initiative, which aims to reduce costs of relief air transportation in a bid to boost capacities of relief organizations.

The breakthrough initiative, he asserted, underscores the UAE's commitment to smooth flows of humanitarian assistance to victims of disasters and catastrophes across the world.

'Millions of people across the world suffer hunger and starvation every day, and the initiative came to alleviate the sufferings of destitute people by utilizing the empty space of the cargo planes to send food supplies by charity organizations', said Sheikh Hamdan. 'Care by Air gives a new dimension to the role of the UAE as one of the leading countries in the region committed to humanitarian and charity work, and makes a qualitative leap in the movement of humanitarian assistance.'

Sheikh Hamdan appealed to government and private airways companies as well as commercial and oil companies to join the initiative so as to boost capacities of local, regional and international relief agencies.

For his part, Buhazza said Care by Air seeks to further develop the promotion of relief efforts in the air cargo industry market, give the relief organizations additional exposure through the partnership's network and marketing activities to encourage potential companies to join, enhance the role of the UAE as one of the leading countries in the region committed to humanitarian and charity work, and to attract international partners, which will help boost the UAE's economy in the long term.

He said that studies show that 30 per cent of the maximum cargo loading capacity of scheduled flights across the world is not used. According to him, Care by Air will have a substantial impact on reducing cargo expenses, which account for 80 per cent of budgets of world charity organizations. He indicated that Maximus has adopted many creative humanitarian initiatives in partnership with the RCA.

Care by Air offers a variety of benefits:

- increase in human relief aid to countries in need of aid around the world;
- increased responsiveness for relief operations (reduced lead time);

- the 'at-cost' approach ensures that no losses will be incurred, so it is possible to sustain and guarantee its efficiency;
- resource efficiency;
- everyone can join;
- establishing a flexible framework for all partners to upgrade the services offered;
- intensifying the cooperation through regular exchange of information.

11 The role of freighters

Past, present and future

With over 40 years' experience in air cargo sales and operations, Stanley Wraight has become one of the industry's leading experts. He has held senior positions with KLM, Atlas Air and Volga-Dnepr – now Airbridge Cargo. His own company, Strategic Aviation Solutions (SASI), founded in 2005, carries out consultancy work for many different companies.

* * *

Cargo was carried on board aircraft right from the very first commercial flights performed by the fledgling new breed of commercial airlines. Boeing's initial commercial service was for the US Post Office – and that was well in advance of any passenger service offering. KLM Royal Dutch Airlines, the oldest airline in the world still flying under its own name, is very proud of the fact that its first commercial flight on 17 May 1919, from Croydon in the UK to Amsterdam, carried two passengers along with a cargo shipment of 50 kg of newspapers.

Most commercial passenger flights in the early days of aviation carried some type of cargo – which was perceived as being very much a luxury item – used for mail or the delight of a privileged few. Air cargo only began to be taken seriously at a commercial level when the true value of the fast delivery of various commodities could be brought down to a cost level that ordinary consumers could afford, and the attendant distribution methods were built to facilitate the processes required. Eventually, that created a business case for developing pure freighter aircraft to satisfy the increased demand, as passenger airliners in their fleet lacked any significant extra space or payload after passenger baggage was accommodated below decks in the bellyhold space.

The McDonnell Douglas DC series of propeller aircraft led the way, starting with the venerable DC-3, with Vickers of the UK and numerous Boeing aircraft contributing as well. But the start of regular freight services, with long-haul jets such as the B707F and DC-8-55F with major airlines such as KLM, SAS, Lufthansa, BOAC, Flying Tigers, Seaboard World, Singapore Airlines and many more who plied the world's trade lanes, started a revolution.

These aircraft offered flights of over six hours non-stop, carrying a full payload of 36–39 tonnes on 13–14 main-deck pallets. Each separate pallet was contoured to allow ground support crews to load and offload a complete aircraft in one hour or less.

It also allowed the IATA and the airlines to introduce standard container rates, or pallet rates, where the shipper could purchase a complete unit and take charge of the whole process. With a simplified pricing structure, coupled with a growing global network of freighter possibilities and logistics companies, manufacturers could now look at air cargo as a viable transport solution, eventually leading to the launch of what became known as global sourcing, global manufacturing and global distribution.

But it came at a price: it was not transparent and a lot of potential customers were wary of the process. Many carriers with well-educated sales forces took to the streets and tried to educate consumers with programmes such as the 'Test of Time', where the total costs including inventory, financing, lead times; packing and insurance were compared side by side with sea freight; and very often air cargo proved to be more economical when everything was taken into consideration. The European airlines were the most sophisticated in this approach – and today every major logistics company or integrator can perform such an audit for its clients.

All-cargo airlines that were not tied to a passenger airline were few and far between at the beginning, with American carriers like Flying Tigers and Seaboard carrying the standard, and soon Cargolux joining the pack. In Asia, it was only the passenger airlines that flew freighters on global routes.

Singapore Airlines started it all in 1972 with the introduction of a new-build B707 freighter, becoming the first serious contender in the Asian market. Others soon followed and Cathay Pacific started its first full-freighter operations in 1976 with a converted B707 passenger aircraft providing the lift. Today, Asian airlines are leading the world with their large fleets of widebody freighters, a complete reversal of the situation just 15 years ago.

Freighter fleets

Asian economies, understanding the value of air cargo and logistics in expanding their economies, have invested heavily in their national carriers, supporting the development of sea, land and air logistics to build export-oriented economies. This rise in Asian freighter capacity challenges the historical dominance of European airlines in the Asian markets. Notable airlines among them have been Hong Kong's Cathay Pacific, Taiwan-based China Airlines, Korean Airlines, Singapore Airlines, Nippon Cargo Airlines (NCA) of Japan and on the mainland of China, Air China, China Cargo and China Southern.

As of September 2012 the cargo fleets and expansion plans for freighter aircraft only stood at:

- Cathay Pacific: 24 total

    - B747-8F: 7
    - B747-400ERF (extended range freighter): 6

- B747-400F: 6
- B747-400BCF (Boeing converted freighter): 5
- In addition, Cathay Pacific has three B747-400BCF aircraft leased out to Air Hong Kong, its 60/40 joint venture with DHL, and three more B747-48Fs and eight B777Fs on order.

- China Airlines: 21 total

    - B747-400F: 21

- Korean Airlines: 27 total

    - B747-8F: 2
    - B747-400ERF: 8
    - B747-400F: 9
    - B747-400BCF: 6
    - B777F: 2
    - Korean Airlines had two Airbus A300-600Fs that are now at Uzbekistan Airlines, though real ownership may still reside with Korean Airlines. Korean Airlines has five more B747-48Fs and three more B777Fs on order.

- Singapore Airlines: 13 total

    - B747-400F: 11
    - B747-400BCF: 2

- NCA: 9 total

    - B747-8F: 1
    - B747-400F: 8
    - Nippon Cargo Airlines has 13 more B747-48Fs on order.

- Air China Cargo: 11 total

    - B747-400F: 3
    - B747-400BCF: 6
    - B747-400BDSF (Bedek special freighter): 2

- China Cargo Airlines: 17 total

    - B747-400ERF: 2
    - B747-400F: 1
    - B747-400BCF: 1
    - B777F: 6
    - MD-11F: 3
    - A300-600F: 3
    - B757-200F: 1

- China Southern Airlines: 8 total

    - B747-400F: 2
    - B777F: 6
    - China Southern Airlines has six B777Fs on order

There are other smaller and still growing players in the Asian market, but the above are the principle carriers.

But what does the future hold for all-cargo airlines and for passenger airlines that also operate freighters, the 'combination' carriers you may hear of? There certainly will always be a need for freighters in various business cases.

The business case

Let us take a look at a few of those business cases for freighters. The use of the civilian fleets of cargo aircraft from US-registered airlines has been a backbone of US and NATO military logistics over the past decades. In the US it is called the Civil Reserve Air Fleet (CRAF), and it has kept many US all-cargo carriers viable where otherwise they would not be. Since 9/11 the massive overseas deployment by the US has required a continuous use of both passenger aircraft and freighters registered in this programme.

Interestingly, the American passenger airlines have divested themselves of their all-cargo freighter fleets, leaving the CRAF market to specialist cargo carriers such as World Airways, Evergreen, Atlas Air and Kalitta. In most cases the American all-cargo operators (other than the integrators like DHL, FedEx and UPS) have a mixed business consisting of aircraft, crew, maintenance and insurance (ACMI), flying, charters and military business.

Figure 11.1 Freighter aircraft
Source: Lufthansa.

Aircraft, crew, maintenance and insurance

ACMI is when an airline leases supplemental lift from a provider to meet short-or longer-term needs for, in this case, all-cargo aircraft. The supplier will provide the aircraft and crew, do the maintenance and insure the aircraft, but the customer who leases the aircraft is responsible for the rest. That includes ensuring the necessary rights and permits are in place, marketing and securing the revenue cargo on board, and most importantly carries the responsibility for the fuel cost.

The American carriers are the traditional leaders in this business for all freighter aircraft types. Companies such as Atlas Air Worldwide Holdings, Kalitta, World Airways, Southern Air and ABX, to name a few, are among the world's largest suppliers. Others exist, notably in Iceland and in the Gulf countries, but these are smaller in fleet size.

Whether it is for a short-term lease to meet a capacity shortfall in peak demand seasons, cover the capacity of an aircraft that is in heavy maintenance or to open a new route, ACMI can be the best solution. Longer term, if only one or two aircraft are required to ensure a viable cargo product offering, airlines tend to choose ACMI as a solution over either dry leasing or purchasing an aircraft.

Charters

The large B747 all-cargo fleets available with a number of the major global airlines usually dominate the charter business for freighters. Charters tend to be used only in cases of emergency, or when a substantial load can be secured and regular scheduled aircraft do not serve the destinations involved. Charters are tailored to the customer's individual needs and there-fore are much more expensive than using the scheduled freighter services offered by airlines. This is because unique handling facilities have to be put in place, the empty positioning of flights either to or from the ultimate destination is involved and the airlines are faced with extra costs that they would normally not incur.

For specialist project work in the outsize and heavy-weight markets, the Antonov AN-124-100 or AN-124-50 is the aircraft of choice. These massive aircraft are 'roll on–roll off' with ramp-loading nose and rear doors accommodating the largest of cargo weights and dimensions possible to be flown with today's technology. These aircraft, due to their unique capabilities and small fleets, are the most expensive option and usually are only used when absolutely no alternative is viable.

While used for commercial project work, the AN-124's primary mission over the past years has been for the military use of the US and NATO commands, as well as disaster relief work for the UN and other government or large NGOs (see Chapter 10).

Fuel

Over the past few years, airlines have been contending with exorbitant fuel prices that have grown faster than crude oil, to reach their highest levels in years. The cost of jet fuel is typically an airline's largest cost and is especially hard on all cargo airlines, which have only one source of revenue, not the multitude available to passenger airlines like passenger fares, tour and vacation packages, duty-free and, of course, cargo and mail.

Having their largest cost so volatile also makes fleet and business planning extremely difficult for the airlines. When jet-fuel prices rise to today's levels, airlines have limited options to mitigate these costs. As fuel prices increase, flights become less profitable, so the natural tendency is to reduce capacity, which is not easy when operating a smaller fleet of all-cargo aircraft. Fuel-hedging programmes are expensive and very risky for all-cargo operators, and many of them lack the scale and financial resources necessary to achieve any relief via this option.

Conversions

Traditionally the largest source or 'feedstock' of aircraft for all-cargo airlines has been older passenger aircraft. In past years a passenger aircraft would always be looked upon as having a second life, and after conversion it could look at another 15–20 years of flying the world's routes as an all-cargo aircraft.

Equipment such as the B727, B757, B767, A300, DC-10, MD-11 and Boeing 747-200 and 400 models were the aircraft of choice. The viability of this second life was always a factor when financing was being arranged for new aircraft, as this second life contributed nicely to the potential resale values.

Four factors weigh heavily in the decision to convert an aircraft, other than the obvious one of what the economic life of the aircraft would be once it was converted. These are aircraft acquisition costs of the feedstock aircraft, conversion costs, maintenance costs and fuel burn.

Technological advances in range capabilities and fuel burn, plus lower maintenance costs of new-build freighters, have been a key factor in the decision-making of many airlines to shun conversions of late. However, to sustain a viable business, the revenue has to justify the expense which accompanies that decision.

A new-build Boeing 747-8F is just shy of $200 million, and a B777F is $170 million. Compare that with a freshly converted B747-400 from either Boeing or IAI industries at less than one-third of the cost. The same holds true for other types as well; there will always be a market for conversions, and it is as cyclical as the market demand that feeds it.

Retirements

As of September 2012 there were 77 B747-400 BCF/SF converted aircraft and 65 B747-200F classics still flying. A large number of older B767-200Fs and MD-11SFs are also still in the air. The question continually rises of whether these aircraft can be operated economically or whether they should be consigned to the scrap heap. Certainly, there is little argument that once the military work (which sustains most B747-200F work) slows down they will be permanently retired. However, the debate still goes on regarding the converted B747-400. Arguments are that fuel efficiency alone will ground these aircraft. Others see a future for them as potential short-haul aircraft to support hub activities. Only time will offer the answer to that question, but I expect the newer-converted B747-400 freighters to be around for quite a while.

The market for smaller 'narrowbody' freighter aircraft will remain small in comparison to larger widebody equipment, and these will mostly serve the express companies. This market is expected to remain a Boeing niche, with the B737 families supplying most of the feedstock.

Looking ahead

It looks increasingly like the future for stand-alone all-cargo commercial airlines may be reaching the end of its life cycle, unless the airlines can find a unique selling point or a niche market that can support the high costs associated with these operations.

Passenger airlines, which treat cargo as a core business, and maintain large widebody passenger fleets, will always need freighters to keep the bellyhold capacity of their passenger fleets full by virtue of transhipment in their hub-and-spoke operations. However, recent technological advances in passenger aircraft, with their huge and hungry bellyhold space, is changing the dynamics of our industry.

Let us look at a few facts:

- Totalling the backlog of production freighters as of September 2012, we find: 54 B747-8Fs; 89 B777Fs; 40 B767-300Fs; and 47 A330-200Fs on the order books of the two main aircraft manufacturers. That amounts to 230 widebody freighters coming on stream in the next four years.
- Using a modest growth level of 3 per cent as a basis, and looking at the freighters expected to come on stream (the 230 widebody aircraft that are on order will lead to a capacity growth of 5 per cent), it looks as if there will be 9 per cent excess main-deck capacity in the market by 2016.
- One of the many quotes circulating in the industry today is: 'I really think the all-cargo airlines are in a permanent circle of decline. I'm just amazed at how the likes of B777 passenger aircraft are changing the game.'
- Passenger growth of close to double digits, with a huge part of that coming from the rise of a consumer middle class in Asian countries, will add even more widebody passenger bellyhold capacity.

The ultimate effect of that appears to be the inevitable bankruptcy of more all-cargo carriers, and exit from the main-deck freighter business of some combination airlines.

The increase in bellyhold freight capability of the current and next generations of widebody passenger aircraft (A330, A380, B787, B777 and B747-48, and the coming A350) is significant. Over 2,300 units of new-build equipment are on the order books, and their bellyhold cargo capacity will offer the lift equivalent of about 450 102-tonne payload B777 freighters. The bankruptcy of more all-cargo carriers, and exit from the main-deck freighter business of some combination airlines, seems the logical conclusion.

But that does not mean freighters are not viable, it just means that the industry has to take a hard look at how those aircraft are deployed, and how they are factored in to keep the bellyholds full with revenue management systems of the large passenger airlines that will still deploy them.

Air cargo: what's in it for passenger airlines?

During a 30-year career with the Dallas, Texas-headquartered carrier, David Brooks served as President of American Airlines Cargo, the air freight division of American Airlines, from 1996 until May 2012. He was also a member of the Advisory Council of GF-X Operations, a company that provides electronic booking solutions for the air cargo industry, and of Cargo 2000, the IATA-led quality organization for the air freight industry. In 2011 he received the Jim Foster Award for Excellence, given by the US Airforwarders Association (AfA).

*   *   *

Many of the world's leading passenger airlines rely on freight as valuable supplementary or ancillary revenue, and a valuable addition to their bottom-line result; for some airlines it means the difference between making a profit or a loss.

Thanks to Orville and Wilbur, most of us would assume that as soon as they had proved their contraption could fly, they would have been selling tickets within minutes of the first landing. Not so. At the beginning of the twentieth century, the idea of groups of people actually getting from A to B by flying through the air was not a sustainable vision. In fact, in the US, long-distance travel was not something people pursued, especially for leisure travel. But in the aftermath of the Industrial Revolution and with rail lines spreading throughout the country, the need for rapid communication was increasing at a rate greater and faster than trains could move letters and parcels over these longer distances.

Even though the new flying machines of the early 1900s were crashing more than they were flying, the US government saw an opportunity to move mail with these new aeroplanes. Over the next 20 years, the government and the military took turns operating a crude airmail service around the country. With little flying experience and no kind of ground navigation other than natural land and water features, these young pilots would get lost, run out of fuel and sometimes simply dump the sacks of mail out the window if they were running late.

Meanwhile, the railroad interests were starting to complain that the government was subsidizing the new competition at public expense. Congressman Clyde Kelly from Pennsylvania responded with what is known as the Air Mail Act of 1925, or the Kelly Act, which authorized the US Postal Service to contract with private parties to fly the mail. These first contracts were awarded to a number of new airlines, which would later evolve into the legacy US carriers with which we became familiar in the modern age: American, Eastern, Continental, TWA, Northwest and others.

Not to be overlooked, as mail took flight during this period, non-mail freight made its first air journey in 1911 – a shipment of silk from Dayton to Columbus, Ohio. So, at least in the US, the commercial aviation industry arose from non-passenger demand.

The military did make use of aeroplanes during the First World War. At the conclusion of the conflict, former military pilots sought to make a living 'barnstorming' the country with their flying displays. These generated interest in aviation among the population. Air fares, however, were too high and passenger cabins too small to make a profit as a commercial venture.

That changed in 1925 with the introduction of the three-engined Ford Tri-motor, and then with the larger DC-3 in the 1930s. Great strides were made in aviation safety with these new aircraft, which together with the in-flight amenities of hot meals, sleeping berths and stewardesses started attracting paying passengers at a profitable level.

But, as is the case today, these early stages of aviation would not have been commercially viable without the combined earning power of both passenger and cargo revenues.

The evolution of air cargo in the US

The air cargo industry kept up with the swift pace of industrial development throughout the twentieth century. Once the commercial framework was established with a mix of passenger and air freight traffic, airlines could expand their franchises in both domains and did so with vigour. The jet age arrived in the 1950s and the computer age in the 1960s; air cargo flourished in both eras, moving high-value and time-sensitive commodities across long distances. Many passenger carriers invested in freighters – the B707F and B747F being the backbone of the modern-day all-cargo fleets.

But no decade brought more transformation for the air cargo industry than the 1970s, when Fred Smith launched Federal Express (now generally known as FedEx). Before FedEx, air carrier service levels lacked what is today a common service standard – time-definite service, meaning delivery of the shipment into the custody of the consignee (the recipient) by a specific time.

The initial FedEx network was very small and concepts such as just-in-time (JIT) inventory were not yet in practice. The venture nearly failed. In fact, it would have, had the government not demonopolized the carriage of documents. Way before the fax machine and then e-mail came along, FedEx could capitalize on the substantial market in the carriage of important and time-sensitive documents by air, as well as other small express packages (see Chapter 13).

The 1980s, 1990s and the early twenty-first century saw significant advances in aircraft technology, particularly in fuel economy, further enhancing a carrier's ability to carry air cargo. Trade barriers fell and global sourcing rapidly expanded, so even when passenger traffic saw cyclical declines, air cargo volumes generally posted annual growth rates of 6–8 per cent throughout this period.

Benefits to passenger airlines

What does air cargo do for passenger airlines? For most large international airlines, air cargo revenue is only 3–10 per cent of the total amount of revenue made from airlines' sales and it is, therefore, often thought to be a 'by-product' or ancillary revenue of the enterprise. Nonetheless, most carriers with cargo franchises know that much of their revenue from freight and mail flows right

Figure 11.2 China Southern B777
Source: SASI.

to the bottom line, depending on how they do their accounting. On long-distance intercontinental flights, this can make the difference between a profit and loss. In fact, some modern aircraft, notably the Boeing 777 and Airbus 340, are designed specifically to accommodate a large amount of air cargo in the space below the feet of the passengers.

So the commercial value to passenger airlines of carrying air freight loads in their bellyhold space is pretty clear. Historically, air cargo revenue helped support the origins of the passenger air service that we rely on today. In fact, it is worth noting that the explosion of world trade enabled by air cargo has been a key source of the increased passenger air travel demand in the twentieth and twenty-first centuries.

Despite the importance of commercial aviation – passenger and cargo – political and regulatory priorities, with the passage of time and impact of events, never seem to quite equate to the industry's needs. Therefore, the challenge for all who rely on a safe and efficient air transportation network is to never lose sight of the need for advocacy and collaboration on behalf of the industry.

History has taught us that air cargo can facilitate the evolution of everything that is important to us, but we must make the investment of time, money and, most importantly, education in order for the air cargo industry and those who rely on it to thrive and prosper.

The world beneath your feet: a personal overview of air freight by Ray Crane, specialist air freight publisher

Ray Crane has spent over 30 years as a publisher of air cargo media. He started with *Airtrade*, the first air cargo specialist air cargo monthly magazine, and later he launched *Air Cargo News*, a fortnightly newspaper which was quickly established as the most read and popular publication in the worldwide air freight industry.

*   *   *

Globally, goods being moved by air have an annual worth of $1.5 trillion, according to IATA. Although only a small proportion, around 1 per cent, of the raw materials and goods moving around the globe travel by air during their time in the supply chain, it is worth noting that 35 per cent by value of all these goods travel by air. It is therefore easy to work out that most of the products travelling by air are of a very high value, or are perishables that require fast transportation to the marketplace – and these shipments all add up to a value of around $60 billion each year in airline revenues around the world for the space they occupy on aircraft.

High-value items such as computers, mobile phones, machine parts or perishable goods like flowers, fruits and vegetables move by air because of the speed of transit which the mode provides – and even fashion goods are described as perishable nowadays, with consumer desires requiring instant satisfaction.

It is also worth noting that while items like fashion goods chase cheap labour costs in Asia, they need to be quickly available in the stores to meet seasonal demand or a change in fashion trends, which often have short time windows. Tropical fruit picked ripe and flown to the consumer is tastier and can, for example, include pineapples from southern Africa to Europe at Christmas, when the consumer is prepared to pay the extra cost.

The air cargo industry has a 100-year track record – and many of these early years were fraught with the danger of the unknown, as well as remarkable achievements by the pioneers. However, it was the advent of the widebody aircraft in the late 1970s and 1980s that had a marked effect on the air cargo product, enabling passenger aircraft to carry substantial cargo loads in their vast bellyhold space, while freighters could lift payloads of well over 100 tonnes. The widebody mainframe and engine manufacturers are now aiming to fly even further with bigger payloads, to cut cockpit crew and save fuel costs, while working flat out and making huge investments in new equipment to preserve our environment.

The modern freighter aircraft

I believe the most successful aircraft over the years has been the Boeing 747 designed by Joe Sutter and his team at the Boeing plant in Seattle. The Boeing 747-100 series prototype had its maiden flight on 9 February 1969, and the latest of five versions of this iconic aircraft – the B747-8 freighter – carried out its first test flight from Seattle on 1 June 2012. The B747-8 has experienced a few technical problems since its initial design in 2008, but Joe Sutter, at the age of 91, was there on the airfield to witness takeoff.

After the B747-100 had certainly revolutionized the way passengers travelled, a full-freighter version came in with the B747-200 series, offering a larger side door and the now-familiar nose-loading cone. The first of these freighters was delivered to Lufthansa in March 1972. I am proud to say I witnessed the first B747-200F in Cargolux livery to takeoff from Boeing Field. The Luxembourg-based company went on to operate a fleet of 14 modern B747-400 freighters, the next rung up the Boeing ladder of progress. Cargolux already operates five of the newest B747-8Fs in its fleet as a launch customer for the aircraft and part of an ongoing upgrade programme.

These freighters are today playing a vital role in world commerce. But apart from providing consumers with the gadgets they use for business and leisure, the food they eat and the clothes they wear, the freighter aircraft is also facilitating some amazing freight movements. Formula One motor racing is a big user of air cargo and widebody freighters, a must-have item when you think of the cargo involved. Even those of you not vaguely interested in motor racing will be aware of the Formula One caravan moving between places like Brazil, Canada, Abu Dhabi, Malaysia, Japan, Australia and many other destinations on the 'fly away' legs of the yearly circuit.

We are talking about many tonnes of cargo worth millions – and by the way, insurance for air cargo is cheaper than for sea cargo as goods are considered to be safer at 35,000 feet. That is certainly why valuable cargo favours transportation by air – including irreplaceable works of art being loaned between museums or the Treasures of Tutankhamen and China's Terracotta Warriors going on a world tour to appreciating audiences.

It's not just at the big airports that these freighters can be spotted. Some international airports such as London Heathrow may be geared up for the passenger market, but many freighter operators look for more cost-effective options which offer specialist cargo facilities, such as a cold store for flowers, fruits and vegetables, safe storage for valuable items and special facilities for live animal transportation, as well as being close to big city main road arteries. The attractively lower landing and parking fees they offer are vital in today's penny-pinching business atmosphere, and night operation can be a big bonus.

Freighters carrying project cargo are always looking for landing spots near the site of construction of a vast infrastructural project or for an airport that does not suffer from congestion. Some of these airports, such as Manston, in the southeast of England, or Hahn, north of Frankfurt in Germany, are virtually unknown to the man in the street, but are appealing gateways to the freighter airlines.

Memories are made of this

Air cargo is a young business, having only really taken off in my lifetime. Having started a publishing business nearly 40 years ago, after ten years with the *Sunday Times* and *Observer* newspapers in London, I found myself questioning some of the business principles in this quite new business – and still do – but one thing I was quick to notice in the air cargo industry is that no matter which country you travel to, the business is full of great characters, possessed of warmth and generosity.

I have always been surprised to notice the different cultures between sea and air transportation folk – or perhaps I just imagine that to be the case. I regard air cargo people as being younger and freer of spirit, but I do believe that the business would benefit greatly at its career entry level from a serious influx of well-educated youth with a smart 'get up and go' attitude to doing business in today's world.

Air cargo already has more than its fair share of intelligent and entrepreneurial individuals among the carriers, the airport staff, cargo handlers, general sales agents, the charter brokers and many other service providers, but we need a bigger influx of 'the right stuff' to be attracted to the business from our universities.

When I came into the air cargo industry at the beginning of 1975, there were no wholesalers, until Tony Realff launched AMI (Air Marketing International) later that year. He worked out of a portakabin office close to London Gatwick Airport, growing into much grander premises as business progressed.

Tony struck a deal with Qantas to guarantee a regular cargo container to Sydney for a fixed rate, and hoped he could fill it with cargo consolidated from a mix of freight forwarders. His customers were initially concerned that he would then go direct to their shippers (the manufacturer customers of the freight forwarder), but he managed to persuade them otherwise and more destinations soon came online.

A great memory that sticks in the mind is when I first travelled to the small undeveloped emirate of Dubai 35 years ago. It was little more than a fishing village and Gulf Air connecting from Bahrain was the national carrier. Dubai was not as well blessed with oil and gas reserves as some of its neighbours, but the ruling Al Maktoum family had a vision and planned to expand the emirate as a trading and financial centre and as an international holiday resort.

Their success with the establishment of Emirates Airline is well documented – it started in 1985 with a fleet of two leased aircraft, and now contains over 120 widebody aircraft and is still growing. Now there are additional airlines established in the region, such as Etihad Airways, Qatar Airways and Oman Air.

So, the next time you fly on your overseas holiday, spare a thought for what is stowed below your feet in the bellyhold space of the aircraft, in addition to your baggage. The air freight being loaded there and on the fleets of full-freighter aircraft around the world is worth $60 billion in additional annual revenue to the airlines. You might also reflect that many of the people who started the modern air cargo business have now reached retirement age – although most will need to be beaten out of the business with a large stick. The world beneath your feet could be the world at your feet for young talent prepared to replace them and make a go of the opportunity.

Outsourcing the non-core business

The air cargo general sales agent (GSA), or more currently the general sales and services agent (GSSA) – denoting that the company will handle other necessary areas of the air freight business over and above the sales function – has evolved since the early 1990s, when airlines began to outsource certain areas of their cargo business, allowing them to concentrate on their core business of flying passengers.

The basic concept of employing a cargo GSSA is to represent an airline within a specific area, which may be a region, a country, or a region within a specific country. The cargo GSSA often works for airlines, which prefer to concentrate on the passenger business, leaving cargo to the specialist. There are also passenger GSSAs and in some cases they will handle both the cargo and passenger business. This may involve just sales, but today is more likely to include document processing, Customs, trucking and insurance – a completely outsourced cargo operation.

The GSSA is remunerated by way of a commission on the sales volume, but may also receive other forms of payment depending on the contract between the carrier and the agent, who will typically sell the product of more than one airline. Carriers normally use a GSSA in areas where they have a small market or even no direct flights, thus allowing them to have a physical sales presence in a country at a much lower cost than opening their own offices. In some cases, the GSSA can take on the entire cargo capacity of an airline client. An airline may also use a GSSA service because of its strong local contacts, historical ties with travel and cargo, or its in-depth knowledge of a country, its culture and the traditional way of doing business within its borders.

When a GSSA sells cargo space in a location where there are no direct flights, it is termed as being 'offline' and any air freight capacity sold is either trucked to the nearest point where there are suitable flight connections, or in some cases the freight is flown to another airport on another airline (inter-line).

All costs related to running the GSSA business are the responsibility of the agent involved, including but not limited to insurance, rent, general office expenses and any travel within the country or region needed to promote and sell the product.

Streamlining the GSSA business

There has been a concerted attempt over the last 30 years to streamline the GSSA business, with the implementation of international standards and regulations.

IATA has also become closely allied to the Federation of Airline GSAs (FedAGSA), which represents more than 100 GSSA companies around the world. For example, the new three-character code launched by IATA is a solution for logistic service providers such as freight forwarders, non-IATA airlines and GSSAs who need to issue their own accountable transportation documents that they wish to be uniquely identified.

In order to satisfy a market need, the airline association launched the new IATA third-party logistics (3PL) code for logistics companies who wish to be identified and recognized by the cargo industry. The 3PL code (three characters made up of a combination of letters and numbers) is used only on cargo or mail transport documents when in conjunction with the provision of transportation services. Companies wanting to issue their own accountable transportation documents for use over their respective supply chains can apply for this code.

Most cargo GSSAs are independent operators who are established experts in the air freight business and well-connected to contacts within their own territory, which is what makes them successful. However, the last decade has seen the emergence of several large multinational GSSA groups which offer their carriers international networks and a greater guarantee of solid business opportunities across several countries. Multi-country contracts help these GSSA groups to compete on a level playing field with the big consolidators, many of which operate their own flights. Companies such as the Air Logistics Group have developed into global GSSAs with around 60 offices in

38 countries. Similarly, the ECS group, with offices in 32 countries, deals with 500,000 tonnes of cargo annually for its airline clients.

The whole business of outsourcing, which has now become so popular, has served the airlines well as they do not have to devote money and resources to a cargo operation in a particular country, as the GSSA does everything. Payment by results is the key phrase to the way the business works. The crisis in the air freight industry during the 2011–2012 recession has had some impact on GSSAs. Cost-cutting by airlines means that the agents, in turn, are under pressure to diminish their costs. The arrival on the scene of fleets of new aircraft with larger capacities is creating an imbalance between supply and demand, with possibly too much capacity on offer.

A view from the market

Howard Jones, CEO of Toronto-headquartered Network Cargo Systems, has been a successful GSSA for over 20 years and he comments on this important aspect of the air freight business.

*   *   *

At first we offered a combination of trucking, warehousing, consolidations and wholesale. As a member of the IATA executive council in Canada, while working for Thai Airways, I made many contacts, which helped me start the company. The biggest element in doing this kind of business is trustworthiness. Your good reputation helps to build a wide portfolio of carriers. I believe the future of GSSAs is bright, as more airlines are moving to this outsourced cargo option.

In order to be a successful GSSA it is necessary to have firm financial backing. The original way was to secure a bank guarantee, which had the effect of keeping the 'cowboys' out. Today at Network Cargo Systems, we work closely with our banks and they have confidence in us after 20 years of success.

GSSAs are the entrepreneurs of the air freight industry and, despite the trend for more bigger airline mergers, they will continue to play an important role.

12 Heavy-lift air transportation

Heavy-weight contenders

There are relatively few freight aircraft that can lift heavy single-piece loads, and there is always an eager demand for their capacity.

During the days of the Cold War, the parents of today's air cargo executive in the UK would worry and whisper quietly that should the Soviets decide to cross the Iron Curtain and storm through the Berlin Wall, 'they will be in London in four days'. Fortunately, that was never to be the case. And all who are familiar with the giant Antonov AN-124 heavy-lift aircraft will know that the information surrounding the whole concern was fundamentally wrong in the first place – courtesy of the backbone of today's heavy-lift air transportation business the Red Army would have been in London in only four hours!

The Antonov AN-124 Ruslan Condor was designed by the Antonov Design Bureau in the Ukrainian Soviet Socialist Republic, then part of the Soviet Union, as a strategic heavy-lift military aircraft capable of flying two fully loaded battle tanks, as well as the infantry and supplies needed to support them in battle, into unprepared airstrips on rough terrain. The aircraft featured a reinforced floor to support the weight it was designed to carry and had nose-door and rear ramps to enable drive-on, drive-off wheeled and tracked access to the main cargo deck. Externally similar to the American Lockheed C-5 Galaxy, it has a 25 per cent larger payload and the capability to 'kneel' on its retractable front undercarriage, allowing full utilization of its front ramp during cargo loading – or initially to unleash its cargo of battle tanks at full speed.

Manufactured in parallel by the Russian company Aviastar-SP in Ulyanovsk and by the Kyiv Aviation Plant AVIANT in Ukraine, the AN-124 is the world's largest serially manufactured cargo aircraft capable of handling heavy loads in its main deck cabin by virtue of a specially reinforced floor. The one-off Antonov AN-225 Mriya (a stretched and enlarged variant of the AN-124), which also operates in the heavy-lift sector, is larger and is covered later in this chapter.

First flown as a military aircraft in 1982, civil certification for the AN-124 was issued on 30 December 1992. Twenty years later, over 20 of the aircraft

Figure 12.1 Antonov AN-124 loading heavy cargo
Source: VIA.

are still thought to be in service with the military and around 20 are in commercial use with various carriers in Ukraine, Russia, the United Arab Emirates and Libya.

With a cargo compartment that is 36 × 6.4 × 4.4 metres – 20 per cent larger than the main cargo compartment of a US-built C-5 Galaxy – the aircraft has been used to carry various types of heavy-lift cargo. Heavy-lift operators love to tell their customers that the length of the cargo main deck on an AN-124 is longer than the distance of the first flight made by the Wright Brothers.

The spectacular loads that the aircraft has carried include locomotives, yachts, aircraft fuselages and a variety of other oversized cargo – it has also become a favourite with the more famous music artists (Michael Jackson, Madonna, Pink Floyd and the Rolling Stones, to name a few), who take complex stage lighting and special effects equipment on their world tours.

The list of cargo lifts made by the AN-124 over the years is endless, but some of the notable lifts include:

• the delivery of new 201 Class locomotives from Canada to Ireland in June 1994;
• the delivery of a whale from Nice in France to Japan and another flight to deliver an elephant from Moscow to Taiwan;

- the transportation of the 160-tonne, 24-metre (78 ft) Obelisk of Axum back to its native homeland of Ethiopia from Rome in April 2005, requiring three trips, each carrying one-third of the monument;
- the shipment of outsized aircraft components like the massive General Electric GE90 turbofan engines to Volga-Dnepr's US-based aircraft manufacturer's assembly line through a contract with Boeing;
- the transportation of astronautical equipment manufactured by the Airbus parent company, EADS, as well as components of the Airbus A380 superjumbo – Airbus Transport International uses Polet Airlines;
- an AN-124 that was used in April 2011 to airlift a large concrete pump from Germany to Japan to help cool reactors damaged in the Fukushima nuclear accident.

To enable the aircraft to perform these spectacular cargo lifts, it has an on-board overhead crane capable of lifting items of up to 30 tonnes onto the main deck of the aircraft, and items up to 120 tonnes can be winched or positioned on board using external cranes.

The original AN-124s were built with a service life of 7,500 flight hours, with a possibility for extension. However, many airframes have now flown more than 15,000 flight hours. In response to requests from commercial users, the AN-124-100 version has been built since 2000 with an improved service life of 24,000 hours, and older airframes are being upgraded to this standard.

Figure 12.2 AN-124 Freighter with outsize cargo
Source: VIA.

AN-124 and the EP-3E incident

In a very high-profile, but somewhat secretive, assignment it was a Polet Airlines AN-124 that was used to transport a US Navy EP-3E Aries II electronic intelligence aircraft from Hainan Island, China on 4 July 2001. The unique heavy-lift operation followed the notorious incident when, operating as a reconnaissance aircraft above the waters of the South China Sea, the aircraft collided with a J-8 interceptor jet of the Chinese People's Liberation Army Air Force that had been despatched to investigate its presence.

The J-8 pilot was killed in the collision but the EP-3E pilot kept the aircraft in the air long enough to make an emergency landing at an airfield on Hainan Island, whereupon its crew was taken into custody and the aircraft seized. A full-scale diplomatic incident ensued. The Americans wanted their highly secret equipment back and the Chinese authorities refused to allow it to be repaired and flown out of the country.

After much diplomatic wrangling it was agreed that the EP-3E could be disassembled and flown back to the US in an AN-124 operated by Polet Airlines. The use of a Russian carrier for the ten trips it took to complete the mission was seen as being significant in the diplomatic negotiations.

Additional retrofitting is being performed to extend its service life to 40,000 flight hours. The Kyiv Aviation Plant AVIANT offers upgrades to the AN-124-100-150 version.

The air cargo operators would like to see more of these heavy-lift aircraft in the skies and Russia and Ukraine have agreed at various times to resume production with an AN-124-150 version. This version of the aircraft would feature several improvements, including a maximum lift capacity of 150 tonnes, but it often seems as though this is wishful thinking that has never borne fruit. In late 2009 it was reported that Russian President Dmitry Medvedev had ordered production of the aircraft to be resumed.

Of the ten AN-124 aircraft that are in commercial use, most are with Ruslan International – a joint venture formed between Antonov Airlines and Volga-Dnepr to create a single marketing and sales operation for a combined fleet of 17 Antonov AN-124-100 aircraft. Polet Airlines has four of the aircraft in service, Abu Dhabi's Maximus Air has one and another aircraft is with Libyan Air Cargo.

The SALIS project

Ruslan SALIS GmbH is a 50–50 joint venture set up by Volga-Dnepr Group (Russia) and Antonov Design Bureau (Ukraine) in 2004 specifically to support the SALIS (Strategic Airlift Interim Solution) project in which member countries of NATO have pooled their resources to charter special aircraft that give the alliance the capability to transport heavy equipment across the globe by air.

The countries have committed to using the aircraft for a minimum of 2,000 flying hours each year and the capability can be utilized in times of urgent strategic or humanitarian need to provide NATO with the outsize and heavy-lift cargo lift it needs as an interim solution to meet shortfalls in its strategic airlift capabilities, pending the first deliveries of the Airbus A400M aircraft.

Under the terms of the agreement two AN-124-100s are constantly based on full-time charter for SALIS at Leipzig/Halle International Airport in Germany, but in case of necessity two more aircraft are to be provided on six days' notice and another two on nine days' notice.

NATO has used the Antonov fleet to support its mission in Afghanistan with weekly flights, to deliver aid to the victims of the October 2005 earthquake in Pakistan and to airlift African Union peacekeepers in and out of Darfur.

Smaller loads

Other than the AN-124, the next largest aircraft available for heavy-lift project work is the IL-76, a ramp-loading 40-tonne payload freighter that has become known as one of the most efficient aircraft when required to operate into and out of airports with undeveloped or underdeveloped infrastructure.

Since 2000, however, the use of the original IL-76 fleet has been seriously restricted by the introduction of a number of strict rules introduced by the International Civil Aviation Organization (ICAO).

Under ICAO's restrictions, numerous Russian-manufactured aircraft equipped with engines that did not meet the new international noise and emission standards were denied the right to operate in the world's largest airports.

Volga-Dnepr Group has been involved in the IL-76TD upgrading programme since 2002, which includes outfitting the aircraft with PS-90A-76 engines and modern avionics that meet the new international noise regulations and safety considerations. The IL-76TD-90VD aircraft has already been to all the countries from where the IL-76 was prohibited.

The transportation costs are estimated at half those of using the Hercules, the only immediate rival of the IL-76TD.

With market research showing a future demand for 15–20 aircraft of this type by 2015, Volga-Dnepr intends to meet the growing demand within a strategy to grow its current fleet of five IL-76TD-90VD aircraft to 15 aircraft in the longer term.

Other heavy-lift aircraft

There is a range of heavy-lift aircraft operating in the lower weight sector of the market, offering specialized lift for heavy pieces of cargo. Many of these aircraft are now very old in commercial aviation terms and many of the modern standard freighters operated by the world's airlines can easily lift heavier items on their main decks.

In November 2011, Emirates SkyCargo, the air freight division of Emirates Airline, set a new record for the heaviest recorded single item ever carried by a Boeing 777 freighter. Weighing in at just under 21.2 tonnes (including packaging), the item – a specialized valve used to seal, control and monitor oil and gas wells – was just short of the aircraft's 21.6-tonne limit.

The AN-26 can carry a 6.5-tonne load and is cheaper to operate than most similar aircraft; however, the Russian-built AN-26 cannot currently obtain traffic rights to fly into certain European countries, such as Germany and Italy.

Although over 900 were built in both military and civilian versions, the 20-tonne payload AN-12 aircraft is banned from operating in EU airspace and a lot of other world regions on the grounds of safety and emissions, severely restricting its use. In terms of configuration, size and capability, the aircraft is similar to the US-built Lockheed C-130 Hercules.

AN-225: the largest aircraft in the skies

Built in 1988 in order to transport the reusable Russian Buran Space Shuttle from its landing strip back to the launch pad, the original objective of the six-engined AN-225 was almost identical to that of the B747 aircraft specially adapted to piggyback the US Space Shuttle.

Two aircraft were ordered, but only one was ever finished. The AN-225 is the largest commercially used transport aircraft in the world and it can carry ultra-heavy and oversize freight, up to 250 tonnes internally on its main deck or 200 tonnes fastened onto its upper fuselage. Cargo carried on the upper fuselage can be 70 metres (230 ft) long.

Owned by Antonov Design Bureau and operated by Ruslan International, the AN-225 is powered by six Lotarev D-18 engines. It has a wingspan of 88.4 metres (290 ft) and a main deck capable of holding 1,220 cubic metres of cargo.

Based on the AN-124, the AN-225 has fuselage extensions added fore and aft of the wings, which received root extensions to increase the span. Two more Ivchenko Progress D-18T turbofan engines were added to the new wing roots, bringing the total to six, and an increased-capacity landing gear system with 32 wheels was designed, some of which are steerable to turn the aircraft within a 60 metre wide runway.

The aircraft's first flight in commercial service departed from Stuttgart, Germany on 3 January 2002, and flew to Thumrait, Oman with 216,000 prepared meals for American military personnel based in the region. This vast number of ready meals was transported on some 375 pallets and weighed 187.5 tonnes.

The AN-225 has since become the workhorse of the Antonov Airlines fleet, transporting objects once thought impossible to move by air, such as locomotives and 150-tonne generators. It has become an asset to international relief organizations for its ability to quickly transport huge quantities of emergency supplies during disaster-relief operations.

On 11 August 2009, the heaviest single-piece item ever sent by a commercial air freight service was loaded on the AN-225. At 16.23 metres (53.2 ft) long and 4.27 metres (14 ft) wide, the consignment – a generator and its loading frame for a gas power plant in Armenia – weighed in at a record 189 tonnes. On 11 June 2010, the AN-225 broke another record when it carried the world's longest piece of air cargo – two new 42-metre (137.8 ft) test wind turbine blades from Tianjin in China to Denmark.

Reliable information on the second AN-225 fuselage has always been sketchy, unconfirmed and surrounded in myth and legend, but according to sources the second aircraft is 60–70 per cent complete, although it would require a large investment to complete construction.

Notable shipments by Antonov aircraft

These are some of the most notable shipments delivered by Antonov Airlines:

- an 88-tonne water turbine for the Tashtakumska Hydroelectric Plant from Kharkov to Tashkent;
- civil engineering vehicles to deal with the consequences of the earthquake in Spitak, Armenia;
- vehicles and systems for resolving the Persian Gulf crisis (mine clearance bulldozers, mobile electric stations, special mine and oil-clearing boats, humanitarian assistance);
- a 135.2-tonne Siemens generator from Düsseldorf, Germany to Delhi, India, air-lifted by the AN-225;
- nuclear fuel in special containers from Habaniya, Iraq to Yekaterinburg (Russia) under the United Nations programme for disarmament of Iraq;
- a 102-tonne locomotive from London, Canada to Dublin, Ireland;
- a 70-tonne generator to Lahore, Pakistan from Doncaster Robin Hood, UK for power station needs;
- a 187.6-tonne power plant generator from Frankfurt-Hahn Airport, Germany to Yerevan (listed in the *Guinness Book of Records*);
- a 95-tonne Putzmeister.

13 Express and mail

Giles Large

Integrators: no time to lose

A quick glance at the worldwide air freight tonnages over the last few years shows the dominance of the express operators over conventional air cargo operations. The mega companies now leading this business – generically known as the integrators because of their fully integrated systems – are able not only to collect and deliver shipments and control them within their own systems, but also offer an accurate tracking service to their customers. With giant fleets of large cargo aircraft, the integrators are removed from the restrictions of using scheduled passenger flights and are able to prioritize these shipments, an ability that is vital to their customers. Conventional airlines, which have in many ways caught up with the integrators, do offer excellent services, but must look after their passengers above all else. Many of the technical systems now in use by freight-carrying airlines owe their existence to the innovation of the integrated express operators.

The rapid development of the international air express sector was probably an unintended consequence of the decision to deregulate the US domestic air cargo market, made by President Jimmy Carter's administration in 1977. Prior to the passing of the Air Cargo Deregulation Act in November of that year, the US domestic air cargo industry was in a sorry state, with carriers reducing service frequencies and, in many cases, dropping routes altogether. A major reason for this was that the US Civil Aeronautics Board (CAB) had been responsible for the economic regulation of all airlines operating aircraft with payloads of over 7,500 lb (3,400 kg). The CAB granted carriers a 'certificate of public convenience and necessity' and also dictated what routes could be operated and what rates airlines could charge for their cargo operations.

Carriers claimed that the rates set by the CAB were too low to support the level of prime-time freighter operations demanded by the market. As a result, the number of US cities served by scheduled freighter operations fell from approximately 50 to about half that figure in the decade before deregulation. There was also a growing tendency for shippers to use contract or charter carriers to move their cargo. Indeed, shortly before deregulation, the CAB itself recognized that all was not well, with its Domestic Freight Investigation concluding that regulated freight rates were 42 per cent below what the industry needed to prosper.

The US Congress took the first legislative steps towards airline economic deregulation in November 1977, when it gave cargo carriers freedom to operate on any domestic route and charge whatever price the market would bear. Congress also declared that one year following enactment of the bill, the CAB could certify new domestic cargo carriers as long as they were found to be 'fit, willing and able'. No longer would there have to be the more demanding, and therefore restrictive, finding of 'public convenience and necessity', as there had been in the past.

Among those taking advantage of this relaxation were a number of major US freight forwarders, such as Airborne and Emery, which leased freighter aircraft and started to develop domestic and, later, international all-cargo services. Another beneficiary was FedEx, which before deregulation had been restricted to carrying express packages and documents in small business jets such as Dassault Falcons. With the lifting of this restriction the company started a programme of rapid expansion, buying a fleet of Boeing 727 freighters, followed by Boeing 737s and the first of its widebody DC-10 freighters.

Deregulation resulted in a huge boost for the air cargo business, both in the US and internationally, but the major winners were those operating in the express package sector. Demand for the overnight delivery of high-value and time-sensitive shipments had started in the early 1970s, but it was deregulation that gave the express operators the freedom to grow rapidly and led to the development of what are now known as 'integrators'.

A simple definition of an integrator is a transport service provider that arranges full-load, door-to-door transportation by selecting and combining the most sustainable and efficient modes of transportation.

Without doubt, integrators are the greatest competitive threat to traditional air cargo operators. US-based integrators increased their domestic market share from 6.5 to 70 per cent in the two decades after deregulation. As their domestic markets neared saturation, these integrators expanded both their geographical reach and their product portfolios to include more traditional heavy-weight international cargo, to the point where they have eaten into the market that was once the preserve of the traditional air cargo operators, such as the airlines and air freight forwarders.

Another key to the success of the integrators was their willingness to advertise heavily and to target specifically those within organizations who are generally given the task of arranging the despatch of documents and small parcels to customers around the world. Whereas before, they would normally have used their own country's postal services, such has been the power of advertising that most will now choose one of the main integrators. Indeed, in much of the international business community, the word 'FedEx' has become a verb, as in the phrase: 'I'll FedEx it to you tonight.'

A good indication of just how dominant the integrators have become is shown in the IATA World Air Transport Statistics for 2011. The top ten carriers of international and domestic cargo, measured in million freight-tonne-kilometres (FTKs) – the tonnage carried multiplied by the distance flown – are:

1   FedEx: 15,939
2   UPS Airlines: 10,566
3   Cathay Pacific: 9,109
4   Korean Airlines: 8,974
5   Emirates: 8,132
6   Lufthansa: 7,674
7   Singapore Airlines: 7,118
8   China Airlines: 5,411
9   EVA Air: 4,882
10 Air France/KLM: 4,702

To an extent, it could be argued that the cosy duopoly enjoyed for so many years by the airlines and forwarders had resulted in industry-wide inertia and the inability to respond quickly enough, if at all, to outside challenges. As an executive of the largest US international freight forwarder, Air Express International (AEI), put it in the mid-1980s, the air cargo industry was a black hole, where 'we dump the freight in and hope it comes out'. As another AEI executive at that time used to tell anyone who would listen: 'Airlines award medals when their flown-as-booked (FAB) hits 90 per cent; integrators fire people if their FAB falls to 98 per cent.' Unfortunately, few in the industry were prepared to listen and even fewer were willing to act on what they heard. AEI was bought by Deutsche Post in 1999, together with the Swiss forwarder Danzas. These two, along with the UK-based forwarder Exel, which was acquired in 2005, now form the basis of DHL's global forwarding and freight division.

DHL

DHL was founded in San Francisco in 1969 by Adrian Dalsey, Larry Hillblom and Robert Lynn when one of the three acted as a courier, carrying a consignment of documents as cabin luggage from San Francisco to Honolulu. In 1971, it became the first US air express operator to offer services to Asia, with a service to the Philippines, followed in 1973 with services to Japan, Hong Kong, Singapore and Australia. In 1976, DHL entered the European market and three years later it expanded its operations to include the carriage of parcels in addition to documents.

In 2000 the integrator signed a strategic agreement with Lufthansa Cargo and Japan Airlines, whereby each airline took a 25 per cent stake in the company. DHL was acquired by Deutsche Post in July 2002, when the German postal group bought the minority shareholdings of the two airlines.

Today, DHL's international network links more than 220 countries and territories worldwide, offering express, air and ocean freight, overland transport, contract logistics solutions as well as international mail services. The Deutsche Post group generates annual revenues of more than €51 billion ($64.25 billion).

International, time-definite courier and express shipments are the core business of DHL's Express Division, with its Time Definite and Same Day services offering a choice of delivery at either a specific time or as quickly as possible. In some markets, this portfolio is complemented by a Day Definite service as well as special services such as Collect and Return and Medical Express. DHL has also increased activities for customers in the life sciences and healthcare sectors, as well as improving processes in clinical trials transport and introducing globally applicable standards. Since 2011, it has tracked all Medical Express shipments in real time, enabling it to respond immediately to any disruptions in the process of transporting these ultra-sensitive shipments.

Other divisions within DHL include Global Forwarding and Freight. DHL Freight is one of the biggest freight forwarders in the European overland market, operating national and international full-truck-load and less-than-truck-load services. It also offers Customs brokerage, warehousing and order fulfilment services.

DHL Global Mail operates one of the world's largest delivery networks, with 38 sales offices and 28 production centres in five continents serving more than 200 countries. It is used predominantly to deliver mail, hybrid mail and parcels, including business-to-customer (b2c) traffic. It currently claims to have a 14 per cent share of the worldwide mail market and is capable of handling six million mail items on a daily basis.

Federal Express (FedEx)

Federal Express, founded by Fred Smith, started overnight services in April 1973 with a fleet of 14 Dassault Falcon 20 business jets operating from Memphis, Tennessee – which still remains the integrator's main global hub. On the first night, it carried just 186 packages to 25 US cities from Rochester in New York state to Miami, Florida.

Federal Express was named due to the patriotic meaning associated with the word 'Federal', which suggested an interest in nationwide economic activity. At that time, Smith hoped to obtain a contract with the Federal Reserve Bank and, although the proposal was denied, he believed the name was a particularly good one for attracting public attention and maintaining name recognition.

Company headquarters were moved to Memphis, a city selected for its geographical location close to the original target market cities for small packages. In addition, the Memphis weather was excellent and rarely caused closures at Memphis International Airport. The airport was also willing to make the necessary improvements for the operation and had additional hangar space readily available.

Today, FedEx Express has the world's largest all-cargo air fleet, consisting of Boeing 777 freighters and MD-11Fs, as well as Airbus A300F and A310F aircraft. The planes have a total daily lift capacity of more than 30 million lb

(14 million kg or 14,000 tonnes). In a 24-hour period, the fleet travels nearly half a million miles, while its couriers log 2.5 million miles each day – the equivalent of 100 trips around the Earth.

In 1965, when he was an undergraduate at Yale University, Smith wrote a term paper about the passenger route systems used by most air freight shippers, which he viewed as economically inadequate. He outlined the need for shippers to have a system designed specifically for air freight that could accommodate time-sensitive shipments such as medicines, computer parts and electronics. Smith also suggested that by using both air and ground transport, package deliveries did not have to take the most direct route, as long as they made it to their destinations within 24 hours. According to the probably apocryphal story, his professor was not particularly impressed with Smith's paper and only gave it a 'C' grade.

In August of 1971, following two tours in Vietnam with the US Marine Corps, Smith bought a controlling interest in Arkansas Aviation Sales, located in Little Rock, Arkansas. While operating his new firm, Smith identified the tremendous difficulties in getting packages and other air freight delivered within one or two days. This dilemma motivated him to do the necessary research for resolving the inefficient distribution system. This led to the development of the hub-and-spoke system for handling air cargo shipments. Every night, a highly coordinated stream of aircraft feed into major hubs, where consignments are sorted and loaded onto aircraft flying to airports nearest to their final destination. FedEx's main hub is in Memphis, while its other major international hubs are at Paris Charles de Gaulle, Dubai and Guangzhou in Southern China. This latter hub replaced the previous major hub at Subic Bay in the Philippines, which FedEx closed in February 2009.

FedEx Corporation provides strategic direction and consolidated financial reporting for the companies that operate collectively under the FedEx name worldwide: FedEx Express, FedEx Ground, FedEx Freight, FedEx Office, FedEx Custom Critical, FedEx Trade Networks, FedEx Supply Chain Solutions and FedEx Services.

FedEx Corporation was formed in January 1998 with the acquisition of Caliber System, which enabled it to offer trucking, forwarding and other services alongside its express product. Through this and future purchases, FedEx sought to build on the strength of its express delivery service and create a more diversified company that included a portfolio of different but related businesses. Caliber subsidiaries included RPS, a small-package ground service; Roberts Express, an expedited, exclusive-use shipping provider; Viking Freight, a regional, less-than-truck-load freight carrier serving the western US; Caribbean Transportation Services, a provider of air freight forwarding between the US, Puerto Rico, the Dominican Republic and the Caribbean; and Caliber Logistics and Caliber Technology, providers of integrated logistics and technology solutions.

In 2006, FedEx Corporation acquired ANC Holdings Limited, a UK domestic express transportation company. This transaction allowed FedEx

Express to directly serve the entire UK domestic market. ANC was then rebranded FedEx UK.

The following year, FedEx Corporation acquired DTW Group's 50 per cent share of the FedEx-DTW International Priority Express joint venture and DTW Group's domestic express network in China. FedEx then launched a domestic express service serving the Chinese market. Also in 2007, FedEx Corporation continued its acquisition of domestic express companies with the acquisitions of Indian express company Prakash Air Freight (PAFEX) and Hungarian express company Flying-Cargo Hungary.

Following the first of several international acquisitions, intercontinental operations began in 1984 with services to Europe and Asia. The following year, FedEx marked its first regularly scheduled flight to Europe. In 1988, the company initiated direct scheduled cargo services to Japan.

Federal Express obtained authority to serve China through a 1995 acquisition of rights from Evergreen International Airlines. Under this authority, Federal Express became at that time the sole US-based, all-cargo carrier with aviation rights to the country.

In 1978, Fred Smith was quoted as saying 'The information about the package is just as important as the package itself.' FedEx now provides customers with access to near real-time information that has led to new supply chain models and efficiencies.

United Parcel Services Inc. (UPS)

Founded in Seattle in 1907 as a messenger company in the US domestic market, UPS has grown into a multi-billion-dollar corporation with its headquarters in Atlanta, Georgia, and total revenues last year of $53.1 billion. Today, UPS is a global company with one of the most recognized and admired brands in the world. As the largest express carrier and package delivery company in the world, it is also a leading provider of specialized transportation, logistics, capital and e-commerce services, managing the flow of goods, funds and information in more than 200 countries and territories worldwide.

Since becoming a publicly traded company in 1999, UPS has significantly expanded the scope of its capabilities, primarily through the acquisition of more than 40 companies, including industry leaders in trucking and air freight, retail shipping and business services, Customs brokerage, finance and international trade services. As a result, the company's relationship with many of its customers has deepened to include much more than the provision of basic transportation services.

The company, also known to many as 'Big Brown' due to the distinctive colour of its truck and aircraft fleet, is most certainly big by just about any measure. It has 398,300 employees worldwide and last year it handled four billion packages and documents, or 15.8 million packages and documents each day. It serves more than 220 countries and territories around the world, including every address in North America and Europe.

UPS operates 1,860 cargo handling and sorting facilities and it has a delivery fleet of nearly 95,000 package cars, vans, trucks and motorcycles. The UPS freighter fleet consists of 226 aircraft and, in addition, it charters a further 297 freighters. These aircraft serve 382 airports in the US and 323 more around the world.

Its main US hub is Louisville, Kentucky, while other major hubs are in Philadelphia, Dallas, Ontario, Chicago-Rockford and Columbia. Its main European hub is Cologne/Bonn in Germany and its Asia Pacific hubs are in Shanghai, Shenzhen and Hong Kong. Latin America and the Caribbean are served from Miami, while Canada is served from its hub in Hamilton, Ontario.

TNT

TNT Express is an international courier delivery services company with headquarters in Hoofddorp, the Netherlands. The firm has fully owned operations in 65 countries and delivers documents, parcels and pieces of freight to over 200 countries. The company recorded sales of over €7.2 billion ($92.96 billion) in 2011.

Formerly an operating division of TNT NV, TNT Express was demerged from its parent company on 26 May 2011, taking a listing on the Euronext Amsterdam Stock Exchange. TNT NV subsequently renamed itself PostNL.

The company operates road and air transportation networks in Europe, the Middle East and Africa, Asia-Pacific and the Americas. It employs 77,000 people and runs a fleet of 30,000 road vehicles and 46 aircraft. TNT Express aircraft operate under the IATA code of TAY (TNT Airways).

On 19 March 2012, UPS announced its intention to acquire TNT Express for $6.7 billion. In July 2012, UPS stated that the TNT Express acquisition was expected to be completed by the fourth quarter of the year. In fact the deal was cancelled.

Postal services

Parcelforce

For over 14 years, Parcelforce Worldwide has provided a vital link for British businesses needing to send express shipments internationally as well as domestically within the UK. It has a long history as part of the Royal Mail Group and prides itself on the dedication of its staff to delivering high-quality services for over 30,000 customers across the country.

Recent years have seen enormous changes in the marketplace and Parcelforce Worldwide has responded with major investments in technology, including the opening of an operational hub centrally located at Coventry, in the UK Midlands region.

Parcelforce Worldwide is part of the Express Mail Service (EMS) network, bringing together the experience and resources of postal services worldwide.

EMS offers customers market-leading services around the globe through its global priority products.

EMS is an international postal express mail service for documents and merchandise, offered by postal operators of the Universal Postal Union (UPU).

The UPU is an inter-governmental organization and the primary forum for cooperation between governments, postal organizations and other stakeholders in the worldwide postal sector. It works to maintain the universal network, establishes the rules for international mail exchanges among its 191 members and improves the quality of service for customers.

The EMS Cooperative was created in 1998 within the framework of the UPU. Its main objective is to promote cooperation between members to allow them to provide customers with a high-quality, competitive EMS service worldwide.

Parcelforce Worldwide is also part of the E Parcel Group (EPG) network, which is ideally suited for b2c and c2c deliveries across Europe, through the use of postal administrations.

The network uses around 400 air and road transport links daily to provide day-certain guaranteed deliveries, which can be tracked from posting to final delivery, with over 12 million parcels handled annually within the network.

China Postal Express & Logistics

Approved by the State Council, China Postal Express & Logistics was co-founded by China Post Group and provincial postal companies as a state-owned limited company in June 2010. The company is the largest integrated express and logistics service provider with the longest history of business operation and the widest coverage in China.

China Postal Express & Logistics consists of 31 fully owned provincial subsidiaries, as well as China Postal Airlines and China Post Logistics. China Postal Express & Logistics is mainly engaged in domestic express, international express, contract logistics and less-than-truck-load freight. Domestic and international express provides premium, standard and economy shipping products in terms of delivery time and also operates some value-added services such as COD (cash on delivery). The contract logistics operation covers the overall process of supply chain management, including warehousing and transport.

United States Postal Service (USPS)

Global Express Guaranteed is the fastest USPS international shipping service, with transportation and guaranteed delivery by FedEx Express services. It features date-certain delivery in 1–3 business days to more than 190 countries, with a money-back guarantee to all destinations.

Case study: the Great Package Race – testing the promises

How do express packages move so quickly around the world? Anywhere in the world in 72 hours, before 10.30 a.m. next business day – there are a lot of proud commercial claims made by the express delivery providers. This book has already looked at the operations of the global express delivery companies, but what are the actual on-time success rates for these expensive deliveries?

Back in 2003, the Supply Chain & Logistics Institute at Georgia Institute of Technology came up with a way to monitor the performance of the big express delivery operators. The findings over the years have proved interesting and a lot of fun for the students taking part in the exercise – as well as sometimes being a little embarrassing for the unknowing contestants in what has become known by many, and feared by a few, as the Great Package Race.

Each express carrier has its own freight network through which a package travels and the experience of each shipment depends on the structure of the network, considers John J. Bartholdi, Manhattan Associates Professor of Supply Chain Management and Director of Global Research, Supply Chain & Logistics Institute at the Atlanta-based Georgia Institute of Technology.

He is the man who first conceived the idea for the Great Package Race as a way his students could reinforce their knowledge of how express delivery packages travel from the sender to their consignee as part of an enjoyable, hands-on learning experience.

He explained:

> Each year we race packages from The Supply Chain & Logistics Institute at Georgia Tech to sites around the world via different international parcel carriers – UPS, FedEx and DHL, and in the later years of the race the US Postal Service. . . . We choose locations to challenge the business processes of the multinational package carriers, then observe the results.

It is remarkable that most packages eventually reached their destinations, even under the difficult circumstances and some of the near-impossible delivery scenarios being dreamed up over the years. There have been notable successes, but there have been some dramatic lapses as well. One package was carried back-and-forth across the Atlantic Ocean nine times before being delivered. Another was sent to Costa Rica instead of Croatia.

One carrier claimed that the destination country on one package did not exist – and there are nearly 200,000 inhabitants on the Pacific island of Samoa who are still a little disappointed by that particular finding.

There have been dramatically close finishes as well. In 2006, UPS beat DHL to Croatia by only three minutes. A race to Singapore ended in a dead heat, when the delivery folk from UPS and FedEx arrived at the door simultaneously, even though the packages had travelled along completely different routes.

'Each race has a theme and we will vary the theme so that one time we will ship, for example, to exotic locales, another time to centres of business, and another time to our mothers', Bartholdi said – and sometimes just to be plain difficult and test the mettle of the competitors to the full.

He added the proviso that the Great Package Race has never been a carefully constructed business experiment: it is an event designed to stimulate student interest and to have fun. Many of the destination choices have not been representative of most international shipping lanes and may not reflect the service levels to be expected from the express carriers to more typical mainstream destinations. Therefore, the results may not be a reliable basis for choice of carrier, he cautioned.

Ready, set, go!

At the start of the race, after local pick-up, each package gets driven to a local freight terminal and then flown to one of the major sorting facilities the carriers operate at major international airports in the US midwest region: UPS is in Louisville, Kentucky; FedEx uses Indianapolis, Indiana or Memphis, Tennessee; and DHL during most of the races used Wilmington, Ohio before relocating its main US hub to Cincinnati/North Kentucky International Airport.

The very first running of the Great Package Race in 2003 involved a straightforward point-to-point delivery from Georgia Tech to contemporary logistics scholars at the Logistics Institute Asia-Pacific in Singapore, with just FedEx and UPS being given packages – and the result of the first contest was extraordinary.

Both packages were processed through a sorting facility in the US midwest on their way to Anchorage, still a major hub for US–Far East air cargo shipments. The UPS package was transported on a B747 freighter from Anchorage to Osaka, then on a B767F to Taipei and finally on a B757 to Singapore. The FedEx delivery routed through a sorting facility in Indianapolis on its way to Alaska, before flying transpacific to Tokyo-Narita and arriving at Singapore Changi International Airport the next day.

The office to which they were delivered in Singapore was open, but not very busy on a Saturday, so the front door was locked. There was a knock on the door and both the FedEx and the UPS delivery men were standing on the step. Legend has it that the UPS courier held the door open for the FedEx messenger – so strictly speaking FedEx arrived first across the threshold. Giving the UPS man extra credit for courtesy, Georgia Tech logistics students declared the event a nose-to-nose dead heat.

Now, Singapore Customs is very efficient and the packages were logged through official channels within minutes of landing. Georgia Tech students found that the UPS arrival scan at Changi showed 17 January at 2121hrs. For FedEx the arrival information read 18 January at 0600hrs. So big pointer was there to be observed by the participating students as they scrutinized the shipment documents online – in the fast-moving word of air freight, more time can be lost on the ground than in the air.

Stepping up the pace

Spurred on by enthusiasm, the pace stepped up considerably the following year, involving deliveries to Lomé (the capital of Togo on the West African coast); Haifa in Israel; and Bangalore (India), well before the local authorities had decided to complicate matters for international package delivery providers by renaming their city Bengalaru.

'We phoned each of the carriers at 1100hrs on 5 April 2004 and asked them to come pick up packages', Bartholdi said. DHL had been selected to join the original UPS and FedEx participants in the contest and, unknowingly, it entered the Great Package Race with great enthusiasm – a driver had arrived within minutes of the shipment request having been placed as he had been in the immediate area, Bartholdi remembered. 'Unfortunately, we did not have the shipping forms ready and had to wait for them to be faxed from DHL.'

FedEx won the 2004 race, delivering at 1540hrs on 7 April 2004 – aided by the integrator's direct air service from its Memphis hub to Israel – and DHL, also with a direct flight from the US to Israel, came in second. Local boy UPS finished embarrassingly far behind, with the shipment entrusted to its care beset by processing errors, rerouting and flight delays. Georgia Tech logistics students recorded that the package to Lomé was finally delivered on 22 June after crossing the Atlantic Ocean nine times and with a shipment 'passport' showing entry visas for Atlanta, Louisville, Philadelphia, Cologne, Paris and Johannesburg.

Another good point for burgeoning logistical intellects to consider for the future – direct flights can be the most effective when time is of the essence.

After a break in 2005, Bartholdi's logistics students sent deliveries in 2006 to Ouagadougou (the capital of Burkina Faso, in west central Africa); Punta Arenas (in Chilean Patagonia and the southernmost city in the Western Hemisphere); Split (on the Dalmatian coast of Croatia); and Surabaya (capital of East Java, Indonesia).

Routing via Atlanta, Miami and Santiago, DHL delivered first to the address in Punta Arenas, arriving at 1626hrs on 18 April.

UPS won ahead of DHL by only three minutes on the delivery to Split – although the recipient was not home to receive the package. 'We consider the race over when the package reaches its destination – even if the recipient is not there to receive it', Georgia Tech said. UPS returned the next day to hand over the delivery.

A keying error by a courier on the FedEx delivery to Split, who tapped in CO instead of CR, apparently resulted in the package first being sent to Costa Rica instead of Croatia. Over the years of the race, Georgia Tech said its findings have brought to light a surprising number of processing mishaps, especially keying errors that have delayed packages.

Demonic intentions

In the 2007 contest, as Bartholdi's students really warmed to the idea of the Great Package Race – and subsequently became more demonic in their intentions – shipments were despatched to Apia (a town on Upulu, one of the islands comprising the Pacific Ocean country of Samoa, which has no street addresses); Florianopolis (a remote island off the coast of southern Brazil); Harare (capital of Zimbabwe, a city experiencing hyperinflation and political unrest); Tikrit (at the time the centre of Sunni insurgency in Iraq and the nearest big town to Saddam Hussein's birthplace); and – a 'curve ball' to confuse the delivery giants – Yangon, the new name for Rangoon, the capital of Myanmar, which even today the British Broadcasting Corporation still refers to as Burma in its newscasts.

'Before starting the race we phoned each carrier and asked them whether they foresaw any difficulties in shipping to our destinations', Bartholdi said. 'FedEx and UPS both claimed that they could not ship to Myanmar, but could not explain why. DHL said that it could ship in to but not out of Myanmar.'

The phone representative at UPS said that there was no country named Samoa (in 1997 Western Samoa changed its name to Samoa, but at the time of the 2007 race it still existed as Western Samoa in the UPS database).

Bartholdi said:

> We ignored the warnings and shipped all packages because in the past the phone representatives have been a rich source of misinformation. We phoned each company at 0830hrs to ask them to pick up our packages after noon. FedEx picked up at 1230hrs, DHL at 1346hrs, and UPS at 1525hrs.

UPS and FedEx initially accepted but later returned the packages addressed to Myanmar. FedEx provided no reason; UPS provided a reason but it was unintelligible ('Invoice and receiver IRS # required'). UPS carried the Georgia Tech package intended for Tikrit as far as Dubai and then returned it stating 'this service is not available'. The Georgia Tech website on the race proclaims: 'After sitting in Louisville for seven days the package was returned. We were billed nonetheless.'

DHL won the contest – the express carrier was first to three destinations on the list and came in a close second in the remaining two.

Important findings made by Georgia Tech logistics students were that the prices of the shipments varied considerably. For example, one carrier charged $94.45 to Apia while another charged $169.10. Prices to Harare ranged from $126 to $336.

Many of the tracking reports were two to ten days behind real time and accordingly not of much use except as historical documents. This was true especially as the packages got closer to their destinations. They concluded that this was possibly due to the limitations of local subcontractors.

Bartholdi added that some of the express carriers had observed – quite fairly, he agreed – that the destinations being chosen in the now well-publicized race were not representative of actual business flows. Therefore, the 2007 race was supplemented with another run from Atlanta to Singapore. Packages were sent on 3 July and all were delivered on 6 July. The results reflected those of the larger race: DHL was first, arriving at 1038hrs; FedEx was next, at 1114hrs; and UPS was third, delivering at 1551hrs.

Hard-to-reach places

Creative thinking continued to run amok as the 2008 race was put together. This time its was themed as 'Hard-To-Reach Places' and packages were despatched to Pitcairn Island (the remote outcrop in the Pacific Ocean, where some descendants of the conspirators of the infamous Mutiny on the Bounty incident in 1789 still reside); Khartoum, Sudan (where the White and Blue Niles meet); Almaty, Kazakhstan (ancestral home of the apple); Uluru, which even some Australians cannot tell you is the big red monolith in the centre of the outback famously known as Ayers Rock; and Gaza City in the Palestinian Territories.

For this event a new competitor entered the race, the United States Postal Service. Packages were sent by priority mail, rather than as expedited mail, which would have been more directly comparable. Yet the logistics students were to discover that some US Postal Service shipments were to arrive nearly as quickly as the express deliveries by the commercial carriers and would cost one-tenth the price of express carrier services.

Bartholdi noted:

> Over several weeks preceding the start, we phoned each carrier several times and asked them whether they foresaw any difficulties in shipping to our destinations. We frequently got different answers, depending on with whom we spoke. Some of the carriers gave us different information each time we called.
>
> We ignored the warnings and shipped all packages because in the past the phone representatives have been a rich source of mis-information. We phoned each company in the morning and asked

them to pick up our packages after 2PM. DHL picked up at 1430hrs, FedEx at 1440hrs, and UPS at 1640hrs. We had to take our packages to the US Postal Services counter.

Confusion followed. None of the carriers offered home delivery in Yulara (the nearest town to Uluru); instead they delivered to the local post office, which held the packages for pick-up. All of the carriers agreed by phone that they would deliver packages to Pitcairn Island, but most returned the packages undelivered citing 'no service'.

Several carriers returned the packages intended for Khartoum, telling Georgia Tech logistics that Sudan was embargoed, but without further explanation. UPS said that it could ship to Gaza, Palestine. DHL lists the destination as Gaza City, Israel. The US Postal Service would not accept our package, saying that they could not find it in their IT system.

In retrospect, Batholdi admitted that the destination addresses chosen for the 2008 race were probably too difficult: no organization other than the US Postal Service was able to deliver to Pitcairn Island, which was too isolated, or to the Gaza Strip, which was in political turmoil. Only the US Postal Service was able to deliver to Khartoum.

Georgia Tech logistics students concluded that the government-run mail provider enjoys greater 'connectivity' than the express package carriers because it hands over to local postal services for the final leg of delivery. This could also be a disadvantage, unless the local postal services were equally as effective, it was noted.

Quite some time after the race had been run, and all but forgotten, on 16 December 2008, Bartholdi said the students at Georgia Tech 'were surprised and delighted' to receive an e-mail from Ms L. Brown of Pitcairn Island:

> Dear Sir or Madam: We received a parcel on the 11th December, this parcel contained Baby Ruth bars which were handed out to the community. . . . The parcel arrived in good condition, all our mail arrives on the supply ship then after the sorting process is finished everyone collects their mail which is normally at the end of the day, so you still have a long wait until you can find out what has been delivered.

The e-mail concluded: 'Our next supply ship is not until March 2009.'

Bartholdi enthused: 'On the basis of this, and its successful delivery to Khartoum, and its amazingly low prices, we have to tip our hats to the US Postal Service.' Today, in 2013, the US Postal Service offers Global Express Guaranteed as its fastest international shipping service, with transportation and delivery by FedEx Express. It features date-certain delivery in 1–3 business days to more than 190 countries with a money-back guarantee to all destinations.

Mongolia bound – or not

In 2009 identical packages were sent to Ulan Bator, capital city of Mongolia; and to Opp, a small town (population 6,000) in southern Alabama whose economy is shaped by small textile and agricultural businesses and the surrounding farms (cotton, peanuts, soybeans), chicken houses and pine forests.

They did not use DHL to send to Opp, because it no longer offers domestic-only air or ground express services within the US. The packages to Ulan Bator included the usual Georgia Tech paraphernalia, but were also packed with peanut butter, oatmeal, books and a selection of sweets for an international team of volunteers working to improve the public health system in Mongolia.

This year they did not pre-announce the start, lest that tempt competitors to anticipate and plan for the race. They took the packages to Kwik Copy, a commercial shipping service that feeds UPS, FedEx and DHL. However, they were not able to accept the packages intended for the US Postal Service – after 9/11 all large packages to be mailed through the postal service must be presented for inspection at a postal facility. They immediately drove to a nearby post office to mail the US Postal Service packages.

In both Kwik Copy and the post office the clerks seemed quite matter-of-fact about accepting parcels to Ulan Bator, but they expressed some incredulity about whether Opp is a real place.

USPS was the only carrier to quote the full cost when the package was delivered to them. The other prices would not be known until the credit card bill was received weeks later.

The package to Ulan Bator seemed to have disappeared within the postal service(s), with no visibility other than recording acceptance of the package. Tracking was lost altogether beginning 10 October as the system was down for 'system upgrades' until 13 October. Even then, there was no visibility until delivery – or rather, pick-up. The package was sent to a branch post office, which phoned the consignee to pick up the package, despite the fact that the main post office was within three blocks of the consignee's address. The consignee reported that this package 'showed more wear and tear' than the others, but nothing was damaged.

The FedEx tracking system showed the destination in Mongolia as 'Maanbaater', which is likely an error in data input (a reliable source of problems in past races). This may be responsible for the fact that, from Japan, the package was sent south to Guangzhou, China, which seemed to be going in the wrong direction. After three days in southern China, the package was returned north, to Incheon, South Korea.

USPS priority mail was the first to Opp and was the cheapest by far to both destinations. But for destinations outside the US you must sacrifice visibility and speed. Another advantage is that USPS prices are known in advance of shipping.

DHL was first to Ulan Bator, more evidence of its strong international network. UPS phoned the same day to ask for directions, but did not deliver until the next day, despite the local representative being only 500 metres away.

For most carriers, visibility diminished as the package got closer to Ulan Bator, which is presumably near the edges of their networks. It was not unusual to go 2–3 days between updates to the tracking system, and one gap was five days. USPS provided no meaningful visibility. DHL seemed best of the group in this regard, with the most frequent updates.

Pointers observed during the 2009 race were that while the tracking systems displayed the actual day of delivery, several listed times that were hours earlier than reported by the recipients. Perhaps the packages were marked as delivered when they were loaded on local trucks.

The tracking systems of two of the four carriers were non-operational for at least part of the time, and a regular source of problems, again, was the inexact transcription of paperwork to the carrier's IT system, when the destination may become garbled.

Preparing to race again

Unfortunately, due to unforeseen circumstances, the 2012 race could not be run but it is hoped to continue again in 2013. Bartholdi observed that Georgia Tech would always welcome suggestions for subsequent competitions, when a set of Georgia Tech baseball caps, T-shirts and other suitable paraphernalia would be sent somewhere – in fact anywhere – in the world.

Georgia Tech has even organized a companion event, the Great Container Race, in which it sent 40-foot shipping containers full of medical supplies by alternate routes and carriers to a hospital in Ghana.

Bartholdi sums up that many of the destination choices have not been representative of most international shipping lanes and may not reflect the service levels to be expected from the express carriers to more typical destinations.

'For destinations, like ours, that are outside the larger channels of inter-national commerce, packages are eventually transferred to local carriers who are subcontracted to the multinationals', which often leads to some lost visibility into the delivery chain, he explained.

Bartholdi concluded: 'Just like the Atlanta Braves football team, UPS is the home team at Georgia Tech and we wish them well; but everyone plays by the same rules and we "call them as we see them" – there are no favourites.'

Ian Martin Jones

14 Technology in air freight

The impact of technology on the air freight process

The acceptance of electronic systems for cargo processing has been somewhat slower by the air freight industry than many others. The leading airlines such as Lufthansa, Air France, Emirates, etc. were quick to see the operational advantages but overall progress has been disappointing. IATA itself is at the leading edge of the drive to engage more operators in electronic cargo processing, thus eliminating paper and waste, while streamlining and creating more efficiency. When the integrators – Fedex, UPS, DHL, etc. – started operating, the adoption of efficient systems was considered vital to their success in order to track the millions of shipments they carried. After much heel-tapping, the conventional air freight community was forced to follow in order to be competitive. The old method of telephone and fax was not only slow, but expensive. While the major carriers and forwarders accepted the new technology and set up their own internal systems, many did not, especially forwarders.

Today's systems provide electronic cargo processing, including EDI, messaging, flight manifests, Customs declarations and compliance, flight schedules, status tracking, web-based tracking and other such electronic features. These systems include use of barcodes and other identifying methods, technology in warehouse handling and monitoring, central databases for control, problem solving, sorting, billing, tracking, tracing and delivery.

Solutions and systems

It is perhaps surprising, given the technological sophistication of the aircraft, handling equipment and warehouse inventory control systems, that the air cargo industry was until very recently dependent on the filling in and exchange of paper documents. According to IATA, each air cargo shipment carried with it as many as 30 paper documents as it made its way from shipper to consignee, via the forwarder, trucker, terminal operator, airline, ground and ramp handlers and Customs authorities. IATA calculated that the industry generated 7,800 tonnes of documents annually, equivalent to the carrying capacity of 80 B747 freighters.

Even where there was a growing use of computer-based message systems, most of these were developed independently and often in-house by the major airlines, with the result that ground handlers were forced to use a plethora of old, cumbersome legacy systems to communicate with their airline customers. The arrival of IATA-led initiatives, such as Cargo 2000 (C2K) and e-freight, coupled with the development of the internet into a universally used business tool, has done much to remove the pen-pushing drudgery from the offices of ground handlers.

Electronic air waybills (e-AWBs) are now commonplace, as are status updates and information on special cargo, such as dangerous goods or express shipments. Evermore stringent security controls mean that more pre-arrival, or pre-shipment, data must now be sent to the airlines and on to Customs and other authorities in the country of destination.

Customs authorities are now requiring entries, as well as security information, in electronic format. In Europe, the most recent Customs development is the Import Control System (ICS). Although the airlines are responsible for submitting ICS data to Customs, most have appointed handlers as their agents and it is now down to these ground handlers to ensure the correct information is obtained in time to make a submission.

The computer systems can alert handlers if ICS data has not arrived, when there are problems with the data, such as errors or inconsistencies, or if Customs has rejected an entry for any reason. The EU's Export Control System (ECS) tends to be more straightforward, as it deals with master air waybills (MAWBs), while the ICS deals with house air waybills (HAWBs). The EU is now considering changing the cut-off time at which ICS data must be submitted before a flight from two hours to five hours, so that Customs authorities can return a 'do not load' message if required.

IATA e-freight

IATA launched its e-freight project with the aim of taking the paper out of air cargo and replacing it with cheaper, more accurate and more reliable electronic messaging.

Benefits of e-freight include the following:

- lower costs, with an average annual saving of between $3.1 and $4.9 billion for the industry, depending on the level of adoption;
- faster supply chain transit times – the ability to send shipment documentation before the cargo itself can reduce the end-to-end transport cycle time by an average of 24 hours;
- greater accuracy – electronic documents allow auto-population, allowing one-time electronic data entry at the point of origin, which reduces delays to shipments due to inaccurate or inconsistent data entry. Electronic documents also have a lower risk of being misplaced, so shipments will no longer be delayed because of missing documentation;

- regulatory compliance – where it is implemented, e-freight meets all international and local regulations relating to the provision of electronic documents and data required by Customs, civil aviation and other regulatory authorities.

By the end of 2011, e-freight was live with 48 airlines in 42 countries, representing over 80 per cent of international tonnage, while 430 airports worldwide offered e-freight. The plan is to have 100 per cent e-freight coverage by 2015.

Cargo 2000

Cargo 2000 (C2K) defines quality standards for the supply chain, improving the efficiency of the industry, enhancing customer service and reducing costs for all participants through implementation of a programme of agreed business and automation standards which are measurable and promote quality competitive performance. The C2K Master Operating Plan (MOP) has been developed based on detailed customer research and with the assistance of leading IT companies. It sits at the heart of an air cargo industry-wide process control and reporting system that in turn drives data management and corrective action systems. By reducing the number of individual processes in the air cargo supply chain from 40 to just 19, C2K is less labour-intensive and improves the processes for managing shipments in a paperless environment. It substantially reduces time spent managing irregularities, such as service failures, cuts the time required for manual track-and-trace procedures and leads to a reduction in service recovery costs. Since 2010, C2K has been offering open access to its standard processes as part of its continuous initiative to improve quality management for customers and service providers across the air cargo supply chain. C2K's quality management system is being implemented in three distinct phases. The key to the MOP is the creation of a unique 'route map' for individual shipments that is monitored and measured throughout the delivery cycle of each shipment.

Phase 1 manages airport-to-airport movements – shipment planning and tracking at the MAWB level. Once a booking is made, a plan is automatically created with a series of checkpoints against which the transportation of every air cargo shipment is managed and measured. This enables the system to alert C2K members to any exceptions to the plan, allowing them to respond proactively to fulfil their customers' expectations.

Phase 2 is responsible for shipment planning and tracking at the HAWB level and provides interactive monitoring of the door-to-door movement.

The third and final phase of C2K manages shipment planning and tracking at the individual piece level, plus document tracking. This provides real-time management of the transportation channel at the piece level. It will also control the flow of information, which will be vital for current and future security requirements. In Phase 3, the control of information is most important as the necessity for paper will be limited to the bare minimum required by law. In the attempt to operate in a paperless environment, the IATA e-freight initiative and C2K complement each other.

A view from the marketplace

One of the pioneers in providing simple and inexpensive systems for freight forwarders was London-based Geoff Stowe, who has, over the years, through his company Redberry Software, developed a wide range of user-friendly products for customers. Here he outlines his strategies and progression until today.

*   *   *

Redberry Software developed computer software for freight forwarders first in 1987, when IBM-compatible computers became prevalent and readily available at what seemed, at the time, good value for money at around £2,000. The Customs Single Administrative Document (SAD C88) had just become a European standard in 1988. This consisted of a header page followed by, if necessary, continuation sheets. However, all Import and Export Customs declarations had to use this single form so which boxes had to be filled in depended on the type of declaration, with thousands of permutations; perfect for a computer system, but difficult for a human being with a typewriter.

This brings us to the backbone of the air freight industry – the typewriter, which is still the rogue of the air freight industry even in 2012. Electronic data interchange (EDI) has always been the goal of the forward-thinking airlines. Unfortunately, some airlines did not think far enough ahead and some developing world airlines are still forcing forwarders to use the pre-printed multi-part MAWB even today. The most important message to the airline when a freight forwarder is sending a shipment is the freight waybill (FWB) message. This message is a précis of the information in the MAWB. The message structure is defined by IATA and is the de facto standard for messaging in air cargo, called Cargo Interchange Message Procedures (Cargo-IMP).

Some airlines still have what are described as 'legacy systems' in operation, written many years ago, working just fine, using early versions of Cargo-IMP messages. However, the messages have been developing in their sophistication. New data elements were added and new versions of the same message were developed, so the current latest version is FWB/16. That is no help to an airline with an old legacy system that can only accept an FWB/6. In order to allow message conversion between different systems using different versions, the cargo community system (CCS) was developed. However, some of these are very regional and others are truly international.

Younger and more fortunate airlines, such as Emirates, were not stuck with old legacy systems, and were able to write their system in a modern language from scratch. At the time of writing, Emirates is still the only airline that will accept an FWB message over the internet by e-mail, and will respond by e-mail with a Flight Status Unsolicited (FSU) message as the freight status changes from booked through to delivered – and this is achieved without using a third-party CCS.

If the airline can be sent the FWB message before the freight is delivered for carriage, then there is no need to retype the data into the airline system, making a great saving. One airline that tried to develop a forwarders system was British Airways, which actually researched our software at Redberry and decided it was too comprehensive for their requirements. They completely forgot that it was the requirements of their customers, the freight forwarders, that they should be looking to fulfil – as well as their own. The system was called Cargo Airline Reservation And Tracking (CARAT). A major part of a freight forwarder's business is creating consolidated freight shipments on a HAWB and putting this on a single MAWB. CARAT did not support the HAWB, so the system had limited success and was abandoned in 1999.

Our forwarders' software, on the other hand, did all that the forwarder required and it could message as well. The major airline communication network is from a French company called Societe Internationale Telecommunications Aeronautiques (SITA). Redberry did a lot of messaging work with SITA in the early 1990s and actually had a SITA address – LONJSXS – to develop this messaging in our software. Unfortunately, joining the SITA network at that time was far too expensive for the average freight forwarder, and while we were able to demonstrate the principle of forwarder to airline messaging and vice versa, it was not a viable proposition in the real world at that time.

What our software was able to do was create a neutral air waybill (NAWB), which is a continuous two-part pre-printed form that could be used for any airline. Some airlines jumped at the chance to save money by not having to hand out pre-printed forms from their airline, others refused to accept them, preferring to continue to use their own stock. Until then we had to use daisy wheel printers to thump through the 12-part set and they, like our old friend the typewriter, were becoming obsolete.

We recommended to our forwarder customers that where the airline refused the NAWB then they simply used the same MAWB number on the airline-supplied cut set and attached the airline copy from the cut set to the back of the NAWB. Slowly these airlines realized they were wasting money and to supply NAWB numbers instead of hard copies of the MAWB was far more cost-effective.

I think that here I should explain what exactly a MAWB number is – it is 11 digits long and the first three digits are unique to the airline, identifying it. The next seven are a rolling number and the last digit is a check digit arrived at by simply dividing the previous seven digits by seven and the last digit is the remainder of the calculation. That is why the last digit of a MAWB number is always between zero and six.

The next major change was the introduction of IATA labelling standards, called the IATA 606b Air Freight Label. This contains a barcode of the MAWB number. European airlines all demanded this label and put in scanners to read the air freight labels' rolling four-digit number that referred to the piece number followed by the MAWB number. The concept was that in the event of a short shipment, the forwarder would know which box was missing and hence be able to identify the contents. I have never yet met a freight forwarder with the time on his hands to match the labels to the box numbering.

In 1998 we demonstrated a plain paper MAWB, which was the logical way to go before the paperless concept that was the industry dream at the time. The airlines were still desperate to receive the FWB message and generally they were not getting them. The use of the internet and communicating by e-mail had now emerged and several CCSs were starting to accept the FWB message in an e-mail and then forward it on to the airlines, usually over the SITA network.

As the FWB message was a small message, we created a blank plain paper page containing a two-dimensional barcode in the format of PDF417, a standard barcode. The idea is that the FWB message is on a plain piece of paper that travels with the MAWB and is scanned on arrival. That really excited the airlines until they discovered that they had all purchased scanners that only read the single-dimensioned barcode in the 606b label and only our demonstration scanner could read a PDF417 barcode and extract the FWB message, while their scanners could not.

Below is a sample FWB message, which is quite readable and small, sent by the freight forwarder:

```
FWB/15
176-74618246DXBMCT/T2K2
RTG/MCTEK
SHP
/EXPOLANKA FREIGHT DUBAI LLC
/PO BOX 28998
/UAE/TEL2990322
/AE
CNE
/EXPOLANKA FREIGHT MCT LLC
/P O BOX 2914
/MUSCAT PC
/OM/OMAN
ACC/GEN/FREIGHT PREPAID
CVD/AED//PP/NVD/NCV/XXX
RTD/1/P2/K2/CM/R80.00/T80.00
/NG/CONSOLIDATION
OTH/P/AWA100.00MCC35.00
PPD/WT80.00
```

/OA100.00/OC35.00/CT215.00
ISU/18OCT10/DUBAI
OSI/PKGS MARKED AND ADDRESSED PLS INFM CGNEE UPON
    ARRIVAL OF CGO REF//10025663/AGT/EXPOLANKAFREIGHT
    D/DXB

Below is a typical FSU message from the airline:

FSU/6
176-74618246DXBMCT/T2K2
RCS/18OCT1815/DXB/T2K2/SYED HASAN

RCS means received consignment from shipper (forwarder).

In 1998 we provided software to a third-party supplier to British Airways that created MAWBs for internal airline freight, called service freight. As it was service freight it did not have to wait for the IATA resolution in 2000 for a plain paper MAWB – plain paper was used from day one. What it did also was to demonstrate the power of the internet. Instead of British Airways putting in a dedicated computer telephone line some 80 miles to London Heathrow Airport, we sent the FWB message to SITA in Atlanta via e-mail. Atlanta then sent it back to Heathrow over the SITA network.

Also, by 1998 several airlines were offering shipment tracking on their websites. We had earlier decided to put all airlines with web tracking on our own tracking website with links directly to the airline's tracking page. Prior to this the first job of the morning would be 'post flighting', phoning up the airline to see if the freight on the previous day had in fact departed. This was a time-consuming and costly process for both freight forwarder and airline. Now the internet had started to speed up and become reliable, more and more airlines offered web tracking. Our own website received a total of 90 million tracking enquiries by late 2012, an astronomical saving in telephone calls for freight forwarders.

Several important events happened in 1999 and 2000; C2K was created as a quality organization measurable and reported on by IATA. This is mainly between a select few airlines and major multinational forwarders, a total of around 80 participants, and the statistics of messaging between parties is reported on a monthly basis on the IATA website. Also, the association created an amendment to IATA Resolution 600a to allow a MAWB to be printed on plain paper. Then, of course, there was, in my opinion, the biggest organized worldwide scam ever, the Y2K compliance designed to cope with the millennium changeover, which hit every computerized sector of every industry. Y2K consultants sprang up from everywhere preying on the general public and even business ignorance of computer technicalities and fear of the unknown.

Early computer programs had limited storage to use, so many programs stored only the last two digits of the date. Our original software did the same, but as we developed it first in 1987, the programme simply stated that if the date is less than 80, precede it with 20 and if it is 80 or more, precede it with 19. We were inundated by 'consultants' who were completely baffled when they were told our current software was Y2K compliant – but not 2080 compliant.

In January 2000 we ran an advert on the back page of the leading industry trade newspaper, *Air Cargo News*, stating that a Y2K consultant was seen in January sprinkling white powder on the pavement in London's Piccadilly. When asked what he was doing he said he was sprinkling elephant repellent. On being informed that there were no elephants in London he replied that this shows how good the powder is and what a great job he is doing. At Redberry we wonder what all the other Y2K consultants are doing now?! The sentiment was met with great support from the air cargo industry.

Also in January 2000 we opened our Asia software development offices. Starting with a completely clean sheet and armed with a history of cargo knowledge, we set up the development of our multimodal logistics package. This was developed in close cooperation with a well-known UK freight forwarder, Signet International.

Signet was one of our pilot sites in 1987 and has now been running its forwarding business using Redberry Software for 25 years. We do not sell our software, we rent it with free updates, so the software constantly evolves with the freight industry. Signet's Managing Director, Richard Newport, has high standards in terms of IT, having worked in senior positions in big-name global forwarders. He says Redberry's solution is able to do everything those larger systems could, and many things better, at a fraction of the cost. Signet received the Queens Award for Enterprise in 2008.

Computer systems are good at removing repetitious tasks. A freight forwarder always has repeat business with the same shippers and consignees. With this in mind, Redberry products are designed to produce shipment documentation with the minimum fuss and key strokes. Provided the operator has a sound understanding of the freight industry, it comes as second nature to use well-written software.

I think I should take the time here to explain shipment consolidation and volume kill, as this leads on to e-freight. Airlines have a volume rate charge set generally at 6,000 cubic centimetres per kilogram and charge whichever is the highest calculation. Now, if a forwarder has two shipments going to the same destination, they would first create each shipment on a HAWB and then a single MAWB to cover both shipments.

In the case of volume kill we can consider two pieces – one very dense and one high volume. Piece one contains drill bits, weighs 100 kg with a volume of 60,000 cc. Piece number two contains a carbon-fibre car wing – it weighs 10 kg and volumes at 600,000 cc, equating at 100 kg by volume. When these two pieces are consolidated to the same MAWB shipment, the total weight in kilograms is 110 and the total volume weight is 110. Each HAWB will carry 100 kg cost, making 200 kg of revenue for the forwarder and 110 kg of revenue for the airline. A computer can calculate both volume and volume kill on the fly as the consolidation builds up to many shipments, showing cost and profit as it goes.

This consolidation paperwork consisting of the HAWBs, a shipment manifest and the commercial invoices would go into a big envelope called a pouch and the MAWB would be stapled to it. On a large consolidation it was quite common practice for the forwarder to pop in also a magazine or the daily newspaper for the overseas import agent to read. This paperwork amounts to a huge quantity of unpaid freight on every flight.

e-freight is not just about saving trees, being green and sharing EDI information, it is also IATA-driven to reduce the amount of unpaid cargo on the aircraft. In the 25 years we have been providing software to freight forwarders, I have seen very little real beneficial change for the forwarder other than the internet replacing telex, fax and telephone. The MAWB, for example, has not changed, only the terms and conditions on the back for the airlines' benefit.

Freight forwarding is by its nature a global product, and global products tend to develop as fast as the slowest global member involved in the process. There also seems to be a direct link between speed of development and amount of corruption in any given country.

That said, I am sure Europe will slowly embrace e-freight – after all, sending PDF attachments of commercial invoices, manifests and HAWBs to your overseas agent by e-mail is e-freight in operation, there is no need for an organized central repository for this information. Other messaging is covered by IATA structures such as the FHL (manifest) that may be sent to a CCS as a structured Cargo-IMP e-mail. There are several web portals that offer to create these messages, but for most forwarders this would be double keying.

This brings us to cloud computing, again a central repository. Development goes in spirals – remember the big central mainframe computers with their dumb VT100 terminals (legacy systems) linked by leased lines? Now we are moving to a big central cloud storage computer accessed by a dumb browser linked by the internet.

My personal preference is to keep sensitive data local and put shared data on a server on the internet where it may be shared without concern. But then I am 'old-school' and have seen it all before. I want my data local on a computer I can see, with back-ups I can control and shared information sent to a web server as required automatically. Incidentally, this is how our software works.

So to sum up, do I expect cloud computing to radically change the way we work? This is most unlikely due to the individual companies not wishing to tie up with service providers who hold their precious data remotely. Do I expect IATA-driven systems to be popular with freight forwarders? No I do not, IATA does what the airlines want.

Do I expect hand-held devices to rule the commercial computer world? No I do not, they are too clumsy and slow to input data. Am I today meeting airlines that still insist on using cut set MAWBs? Yes. Do I expect to meet airlines that still insist on using cut set MAWBs in 2022? Yes, I am afraid I do. Can an ancient Olivetti typewriter that deserves to be in a museum send an FWB message? I leave you to decide.

Am I a grumpy old man or a realist with over 35 years of experience with freight and computers? I leave you to decide.

e-freight solutions

There are now a number of global technology companies offering cargo operators bespoke and off-the-shelf solutions for electronic cargo processing. SITA, based in Geneva, provides a range of IT and telecommunications services to airlines and works very closely with IATA.

Traxon Europe, now part of CHAMP Cargosystems, which is a subsidiary of SITA, provides a neutral communications platform through which forwarders could access airlines. The airlines themselves offered their own systems but were not all compatible or accessible.

Traxon, headquartered in Frankfurt, was founded in 1991. The company provides comprehensive, leading-edge electronic communication solutions and services to the air freight industry. Traxon Europe's innovative products help the different partners of the air cargo supply chain to electronically manage air shipments and meet C2K, IATA e-freight, WCO (World Customs Organization) and postal requirements. They optimize global process quality, increase on-time delivery and document accuracy by eliminating sources of error.

CHAMP's Cargospot new-generation application suite is a key business enabler, integrating systems and processes on a network-wide basis for optimal operational and commercial agility. Cargospot also provides a modern software platform for airlines, the general sales agent (GSA) and the ground handling agent (GHA) needing a complete solution to automate their cargo business or replace their current legacy system. CHAMP Cargosystems offers its advanced cargo management systems on both a licensed and software as a service (SaaS) basis.

Descartes Systems Group has, by working with IATA, developed a technology bridge that helps air cargo messaging participants easily transition from legacy messaging procedures to cargo-XML standards. The solution provides bi-directional translation and message version control between legacy Cargo Interchange Message Procedures (Cargo-IMP) and the new Cargo-XML scheme.

Companies in the air cargo industry are saving thousands of dollars and improving service every single day using Descartes' end-to-end shipment management solution, Descartes CargoBooker. Descartes CargoBooker is a basic air freight electronic booking service aimed at small- and medium-sized air freight forwarders. It enables forwarders to access air cargo carrier information, to make electronic bookings 24 hours per day, seven days per week, via a simple web browser. As part of the Descartes GF-X Exchange, users have access to one of the largest electronic information and reservation systems in the air freight industry.

In Dubai, Calogi targets smaller operators and assists them in adopting electronic systems for supply chain logistics, messaging and e-commerce. CargoWise, based in Sydney, Australia, offers a range of supply chain management and integrated logistics solutions.

UNISYS, a worldwide IT and technology innovator, offers a cloud-computer-based logistics management system for air freight transactions. It handles around 35 per cent of world air freight.

In the future, the air freight industry will be forced to accept fast, accurate and efficient e-communications systems in order to survive. The days ahead are going to be tougher than ever, with high security and cost cutting combining to squeeze the profits of everyone in the logistics chain.

The evolution of air freight technology

Jean François Bouilhaguet presides over the express handling facility at Paris CDG Airport. His company, Sodexi, a division of Air France/KLM Cargo, handles express shipments for the 16 airlines which form the Skyteam Alliance. In addition, as a neutral intermediary, the company handles shipments for integrators such as FedEx and UPS, as well as other airlines using CDG as a convenient transit hub. In order to achieve the required levels in efficiency, security and speed, it has invested heavily in creating its hi-tech warehouse and systems, introducing a whole range of state-of-the-art technologies, all based on electronic management of the processes. He has been one of the innovators in modernizing the industry and is, at the same time, highly critical of the progress and attitudes of many of the operators. He was recently appointed President of the Cargo Information Network (CIN). This initiative combines the information from all the participants in the Paris air freight community with the purpose of streamlining security, efficiency, Customs data and revenue collection, thus helping exporters. Paperless cargo processing is his main objective. He reflects on 25 years of activity.

1987–2012: 25 years of geopolitical, economic and technical development

It is difficult to think back over the amazing changes of the late 1980s without a little nostalgia. I was, at that time, in China promoting high-technology products. It must be remembered that in this era telephones, cars and consumer goods were reserved strictly for the Party dignitaries responsible for state organizations, the same applied in the USSR. It was in this region where the birth of change of the aviation world, and especially cargo, started and accelerated. During the 1980s the world economy opened up and resumed its business activities – between China and Western Europe, Japan and North

America, with Latin America sharing its development with the US, Africa with its old colonial powers and the Middle East re-distributing its petro-dollars between three poles – US/Canada, Japan and Europe.

The commercial activities which nurtured air freight paralleled closely this global economic pattern. The US dominated the market with a number of international airlines which supplied its powerful domestic market. France and Britain had the luxury of three airlines, while Germany, not yet unified, relied on the all-powerful Lufthansa, the leader of international cargo. Japan Airlines, meanwhile, took advantage of the burgeoning electronics industry exporting its products 'made in Japan' throughout the world. Whereas the number of airlines visible within the air freight sector was limited, airports which benefited from powerful cargo infrastructures were limited to several regional hubs. The special status of Hong Kong under the British protectorate allowed it to achieve a strong position within Southeast Asia. The local airline, Cathay Pacific, was the only one in the world to generate higher cargo turnover than passengers. Singapore would eventually follow the same model.

While the number of carriers to be seen in the air freight sector was limited, the airports benefitting from significant cargo infrastructures were equally few and far between. Within this environment, where the number of operators was so limited, it was possible to manage freight operations through the use of paper documents and manual control. The supporting documents were simply those between shipper and consignee relying on the general principle of agreement and confidence. And then terrorism took its first life-changing steps.

The air waybill (AWB) introduced in the 1930s wielded the supreme power in air cargo. Each new employee would undergo training to become familiar with the hundreds of case studies which illustrated the function of these documents. The AWB, which sealed definitively the confidence between operators, at the same time would become the main barrier to the modernization of air freight. For more than ten years the operators have run aground on this attempt to make the industry paperless, while any one of us wishing to travel on a passenger flight can deal with the whole process in a single click.

What was it that kept the industry reliant on this same technology for 25 years? Over this period, aircraft manufacturers considerably improved aircraft technology, and in doing so increased capacity and reduced fuel consumption. But it was the passenger sector which monopolized the means and resources for this progress, while cargo remained almost invisible. Only the integrators invested seriously in innovation. In 1985 Dell created its first computer and at the same time, the fax. In 1988 CDs overtook the sales of vinyl discs. By the 1990s everyone was using digital technology. At the same time, the standard use of barcode labels was adopted for a speedier distribution of packages.

FedEx and UPS were the great innovators and imposed their own system of codes to cover the transaction from client to consignee, at the same time demonstrating the quality of their services. The equipment evolved rapidly during 1990–1995 and led to the various centres for automatic sorting, tracking the shipments onto the integrators' aircraft. At this time, 90 per cent of cargo airlines did not use this system during loading, with the operators visually controlling and using written labels. Even today, some operators still work with this method. Certain traditional airlines justified this archaic procedure but eventually were obliged to accept the new technology.

Radio frequency identification (RFID) has been established for a number of years and has become an essential element in many different industries and activities. In logistics, the radio frequency electromagnetic field label is used in warehousing, inventory control and sorting in the handler's warehouse. Data stored on the tag can be accessed through radio waves. The energy necessary for good reception requires an enlargement of the label, which receives the signal and in turn re-transmits the response. A radio signal can reach several labels simultaneously. For logistic purposes a signal must be simple and used throughout the entire world in places often far from the terminals. Signals between containers on board an aircraft are perfectly accessible with barcode readers.

While supermarkets generally use the barcode system, some members of the air cargo industry are moving away from the RFID system. The potential

Figure 14.1 Sodexi handling warehouse
Source: Sodexi.

health risks from the pollution it generates means that the trade unions feel the risks are too great for operatives. We will not convert to RFID as we do not want to adopt a system which contains the risk of radiation and heavy metals, etc., and could create legal and regulatory problems. Barcode technology uses paper labels or recyclable boxes. Reading by video is replacing lasers. This technology can calculate the volume of a package and perform a number of other tasks, such as calculating costs. Video processing is certainly the future. One camera will perform identification and control of security of the warehouse and flights, personnel and goods. The control of national borders has forced this development very quickly. It must be remembered that prior to the tragic 9/11 terrorist attack, smoking on or around aircraft, even by engineers, was allowed. Furthermore, no identification or badge was required for people working in an airport and people could freely carry a sports bag, containing anything, without any control either at entry or exit. Anything was possible at this time.

Since 2001 everything has changed. The technology of screening, badging and biometric identification has been obligatory within the freight area of an airport. Also, the identification of the merchandise has become necessary to guarantee the aircraft's security. Little by little, different countries imposed operational controls on the invisibility of shipments consolidated by forwarders and covered by the sanctified AWB, as well as the details of the package, the shipper, consignee, nature of the goods, weight and name of carrier.

In fact, air freight is forced to follow shipments in exactly the same way invented by integrators 25 years ago. In the very near future each operator will have to guarantee these exact details from the moment of collecting the shipment, through Customs, arrival at the airport and loading of aircraft. This chain of activities was normally handled by the different players. It demands the installation of a cargo community system (CCS) which collects together the different processes to guarantee a complete result.

These systems are already in place with Customs authorities in different countries and, based on this data, permission will be granted, or not, to allow the loading on the originating airport. Therefore, each state can retain any suspect or risky shipment. Cargonaut in the Netherlands and CIN in France are two examples of these CCSs.

Let us not forget that we rely on the geo-localization by GPS in our cars, which allows us to find our way and avoid radar traps (SatNav). This technique has found an application in the monitoring of vehicles at an airport. XOPS is certainly the most practical solution. Movements of aircraft and vehicles are controlled in real time by a single monitor. Each vehicle is continuously supervised over 24 hours and can be automatically diverted to optimize usage, whether cargo or baggage. Any anomaly is automatically noted. In an aviation environment which is so competitive, every part of the operation must become faster and more effective. This is true of both handling the goods and ensuring security.

In conclusion, cargo operators have witnessed over 25 years a growth linked to the enlightenment of developing countries, mainly China. As airport

Figure 14.2 Completely computer-controlled express Sodexi handling warehouse

infrastructures are extended, the strong expansion of airline route development has made operations completely dependent on new technology and IT.

Mobile phones, satellite positioning and video techniques combine to produce solutions for the monitoring of activities in real time. On the other side of the world, each airline and each client will be able to track his shipments throughout adequately equipped airports. Once again it is China which produces the most mobile phones with the greatest number of users. The low number of airport projects within Europe will not, unfortunately, create this technological dynamism. Cargo operators, already hit hard by a crisis without precedent, will be obliged to adapt in order to respond to the regulations controlling the flow of goods.

Concerning the CIN at CDG, my task is to manage and promote this highly complex and technology-based system which, in today's multimodal, multi-national market, will be increasingly vital in order to compete realistically with stiff competition from Asia and the Far East. It is a challenge but I am convinced it will reap rich rewards.

15 The environment

Cut the noise and clean up your act

The aviation industry wants to expand – others say it needs to expand to handle growth forecasts. In a modern society, passengers are demanding access to all parts of the world and global industry is setting new parameters of source and supply that makes air cargo transportation a fundamental part of the way it wants to work. Aviation, however, is under attack from the environmental lobby over the amount of carbon-based emissions it releases into the atmosphere, adding to the 'greenhouse gas' (GHG) effect and hastening global warming.

On the upside of the argument, in a massively capital-intensive business, billions of dollars of investment are being made by the airlines in quieter, more fuel-efficient aircraft. No other commercial sector has worked harder than the aviation industry to clean up its act.

Aircraft fuel efficiency has improved by 75 per cent in the past 40 years, through improvements in airframe design, engine technology and rising load factors, where improved yield management techniques are seeing more people being moved on each flight. Upgrades in aircraft and engine design mean that air transport is now 75 per cent quieter than it was four decades ago.

Aviation claims to be the only globally active industry to agree tough targets for emissions reduction, and by 2020 it is estimated that 70 of the world aircraft fleets will comprise advanced technology equipment added since 2002.

Speaking on 11 June 2012 at the 68th Annual General Meeting of the International Air Transport Association (IATA) held in Beijing, Tony Tyler, CEO and Director General, outlined: 'Our planet is more connected than at any time in its history. In 2011, some 2.8 billion people travelled on 35,000 routes connecting 3,800 commercial airports.'

He continued:

> Aviation is a vital component of the global economy. We support 57 million jobs and US$2.2 trillion in economic activity. Some 48 million tonnes of cargo with a value of $5.3 trillion was shipped by air. That's over a third of world trade (calculated by the value of goods in transit). The benefits of global connectivity touch virtually every modern business.

As head of an industry body that represents some 240 airlines comprising 84 per cent of global air traffic, Tyler emphasized: 'With about 100 years of history, air connectivity has established itself as a powerful force for good in our world. And our potential is almost without limit.' In fact, he went on to note that by 2030 twice as many people will travel and cargo loads could triple to nearly 150 million tonnes per year – a level of connectivity that has the potential to support 82 million jobs and $6.9 trillion of global GDP.

But one factor that does threaten the future growth of the aviation industry is the perception that emissions caused by aircraft irreparably harm the planet. There is also concern on the perceived environmental impact of air freight and the noise its activities can generate, particularly when many cargo-carrying airlines need to operate through night-time takeoff and landing slots to make their business models sustainable.

'Cash cow' taxation opportunity

There is a real worry within the air freight industry that too often governments see aviation as a luxury item and tax it as a 'cash cow', ignoring the fact that connectivity by air is vital to the infrastructure of the global community and the way international commerce functions and the methods by which it wants to see its cargo move on, unrestricted and intercontinental.

To keep air cargo in the skies as a sustainable business, there must be a thoughtful and comprehensive approach to the expansion of the aviation industry focused on building competitiveness in order to maximize aviation's economic and social benefits to their full potential.

Globally, aviation produces around 2 per cent of man-made carbon dioxide (CO_2) according to the United Nations Intergovernmental Panel on Climate Change – but with the forecast growth in demand for air services, these emissions will grow if action is not taken. In response, the aviation industry has developed a set of targets aimed at limiting its climate impact, while enabling it to continue to provide a key vehicle for economic growth. The targets include: improving fleet fuel efficiency by 1.5 per cent per year until 2020; capping net aviation emissions from 2020; and most ambitiously, to halve aviation CO_2 emissions by 2050, compared to 2005.

The Air Transport Action Group (ATAG), a Geneva-based coalition of independent member organizations and companies spread throughout the global air transportation industry, says these targets were set after careful analysis and follow the industry's track record of measured progress, while also being far-reaching. But these ambitions cannot be achieved by technological or operational improvements within the aviation industry alone; governments will also have to play their part in ensuring that aviation can operate in the most efficient skies – with the introduction of much-needed improvements in air traffic control infrastructure and management.

In the Beijing speech, IATA's Tyler went on to state that airlines would achieve carbon-neutral growth from 2020. He noted: 'Our goal is to cut net emissions to 320 million tonnes by 2050. That would be half of our 2005 emissions in a world that will be demanding much more connectivity.' And he noted: 'Success will need the support of governments.'

Where there's smoke . . .

Aircraft produce several types of emission that can contribute to climate change and it is calculated that some 2 per cent of global man-made carbon emissions can be directly attributed to aviation.

First, and producing the biggest percentage share, there are the emissions of CO_2 that are produced in direct proportion to the amount of jet fuel used to fly over any distance.

Then there is water vapour created by burning jet fuels. At altitude, condensation trails form, comprising frozen ice crystals that deflect a small amount of sunlight away from the surface of the planet and reflect more infrared radiation back towards Earth. This has an overall warming effect on the atmosphere of the planet.

Next, the combustion of atmospheric nitrogen and oxygen in jet engines produces nitrous oxide, which catalyses the production of ozone and the destruction of methane. The ozone layer prevents damaging ultraviolet light from reaching the Earth's surface, and methane is another GHG, so perhaps the news from that area is not all bad.

Finally, some extra emission of GHGs is caused by trucks operating on behalf of airlines carrying air freight as they shuttle to and from the cargo warehouses. There are also carbon emissions caused by auxiliary power units that serve the cargo facilities, like cool rooms at the airport.

About 10 per cent of aircraft emissions of all types, except hydrocarbons and CO gas, are produced during operations on the ground and during landing and takeoff, with the bulk of emissions (90 per cent) occurring at higher altitudes. For hydrocarbons and CO, the split is closer to 30 per cent at ground level and 70 per cent at higher altitudes.

There has been a speculative idea that aircraft could cut carbon emissions by harnessing energy from the wheel rotation of their landing gear and braking system on touchdown to generate enough electricity to power their taxiway propulsion to and from airport buildings, reducing the need to use their jet engines when actually on the ground.

The noise caused by aircraft on the ground or during takeoff and landing is considered a major source of environmental pollution and can be a serious nuisance for people living close to airports, causing distress to residents and plummeting house prices. Early in 2012 this concern resulted in the German high court upholding a temporary night-time ban previously imposed by a state court on flights between 2300 and 0500 hours at Frankfurt-Main International Airport. Frankfurt is Germany's biggest air freight gateway and the main hub of Lufthansa Cargo, one of the world's largest cargo-carrying airlines with a fleet of MD-11 freighters operating schedules that depend for their commercial success on flying night-time schedules.

While undoubtedly there are savings to be made in terms of GHG emissions for long-distance freight movements, a voyage by sea is significantly longer. It can take almost four weeks for a large containership to sail from London to Singapore, compared with about 12 hours by air, and in many cases there may be a number of economic or time-sensitive advantages for the use of air freight in the first place – so keeping cargo-carrying airlines in the skies 24 hours per day is of vital economic importance for many in the industry.

Alternative fuel sources

Many efforts are being made to encourage the development and use of a new sustainable source of fuel to power aircraft. Such a move is considered to be one of the primary means by which the industry can quickly and effectively reduce its carbon footprint.

Modern jet aircraft use a petroleum-based fuel commonly known as 'Jet A' or 'Jet A-1'; the emissions problems associated with their use is discussed earlier in the chapter. Alternative fuel that is not derived from petroleum can be classified into three main categories: biofuels, synthetics and other sources like hydrogen, natural gas, ethanol, methanol and propane (LPG).

The industry body, IATA, has called for 6 per cent of jet-fuel demand, or 8 billion litres per year, to be met by biofuels by 2020, adding that it expects airline demand to be 2 per cent or less over the next few years as it is as yet uncompetitive on cost and will be bought by airlines solely to 'improve their environmental credentials and to gain experience of biofuels technologies'.

If governments expect their airlines to operate in a more environmentally friendly way with the use of biofuels and convert to using a significant proportion of non-fossil fuel in their aircraft engines before 2020, these administrations will have either to subsidize biofuel production for their airlines or introduce tough legislation requiring carriers to use a certain percentage of sustainable biofuels in their mix and force them to pay the bills.

But the production of biofuels in large commercial quantities is going to be a costly exercise, so those governments that do impose mandatory requirements for airlines to use it without providing any subsidy will have to weather the storm generated by the soaring cost of passenger tickets, rocketing air freight charges and the resultant increase in high street prices. If they get it wrong, the legislators can then sit back and watch their passenger and freight carriers go out of business – while preparing themselves to hand over to the opposition at the next election.

Biofuels

It is estimated that sustainable biofuels alone have the potential to reduce the carbon footprint of the aviation industry by up to 80 per cent and by mid-2012 a variety of 'drop-in' biofuel products had been used to power more than 1,500 commercial flights – these are biofuels that are completely interchangeable with conventional fuels. But to increase the use of these, the costs of production need to come down notably and the level of supply needs to increase dramatically.

Biofuel can be made from the oils contained in crops and feedstock, such as soya beans and canola seeds, to produce petroleum-like oil that can be transformed into fuel similar to diesel fuel. This is a renewable fuel source, but conventional crops and feedstock require significant quantities of arable land to produce enough biofuels to supply scalable and sustainable fuel needs.

Biofuels have now been around for a few years in the aviation world and have been used to some considerable effect on test and now commercial flights. In February 2008, the UK's Virgin Atlantic Airlines operated the very first biofuel test flight between London and Amsterdam, using a 20 per cent blend of coconut and babassu (a palm tree oil) biofuel in one of the engines of a B747-400 aircraft from its fleet.

In the next few years, various other test flights were carried out by a number of world airlines using a variety of biofuel mixtures before KLM flew the world's first fully biofuel-powered commercial service, a twin-engine B737-800 carrying 171 passengers from Amsterdam to Paris in June 2011.

In the same month, aircraft manufacturer Boeing flew its brand-new B747-8 freighter straight from the assembly line in Seattle to the Paris Air Show with all four engines burning a 15 per cent mix of biofuel produced from *Camelina*, a genus within the flowering plant family Brassicaceae native to Mediterranean regions of Europe and Asia.

Although aviation body IATA recognizes that aircraft are long-lived assets and will be using kerosene or kerosene-like fuels for many years to come, it believes a 6 per cent share of sustainable second-generation biofuels can be in use by world airlines by 2020 and Boeing supports a target of 1 per cent of all aviation fuel used globally to be coming from the same source by 2015.

Synthetics

Synthetic kerosene can be obtained from coal, natural gas or other hydrocarbon resources and can be produced by first turning the resource into gases, which are then recombined to form hydrocarbon liquids. However, synthetic fuel production is an energy-intensive process that produces significantly higher CO_2 emissions than the production of fuel derived from petroleum.

Other

Quite a few alternative options have been considered for a new source of aviation fuel, but all represent significant challenges and would require the cost-prohibitive production of new aircraft and fuel delivery systems. Hydrogen and natural gas must be used in their liquid form, which requires storage at extremely cold temperatures. Hydrogen burns cleanly, but its production is very energy intensive and it emits large quantities of water vapour with uncertain effects on cloud formation and the atmosphere.

Sabre-rattling policies

Governments have stepped in with improved environmental legislation in their attempts to cut GHG emissions – although the Emissions Trading Scheme, first introduced by the EU in 2005 to combat climate change, caused a storm when it was applied to the aviation sector in January 2012. The scheme applies to all airlines that fly in and out of the EU member states, capping their emissions at 95 per cent of historical levels. Non-compliant airlines must purchase ETS credits to make up for any deficit and revenues will be retained by EU member states.

The introduction of ETS was immediately seen by some as just another disguised tax on aviation and a target for retaliation, with aviation organizations claiming it is a unilateral and extra-territorial approach that would be seen by non-European states as an attack on their sovereignty, with the potential for resultant trade wars or bilateral air limitations.

India and China said they would not allow their carriers to participate in the ETS programme and the US Senate Commerce Committee passed a bill to prohibit US carriers from participating in the scheme. Significantly, the US legislation makes specific provision for its officials to use their authority to conduct international negotiations to pursue a worldwide approach to address the problem of aircraft emissions.

Such an agreement, however, is not seen as being possible under current conditions, when Europe seems more committed to implementing its ETS unilaterally than to negotiating a multilateral agreement – and for many international countries it's like being asked to enter talks with a gun to their head.

The situation could lead to non-compliant airlines being banned from flying to European countries. However, the first ETS credits are not due to be submitted by airlines to the EU until April 2013, so there is a short breathing space to sort out the matter.

There is, however, some common ground. Everyone – including Europe – agrees that the only real solution is a global agreement brokered through the International Civil Aviation Organization (ICAO), a specialized agency of the United Nations created in 1944 to promote the safe and orderly development of international civil aviation throughout the world.

While everyone credits Europe for moving the item up the global agenda, the onus is now on Europe to seize the moment and to take credible action to defuse the situation and get on with finding the global solution that everybody is hoping for to solve the problem.

Both sides of the argument

On another side of the discussion, environmental campaigner Greenpeace foresees catastrophic climate change if the aviation industry is allowed to go on expanding at its current rate. In passenger terms it states that flying is ten times more harmful for the environment than a traveller taking the train. IATA claims, on the other hand, that it can often be considerably cheaper than some modes of surface transport. The association notes that a web search priced economy fares for the 22,000 kilometre round-trip from New York to Beijing at around $1,500 – seven cents per kilometre. A New York taxi ride costs $1.25 per kilometre, or 31 cents if four passengers take the same vehicle.

In the US, the Federal Aviation Administration (FAA) notes that the aviation industry plays a key role in the economic prosperity and lifestyle that Americans enjoy and the nation's economy benefits greatly from the ability to move people and products all over the globe. Regulatory frameworks have developed to constrain the growth of aviation emissions of many aviation sources and improvements to the efficient aviation network have had a positive effect on the environment, the FAA maintains.

As part of the US Department of Transportation and the national aviation authority of the US, the FAA points out that aviation has progressively improved its environmental performance and technological advancement in new aircraft design, with improved aerodynamics and reduced weight cutting aircraft fuel consumption and emissions significantly over the last 30 years. This improvement is expected to continue in the future.

Greenpeace, however, claims that the aviation industry has produced 'a completely reckless response to climate change' and in the UK alone the campaigner is calling for an end to all domestic short-haul flights, a cap on long-haul flights and an end to the government's airport expansion plans in the country.

Between 1990 and 2050, Greenpeace says emissions from aviation are set to quadruple, which could wipe out all other savings made in every other sector of effort – but anyone who has ever gazed out of the window of a high-rise Shanghai hotel above the smog line, tried through the industrial haze to watch the sun set over the Caspian Sea oil shelf or wrestled through the rush hour in any of the world's major industrial cities will be aware that there are some other far more virulent areas of atmospheric pollution where not enough effort is yet being made. These need to be cleaned up urgently for major environmental improvement to work on a global scale in line with the Kyoto Protocol – a series of formal agreements to the UN Framework Convention on Climate Change struck in the Japanese city in 1997 that gives ICAO the responsibility for overseeing international aviation emissions.

This method of working to solve the problem would enable ICAO to manage aviation emissions on a global scale and ensure a level playing field. The approach consists of three main elements that would enable: full accounting for aviation's emissions as a global industrial sector, not by individual state; global coordination of economic measures to ensure that aviation will not pay more than once for its emissions; and access to global carbon markets.

In his Beijing speech, IATA's Tyler concluded:

> Aviation is a force for good – supporting jobs for 57 million people, uniting families and friends in a global community, facilitating access to global markets, spreading wealth and prosperity, and fostering business, educational, and cultural opportunities in every corner of the world.

The way aviation is allowed to grow to accommodate the needs of developed and developing nations, while not losing sight of its global social and economic responsibilities, will be of vital importance to the future wellbeing of the air cargo market and the effectiveness of the way world trade and industry functions.

16 Crime in air logistics

Pirates attacking merchants at sea and on land, and highwaymen robbing stagecoaches, have all been part of society for centuries. It is no surprise that today's supply chains are under similar threats from modern-day criminals.

Air freight's main reason to exist is to move high-value goods around the world. Given this fact, it is safe to assume that a large proportion of shipments are worth considering as targets for possible theft. Sooner or later, any shipment will either start or end its journey in a vehicle or a warehouse where it is at its most vulnerable. As they say, 'Cargo at rest is cargo at risk.' For several decades, certain consignments have been easily targeted by the criminal fraternity and in most cases their task has been made easy by lax security and inside help or tip-offs. The big 'heists' often make the news and in some cases have even been the subject of films or TV programmes. Smaller and less sensational robberies continue to occur and although they do not make the headlines, they cost the industry and insurance companies billions every year. A few examples of the more spectacular robberies are as follows.

In 1967, $429,000 in cash was stolen with ease from the Air France warehouse at New York's JFK Airport. The airline regularly transported large amounts of American currency being returned from Asia. This was well known by the cargo staff and it was the security guard who was forced to hand over the key which helped the robbers gain access. The robbery, allegedly organized by the Mafia, was regarded as an uncomplicated hit. In 1990 the film *Goodfellas* was produced based on these events.

In 1978, a similar, but more violent, attack was made on the Lufthansa warehouse at the same airport and was also Mafia-inspired. This time $5 million in cash and $1 million worth of jewels were snatched by six armed robbers with inside help. The whole robbery took exactly 64 minutes. In this case, most of the robbers subsequently met a violent and untimely death.

In 1983, thieves broke into the Matt-Brinks security warehouse at London Heathrow. Expecting to find a haul of around £3 million in cash, they were astonished to discover gold bullion, jewels and cash worth £28 million, which, with some difficulty, they stole. The police, recognizing an inside job, quickly arrested the main culprits who were imprisoned for 25 years.

In 2005, at Schiphol Airport in the Netherlands, robbers escaped with a truck load of uncut diamonds valued at $118 million. A similar robbery had occurred six months earlier.

All of these cases share some common factors. They were betrayed by dishonest employees with criminal contacts, which police quickly identified. Security in every case was lax and almost non-existent and there were many opportunities to escape with the loot. There have been countless other criminal assaults on cargo shipments of cash and valuables over the years, but nowadays, considering the high value of goods such as computers, mobile phones, fashion and pharmaceuticals being shipped around the world, cash or gold is not always the target. The temptation and opportunities are greater than ever and the problem is exacerbated in many cases by reluctance on the part of the victims to report the crime or even acknowledge its occurrence.

Cargo theft affects everyone as it damages economies and companies, forces up prices and feeds the world's black markets that are often sources of funding for terrorists and large criminal gangs. In the US alone, it is estimated that some $30 billion worth of cargo is stolen annually by highly sophisticated and well-organized gangs. In the US there are often Cuban crime syndicates involved, which find unlimited markets for the stolen goods throughout Latin America. In Canada it is the Chinese Triads that have been linked to many cargo thefts. Recession has created an unprecedented demand for cheaper black market goods, which are sold freely through open markets, car boot sales and internet sites. Consequently, there is no shortage of demand for goods stolen from air freight shipments. Goods stolen in transit will also deprive retailers of the sales and may lose their customers to a rival. Trucking companies may respond by raising prices or employing expensive security guards, the costs of which will be passed to the consumer who may consequently seek cheaper goods from the black market. Governments will in turn miss out on tax derived from the legitimate sale of goods.

In addition, while illegal merchandise such as drugs, fashion items and ivory have always been part of the problem, counterfeiting is becoming not only a commercial threat to the manufacturers of branded goods, but can also be dangerous or even lethal. Phoney pharmaceuticals, shoes, cosmetics and toys, for instance, threaten people's health and severely damage the financial performance of the manufacturers. In many cases these items are crudely presented and easy to spot, but beware of the clever forgers whose products are almost undetectable.

The tragic 9/11 attacks suddenly focused the aviation industry's mind on the whole security issue and a raft of new rules and regulations were introduced globally in an attempt to combat future threats. The air cargo sector was also included in these sweeping measures. Whereas in previous decades free access to on-airport areas, warehouses and even aircraft was open to all kinds of unauthorized people, today access has become severely curtailed. Strict registration of staff, including police background checks, makes it much more difficult to obtain a job within secure zones. Although these new conditions have definitely tightened security in cargo warehouses and handling areas and were primarily directed at securing aviation, many of the measures have also hit criminal activities. Today's crooks, however, are up-to-date with all the latest equipment and technology to outsmart the industry security experts.

What are the solutions available with which to fight back?

The movement to introduce electronic processing of cargo can do a great deal to stop crime. Secure cargo identified with barcodes can be tracked throughout its journey with GPS trackers and alarm systems fitted to vehicles which can be immobilized. A range of hi-tech systems and solutions are available to companies. Low-tech solutions like better locks and seals which are alarmed can also be very effective. Any suspicious activity or person should be investigated quickly as prospective thieves may be testing the security system. A company's efficient cooperation with any outside contractor is vital so that no unknown vehicles or drivers are permitted without close scrutiny. The screening and training of all staff should be fundamental to the entire security effort.

One organization which is working hard to prevent theft is the Transported Asset Protection Association (TAPA), a forum that unites manufacturers, logistics companies, carriers and law enforcement agencies with a common aim to reduce theft and subsequent losses from the international logistics industry. TAPA sets out to identify problem areas and develop solutions. With thefts increasing every year, companies which apply the TAPA standards are reporting significant reductions in losses. The biggest risk is always when the high-value cargo is at a standstill at airports, in warehouses or truck stops. There are a number of other alliances and groups which airlines, handlers and forwarders can join whose aim is to share information and research better ways of combating crime, including: Cargo Security Alliance, Freight Watch, Security Cargo Network and many more. Insurance companies, which have clearly born the brunt of much of the losses, are working in collaboration with these groups.

Cybercrime, which is becoming a global menace for everyone, is also part of the air freight security problem. The ability to hack into company systems, identify rich targets, track their location and even forge necessary documents and permits frequently outwit the experts working on the inside for the operators. The European Cybercrime Centre, part of the EU's police body Europol, has to deal with billions of internet protocol addresses when attempting to trace possible criminal activity. Some intelligence services and large companies are being targeted to steal online data which could lead to trading advantages. Clearly this type of crime will increase in proportion to the logistics industry's efforts to make cargo more secure. As we go to press with this book, we have learned of another armed robbery which occurred at the TAM warehouse in Viracopos International Airport in Sao Paulo. Five armed men subdued and locked up eight security guards and got away with $1.75 million worth of consumer electronics. With the Christmas season starting, crimes like these are on the increase. What is certain is that there are no victimless crimes. Every mobile phone that goes missing has to be paid for by someone.

17 Careers in air freight

The logistics of attracting talent

Having worked in supply chain management for over 22 years, Matthew Marriott, Commercial Director of Hellmann Worldwide Logistics UK, is well-placed and able to offer an informed opinion on the career opportunities in the air freight industry available to young people undertaking higher education.

*   *   *

When asked what they want to do when they are older, children normally say things like 'footballer', 'astronaut', 'actor' or 'ballerina'. They invariably aspire to professions that offer a glimpse of glamour, a frisson of danger or the opportunity to be widely recognized in a variety of professional and personal contexts. Unfortunately, in the unforgiving realities of the real world, and particularly in an economic climate that has truly squeezed employment opportunities, there is little scope for finding that elusive position that offers all the glamour, glory, repute and excitement anyone could ever want. In fact, that job exists only in films and perhaps in the minds of the most idealistic fantasists.

Indeed, such expectations, apart from predicating a sharp reality check, can actually make it extremely difficult for certain industries to attract the talent they require. I write this from the perspective of an industry that has to face up to precisely this issue. When was the last time you heard a child, or indeed anyone, say, 'Mummy, when I grow up I want to coordinate freight forwarding operations!'?

This might be a slightly glib way to illustrate the point, but the underlying fact remains: there is a serious gap in young people's knowledge in regard to some of the world's major industries, and particularly that of air freight. Indeed, this is even more of an issue when you consider that, despite perceptions, the wider logistics industry actually has a number of attributes that would almost certainly appeal to ambitious graduates; our industry simply needs to find a way to convey this message if it is to attract the top talent that it really needs.

However, before I, or indeed anyone else, can begin to extol the oft-concealed virtues of the work, there are some quite serious issues to conquer first. In March of this year, multinational professional services company PricewaterhouseCoopers (PwC) released a report that outlined a number of extremely worrying conclusions about the current state of the global transportation and logistics industry (http://www.ukmediacentre.pwc.com/ News-Releases/Transportation-Logistics-industry-is-just-not-hip-enough-to-attract-talent-PwC-report-says-1218.aspx). They were conclusions that made clear that it is not merely problems of perception that the industry should be concerned about. In comparison to other industries, salary levels are low, while training and development is insufficient in terms of providing the type of opportunities employees might look for. Indeed, the report found that there was only a 36 per cent probability that people will find the sector 'attractive' to work within by 2030. Translated into commercial terms, this means that the industry needs to undergo a substantial overhaul to stay competitive in the coming decades. It is certainly sobering stuff.

And yet, in the words of Klaus-Dieter Ruske, PwC's global transportation and logistics leader, despite the 'poor image, poor pay and poor prospects' that currently choke the industry, the reality is that there are 'rewarding, multinational opportunities out there that need tapping into'. Quite! These 'multinational opportunities' might well be one of the industry's greatest attributes in terms of drawing in talent.

Logistics and freight forwarding, by its very nature, is a truly global enterprise. Even for small companies that transport primarily within a particular country, they will most likely have to develop international business relations, while bigger companies will have offices across the world. From the perspective of a young graduate, or indeed anyone looking to forge a career, this is often a hugely attractive prospect, providing a glimpse of opportunity and possibility that can be as inspirational as it is exciting.

As someone who has worked their way up through a wide range of industry roles during the course of my career, I suppose I'm well placed to emphasize the virtues of the work. I can say with clarity that I've had (and am still having) an extremely rewarding career in the industry, including my fair share of globetrotting; but while individual personal circumstances can offer a certain degree of insight, they only really offer a very partial and insular perception of the opportunities available. That said, in the interest of perspective, and in the context of this chapter, I do find it revealing to compare the state of the industry's attitude towards recruiting now, to that of when I first began working in air freight in 1987.

I entered the industry via a scheme that was designed to combat the rising rates of unemployment among unskilled young people emerging from school; a situation that, despite the radically different times, is not radically dissimilar to the world's current employment predicament. The Youth Training Scheme (YTS) was what brought me to the industry: a Margaret Thatcher-championed on-the-job training course that allowed 16- and 17-year-old school leavers to get a taste of the workplace. It was a scheme that faced strong criticism for what some called 'exploitation' of the young workforce (I can attest that the pay scales were challenging, to say the least), but beneath some of the more apparent flaws of the scheme there were some of the raw ingredients to maximize young talent – ingredients that go far beyond any short-term political capital and actually had enduring merit.

For example, my two-year period on the scheme gave me access to a mentor; a steadying influence who was able to impart the crucial employment wisdom that can, in hindsight, seem so obvious, and yet to young people in the workplace can be so valuable. The hands-on approach taken by my mentor, and the training and working methodology that I quickly became accustomed to, entrenched some very fundamental skills. It was a process of workplace osmosis; by working in a professional atmosphere, and adhering to employment standards and requirements, you invariably, without necessarily always being aware of it, become a more professional employee.

Now, even though I found my way into air freight and then the wider industry as a whole through this scheme, the distinction needs to be made that this was a general nationwide initiative, and that in order for any of the positive elements to be applied to the logistics industry, the whole process needs to be distilled and refined quite considerably. Indeed, two issues stand out in particular: carving out the niche specificity to highlight the range and potential of careers that something like air freight can offer; and attracting a far bigger segment of high-performing graduates, college leavers and young professionals.

Both issues need to be grasped by the industry at all levels. The former can begin to be addressed by the large air freight and logistics employers putting resource towards providing clearly defined employment pathways; pathways that explain the development and opportunity of both company and industry. At present, too many freight forwarders are content to simply recruit, rather than looking to the longer-term challenge of attracting the best talent. Indeed, somewhat of a natural measure in this regard, and something that addresses the latter of the two aforementioned issues, is to increase the industry connection to higher education. It could take many forms, from offering guest lectures, inviting students to site hubs to having a consistent presence at higher education (HE) fairs – preferably all of the above!

It is at university, and to a lesser extent college, where young people make decisions about their future, and logistics must work to make itself a serious consideration. It's not enough (and the last decade has really proven so) for people to just stumble into air freight as I did over 20 years ago. We need to engage the ambitions and aspirations of young people so that the industry can move forward, as it must, over the next decade.

Aside from my own experiences, and part of the reason I can speak so forcefully on this issue is that my own company has in the last five years started to take action. The Hellmann Account Manager graduate scheme began in 2008 with the express aim of developing a select group of young people, graduates or otherwise, into fully trained, fully equipped account managers. Obviously, the scheme is still in its relative infancy, and yet the process has already produced some extremely promising candidates. One employee, who was part of the original 2008 intake, is now a senior manager and a mentor for eight other graduate employees.

Hellmann is certainly not alone in introducing such schemes, but I would hesitate to say that this is widespread practice in the industry, despite the fact that it patently needs to be. There needs to be a commitment to invest in talent. There needs to be an assessment of recruiting processes and, perhaps even more importantly, the systems that they have in place in terms of developing employees.

Graduate programmes and management schemes cost money to implement, but not only do they offer the company the chance to develop the skills that its personnel require, but they demonstrate the sort of commitment towards employee training and wellbeing that can really help fight against some of the superficial, yet powerful, negatives of external perception.

Those who come through company schemes and go on to have dynamic careers within the sector will be walking exponents and advocates of the logistics profession. It is an incredibly effective method, and one that benefits the sector at every level.

This is certainly not an issue that the air freight and logistics industry faces in isolation, but nor does that diminish the importance of taking action now and turning attitudes around. Children might not have to say they want to grow up to be a freight forwarder, but graduates and young professionals really do – and it is up to those within the industry to make sure that is the case.

Hellmann Worldwide Logistics is one of the largest privately owned and family run logistical global networks, currently employing over 16,500 people to serve customers worldwide and operating from 443 branches across 157 countries.

Air logistics: a first-class career

John Lloyd has over 26 years in air cargo, joining Virgin Atlantic Cargo in 1987. He has steadily progressed throughout the company, serving in various supervisory and management positions. He was appointed as Director of Cargo in May 2000. During his time in this capacity, Virgin Atlantic Cargo has won 11 International Cargo Airline of the Year awards.

*   *   *

Ever thought of a career in air logistics? Well, it's time you did because it's air logistics that keeps the world of business moving.

Logistics is one of today's fastest growing and most dynamic business sectors, and although you may not realize it, you rely on it every single day of your life.

So many everyday items move within air logistics supply chains, often from one side of the world to the other within a matter of hours, on behalf of the majority of the world's leading consumer brands.

While the majority of goods are transported on ships and trucks, air logistics is the preferred mode of transport for manufacturers moving high-value, time-sensitive products across the globe and whose success is based on combining the quality of their products with speed-to-market. They depend on the predictability and security of moving their products using air logistics, and it's the speed and reliability our industry delivers that makes it a premium service.

Computers are a great example. Thanks to air logistics, major manufacturers don't need to build computers to the specification they think people want and store them in a warehouse hoping someone will buy them. That ties up money and is a high-risk strategy because of the speed with which new technologies are developed. Today, highly knowledgeable consumers want to configure their own computers and that demands flexibility and speed on the part of the manufacturer in terms of both production and delivery. By using air logistics, companies now build-to-order and still get the product to their customer within 24–72 hours, wherever they are in the world.

Another big advantage for manufacturers is that by taking this approach to manufacturing, they are paid by the customer before they've finished making the product and this produces a vital cashflow advantage.

And, of course, that's great news for air logistics companies. When Apple launched its iPhone 5, even the US Federal Reserve acknowledged the vital role played by our industry. In its quarterly report on the US economy, it stated: 'Air cargo companies saw an increase in cargo volume tied to the launch of various smartphones and computer tablets, which favor shipment by air over other modalities.'

It is the speed of air logistics that customers love. Manufacturers realize that even the best products in the world lose some of their competitive advantage if they don't reach the market quickly, and when demand for a product soars they have to be able to keep inventory levels high or risk losing sales.

Most consumer electronic products, smartphones and all manner of other hi-tech goods will have flown on board an aircraft at some point in their life. Other regular cargoes include fresh fruits and vegetables, meat and fish, high-fashion garments and accessories, pharmaceuticals, books and magazines, parts for cars . . . and even family pets.

More often than not, these cargoes will be flying with you on passenger flights, carefully stowed in the cargo hold below the passenger cabin. Although there are cargo-only aircraft, the majority of freight is carried on board passenger services – and it needs to because on many routes, without the revenue generated by air cargo, services could not survive. So, no air cargo would mean significantly higher ticket prices for passengers or a severe reduction in the number of routes airlines serve.

Air logistics is big business. Every year, the air logistics industry delivers 48 million tonnes of cargo and the value of these goods exceeds $3.5 trillion – that's 35 per cent by value of all the goods traded internationally.

At Virgin Atlantic Airways we are an airline that truly understands the value of air cargo and its importance to our overall success. The 2011/2012 financial year was the second consecutive year of record performance for Virgin Atlantic Cargo, with a 39 per cent increase in revenues to £224.4 million and a 17 per cent growth in the amount of cargo carried to 227,000 tonnes across our global network of routes. Today, Virgin Atlantic Cargo's growing network expands to more than 350 destinations worldwide, supported by global interline agreements with other airlines and trucking partners.

We also help other airlines to grow a successful cargo business that makes a strong financial contribution to their bottom line. A perfect example is Virgin Australia. Virgin Atlantic Cargo sells the cargo capacity on behalf of Virgin Australia on its international passenger flights and has grown this business 25 per cent in the last financial year.

To really appreciate the role of air logistics, you have to look at the big global picture. The air cargo supply chain not only involves airlines. The successful movement of products around the world is a complex and sophisticated process that involves freight forwarding and logistics companies working on behalf of manufacturing customers, cargo handling companies, airports and trucking operators.

It is an industry that is strictly regulated in terms of security, Customs regulations and the environment, and that relies on fast and accurate technology to ensure goods move quickly and seamlessly between cities all over the world.

Figure 17.1 Loading cargo on a B747 passenger plane
Source: Virgin Atlantic.

But there is a world beyond this frontline activity that also exists and prospers because of air logistics.

Farmers in Africa, for example, now supply major supermarkets in the UK with fresh fruits and vegetables. They have worked closely with buyers to ensure they are growing the right fruits and vegetables to suit British tastes and have become increasingly sophisticated in meeting the demands of consumers. Nowadays, produce grown and picked in Africa is also prepared, quality checked and packaged before being loaded onto a flight so that when it arrives in the UK, all the customer needs to do is label it and put it on the supermarket shelf.

The same can be said of the millions of red roses that are flown in to meet excess demand on St. Valentine's Day and thousands of other products throughout the year.

Manufacturing is a global business. To boost their profits, companies need to make high-quality products for the lowest possible price. All over the world, companies are able to source skilled workforces at a lower cost than in their own countries and then use air logistics to import finished products. This can mean a constantly shifting picture as one country becomes more competitive than another, so a company that manufactures in China or India is just as likely to move production to Vietnam or Indonesia if it is economically sensible to do so. Air logistics makes this possible.

All over the world, entire communities are being employed by companies that are growing successfully because they are part of an air logistics supply chain and the income and prosperity this generates also makes a vital contribution to local and national economies. So, air logistics is also a respected engine of economic development.

That's why it offers so many great career opportunities.

If you are interested in sales and marketing, IT, customer service, engineering, research and analysis, international trade, business administration, finance, human resources, etc., air logistics offers a great career path for you. And it can be a career path that will help you to see the world as companies look to fast-track talented recruits and give them a broad range of experience across their business divisions and international networks.

If you have the drive, energy and motivation to build a career, the air logistics industry offers you a world of opportunity.

To that list of attributes, I will add one more requirement: passion. As an employer, Virgin Atlantic wants its team members to want to be the best. We don't aspire to be the biggest airline in the world, but we are passionate about delivering the highest possible levels of customer service and offering customers another choice to major markets around the world. It is this passion that has earned us 11 international 'Cargo Airline of the Year' awards since 2002.

Every day we challenge ourselves to be the best. If you're ready to do the same, you can build a great career in the air logistics industry.

I wish you every success.

Epilogue
The future

Ram Menen began his career in aviation in 1976 at Kuwait Airways. He later moved to British Airways to head its cargo operations in Kuwait. In 1984, he joined the Kuwaiti aviation group Alghanim Al Qutub Shipping Agencies to set up and manage its air freight forwarding unit in Dubai. He has headed the cargo division of Dubai-based Emirates Airline since it first took to the skies in October 1985.

He is one of the founder members of The International Air Cargo Association (TIACA), the premier organization for the entire air logistics business, serving as Vice President in 1993/1994 and as President, CEO and Chairman of the TIACA board in 1995/1996. He continues to be involved with TIACA as a trustee and a member of the Chairman's Council.

Menen is the current Chairman of the IATA's Cargo Committee and is also involved in an advisory capacity with several other air cargo groups. He has been a resolute champion of the air logistics industry and is actively involved in the development of various IT initiatives to address the needs of the industry. He has helped focus attention on cargo as an integral part of the world trade process.

Trained as an engineer, Menen spearheaded the concept and development of the LD-36 (AMF) type unit load device (ULD), which increased the usable space on each lower-deck pallet base by 33 per cent.

He is a Fellow of the Chartered Institute of Logistics & Transportation (CITL) and the recipient of a number of achievement awards for his contribution to the air cargo industry.

* * *

The most crucial defining factors of the air freight industry have proved to be the globalization of production and markets, which have led to the creation and development of the science of supply chain management (SCM). This has resulted in air freight being used as a planned tool rather than a default mode of transport to be called upon in response to emergencies such as production delays, missed sailings and so on. When time is factored into any business decision, the higher price of air transportation can bring better cost-efficiency in the overall end-to-end process. Inventory management and logistics are key components of any modern supply chain operation.

Vendor managed inventory (VMI) is becoming the order of the day, as manufacturers are able to economize by decreasing the inventory held on their books. Components and parts are only produced on demand and on a just-in-time (JIT) delivery basis. Speed to the customer is vital, as is getting the product to the market and gaining an edge on competitors. Management of inventory-to-sales ratio is becoming a science in itself and is key to achieving optimal cost efficiency in inventory management. Today, the supply chains of a product, rather than the product itself, are the competitive edge.

Furthermore, markets are mostly global and the constant chasing of skilled operators at economic cost has led to the various components being made in different countries and regions. Final assembly is often carried out in locations other than the main production site. Hence, efficient logistics and transportation are critical within supply chain operations.

The air cargo trade has become a barometer of business health and economic activities can be accurately forecast with reasonable confidence at six weeks to three months in advance.

The challenges

There are a number of factors that have been hindering growth in air cargo traffic in recent years. For example, the eruption of the Icelandic volcano Eyjafjallajökull and its destructive ash cloud, which shut down European and subsequently global aviation activity for many days in April 2010. In addition, various acts of international terrorism have resulted in the heightening of security-related aspects, which in turn tend to disrupt efficient supply chain operations, especially since the 9/11 terrorist attacks on the US in 2001.

High oil prices have also been a challenge, not only by increasing the actual cost of transportation, but at the same time by diminishing consumer demand for all the normal day-to-day goods. Transportation costs have a major impact on the price of household goods, thus reducing disposable income. Oil prices are no longer demand-driven. Speculative trading, hand-in-hand with profiteering, is keeping the oil price high and unpredictable.

This is a major factor in the emergence of frequent economic downturns. In the closing decades of the twentieth century, the economic cycles were usually four to five years apart in a very predictable pattern. The advent of communication and internet technology has made information instantly available in real time, exposing weaknesses and excesses very quickly and throwing economies into very turbulent and erratic patterns, as witnessed in the first years of the twenty-first century. The disastrous financial crisis of 2008/2009 forced an immediate impact on world trade in practically every region. Failure of confidence coupled with considerable financial turmoil had a knock-on effect on consumer confidence. With very few goods being purchased, transportation demand fell dramatically. The subsequent crisis within the Eurozone, which has manifested itself in the collapse of the Greek economy as well as affecting several other Eurozone countries, is taking its toll on air transportation traffic and profitability. Running in parallel with this, the widespread political upheaval within the Middle East during the early months of 2011 – the Arab Spring – has further exacerbated the situation.

New culture

To combat these negative factors, the air freight industry is taking steps to address the situation. A decision was made in 2011 to form the Global Air Cargo Advisory Group (GACAG). The aim is to create a common voice, leading to a further loosening of market access, thus creating a more open and cost-effective basis for air transportation.

Overall, our world, our industry is going through a renewal process. The old rules do not apply and the new rules are not yet written. In such an evolutionary period, rigid procedures may be impracticable; any framework of rules thus created would need to be immensely dynamic so that they can be modified and be proactive to handle changes as they actually occur.

Technology is bringing in more efficiency in the movement of cargo by making information more transparent and available when it is needed. E-commerce will also facilitate better profiling and help to speed up security procedures as well as border control and clearance processes. Attaching X-ray images of the shipment being transported will become a mandatory requirement in the next eight to ten years. This will mean that any official wishing to see what is inside the cargo boxes will have appropriate access at any stage during the transportation process. Technology will be developed to reconcile images automatically without the need for too much manual intervention, which will help in speeding up the Customs clearance processes. E-freight will become a norm and in the next five to eight years the complete trading cycle will become 100 per cent electronic. This process will automatically incorporate electronic shipment tracking and it is likely that updatable radio frequency identification (RFID) chips will be inserted by the manufacturer at a point in the production cycle – thus everybody who handles the shipment will be able to update the data as it progresses through various parts of the transportation chain. E-freight will also facilitate the interaction between various transportation modes, making seamless multimodal transactions a reality.

Regulatory approach

The aviation industry, being one of the world's most regulated businesses, will continue to be held hostage to various government institutions, which consider this industry as a cash cow for easy funds. This is mostly driven by political agendas, with governments being forced to reduce taxes in other areas in order to gain votes and political strength. Taxation on oil prices and the lack of government support in tearing down oil cartels, together with ongoing speculative trading, forces the transportation industry to always be on the lookout for fresh cost-efficiencies. Engine technology will continue to improve, with engine and aircraft manufacturers continuing to invest in research and development (R&D) of new and more economical fuels. Over the next years the current EU environmental taxation agenda and the resultant political standoff will force governments to find more palatable solutions. The International Civil Aviation Organization (ICAO), meeting on 2 November 2011 in Montreal, has also endorsed the declaration, expressed in working papers (www.ainalerts.com/ainalerts/alertimages/ICAO.pdf) advanced by 26 countries. ICAO aligned with the international airline industry and a collection of countries including Brazil, China, the US, India, Japan and the Russian Federation in fighting and opposing the EU's 'unilateral' action to include non-EU aircraft operators in its Emissions Trading Scheme (ETS) as of January 2012.

All opposing parties have indicated that they would be in support of a global initiative led by ICAO. As of mid-2012, ICAO had not put forth a proposal for such an initiative; however, it has undertaken to look at and develop a proposal over the coming years.

Changes in manufacturing

Although aircraft technology is constantly improving, this is unlikely to impact payload capability in the near future. However, over the next 20–30 years it is possible that aircraft or flying machines capable of transporting 300–400 tonnes will emerge from the drawing board.

Accurate prediction of the immediate years is a major challenge. It is certain that air cargo will be a continuing growth segment of total transportation capacity, as commodity lifecycles are going to remain short, and will in fact get shorter because of the evolution in technology. Globalization is here to stay. However, there will be a plethora of changes in manufacturing, assembly and distribution. Driven by the need to balance trade deficits better, we will start seeing final assembly work being carried out within the actual countries that comprise the larger consumer markets – for example, the US, Mexico, Brazil and so on. However, the ongoing struggle to find cost efficiencies will mean that the manufacture of components will remain concentrated in places like China, India, Vietnam and other such locations. Hence, there will still be a demand for long-haul air cargo transportation.

Although production, markets and brands will all be global, marketing and sales activities are likely to be more regionalized and localized. In short, we will see the rise of 'glocal' (globally local) activities in order to cater to ethnic and cultural requirements.

The internet era has created acceleration in technology evolutionary process, causing a compression of time, leading to the lifecycles of products being greatly reduced. The integration of time – the fourth dimension – with the other three has brought with it variability that can be clearly seen in how inventory is managed nowadays.

Security and other border control challenges will continue to plague the air cargo business, at least in the foreseeable future, as screening technology continues to struggle to keep pace with regulatory requirements. During the next decade, we are going to see significant developments in this field and we will start benefitting from some of the efficiencies created by logistics management. VMI processes are here to stay and three-dimensional (3D) printing will change some of the procurement behaviours. How this will actually change is something that remains to be seen. I predict that some of the less complex parts will be manufactured via this mode and the 3D printer is likely to become a household item within the next four to five years.

The current range of PCs in general use will become largely redundant by 2020 – even tablet technology will start fading – with newer communication tools emerging as technology evolves. Semiconductors, and their technological offspring, will continue to be the typical cargo transported by air. Furthermore, because of compression of time and acceleration of evolution, these hi-tech products will become quickly obsolete. Of course, growth in this area will also mean that the commodity sizes will continue to diminish. The involvement of artificial intelligence will shorten research and development cycles over the next ten years. Prototypes are going to be computer-simulated and extensive testing cycles will be greatly reduced. Survival for companies will depend on how quickly they can develop products and get them into the market.

The future of freight forwarding

Production of pharmaceuticals, flowers, fruits and vegetables will remain global, and this sector will grow in its share of the total air cargo business. The investments currently being made in maintaining unbroken cool chains will bear fruit and temperature-controlled logistics operations will continue to grow in double digits for the foreseeable future. These commodities are – and remain – less sensitive to economic cycles. Environmental issues will remain centre-stage. The automotive industry, currently a major user of air cargo, will continue to thrive as more fuel-efficient vehicles are introduced. Over the next eight to ten years, barring some pockets of less-developed countries, the current worldwide fleet of vehicles will need replacement. This will stimulate air cargo traffic in automotive components and spare parts. In 10–15 years' time we will start seeing more personal flying machines in use, which will create a new segment of business related to the automotive industry.

Up until the time the world finds an alternative to fossil fuel, oil prices are likely to remain high and create challenges. We are probably some 15–20 years away from a viable alternative to aviation fuel, leaving the industry in a perpetual struggle. Aviation assets will remain highly capital intensive and will force consolidation – and some of the current smaller, less efficient carriers will fade away into the sunset.

Within the next ten years, the shape of aircraft is likely to stay largely the same. However, they will be flying longer distances. All the old classic freighters (such as the B747-200 and the early B747-400 series, as well as the DC-10 and DC-8) will disappear as the fuel costs required to fly them will no longer be affordable. There will be more demand for the 80–100 tonne payload, longer-range freighters, as regional distributions will be catered for by either road feeder services (RFSs) or, in many cases, the bellyhold capacity of the large, widebodied passenger aircraft.

The freight forwarding segment of the logistics business will evolve into outsourced procurement and logistics operations within the supply chain. The larger multinational forwarding companies will transition into full-fledged supply chain managers. There will be remnants of traditional forwarding, but they will be very localized and operating in niche markets. With Customs and border control processes getting more sophisticated and seamless, the demand from the forwarders or logistics suppliers will be on a full-service basis in about ten years' time. Thanks to the considerable development of electronic cargo processing, traditional relationships between airlines and the forwarding industry will evolve. This will create better transparency in all processes and costs, and replicate the ocean side of our business. Overall net costs, calculated with the margins added at the end of the transaction, will show the true cost of logistics within the supply chain. In about five to eight years' time, credit terms are going to be shorter and transactions moving more towards a real-time and online basis; very similar to the online purchasing of services currently in use today.

Manufacturing powerhouses

China and India will remain the factories of the world, supplying the global economy. These nations will be joined by Brazil and a few other progressive countries such as the Philippines, Vietnam, Cambodia, Myanmar and some African states. India and China will have larger skilled workforces and as their own regional and metropolitan economies strengthen they will keep on moving inland to find cheaper labour.

The pattern of production will shift slightly from finished products only to components manufacturing, which will then flow to regional manufacturing centres in or near the points of consumption. During this ongoing process, their own national consumer bases will continue to generate strong buying power, which will help to develop robust domestic economies, thus partially insulating them from exterior economic pressures.

The current status of North America as the world's largest consumer market will be challenged by the new breed of young consumers in India and China with money to spend.

Future career opportunities

Career opportunities in SCM will be extensive. The cargo industry will no longer be the stronghold of male domination. As the science of SCM grows and develops, it will attract both genders into its fold; this is already happening to a large extent. SCM is now becoming a boardroom discipline and logistics experience will be an advantage for future company CEOs. This culture is also driven by the fact that there is now more emphasis placed on academic qualifications for company executives and future directors.

Logistics has become a degree course, from undergraduate through to PhD levels, and is recognized in universities throughout the world as a professional career path. Some universities are now offering SCM in conjunction with transportation and logistics as an engineering course – and this is happening on a global platform. All one has to do is to search on the internet using the keywords SCM or logistics and to see the extent of programmes available.

This will create new industry professionals, who could possibly be called the 'logisteers'. There will be an abundant supply of qualified logistics professionals in future years.

However, for jobs requiring lower levels of academic skills, the recruitment challenge persists. The wage levels offered by airlines, airports and freight forwarders may not be in line with expectations. For this purpose, greater efforts must be made by companies and the air freight industry as a whole to attract school leavers who for some reason will not pursue a university qualification. Drawing them into an apprentice programme will help develop the specific skills required by the industry. The air cargo industry has to focus more on creating such apprentice schemes to ensure a constant supply of skilled applicants at all levels. We must not forget that the physical operations at the cargo warehouse, on the airport ramp and so on will remain more belt-and-braces than anything.

Conclusion

Overall, the global movement of air cargo will remain a growth industry. As the world goes through the current renewal process, where all past definitions of trend analysis have to be redefined, the anticipated growth, which was forecasted by Boeing at around 5.4 per cent per year over the next 20 years, might actually track slightly lower. This is driven by more technological and global regionalization of production. Management during the next few years of evolution must base its thinking on what can happen and be realized in the future. The past is past; it is firmly consigned to history, and the trends of the past cannot be used to manage the industry today and forecast its prospects for tomorrow. Today has got to be managed with the possibilities of what can be tomorrow. Visions of grandeur are great, but today has got to be managed viably so we can all be there in the years ahead. The future is where we all want to be.

Note: At the time of publication, the ETS initiative has been postponed pending international agreements.

Freedoms for airlines

Freedoms of the Air (air traffic rights) apply to commercial aviation, carrying paying passengers, cargo or mail.

Freedom	Description	Example
1st	To fly over another country without landing	Qantas: Sydney to Singapore, overflying Indonesia
2nd	To make a technical stop in another country	Air New Zealand: London to Auckland, via Los Angeles
3rd	To carry traffic from the home country to another country	Emirates: Dubai to Mumbai
4th	To carry traffic to the home country from another country	Emirates: Mumbai to Dubai
5th	To carry traffic between two countries by an airline of a third country on a flight with either originates or ends in the airline's home country	Iberia: Madrid to Bogota, Colombia, and Quito, Ecuador
6th	To carry traffic between two countries by an airline of a third country via the airline's own country	British Airways: Houston, US, to Lagos, Nigeria, via London
7th	To carry traffic between two countries by an airline of a third country on a route outside its own country	FedEx: Caribbean feeder services
8th	To carry traffic between two or more airports in a country on a service that originates or ends in the airline's own country	Cathay Pacific: Hong Kong to Cairns and Brisbane
9th	To carry traffic on routes within the airline's own country	Aeroflot: Moscow to Vladivostok

Glossary of common terms

ACMI	Aircraft, crew, maintenance, insurance (wet lease)
Air cargo	Goods carried in an aircraft
Air freight	The lading, or cargo, in an aircraft (often synonymous with air cargo)
Airside	Those parts of an airport controlled by the Customs authorities that are inaccessible to the public
All-cargo carrier	An airline that does not carry passengers
Apron	Aircraft parking area, for refuelling and the handling of cargo, baggage and mail
AWB	Air waybill, giving full details of the cargo
Block space	Air freight forwarders pre-book space with airlines
Break-bulk	Sorting consolidated cargo into individual consignments. Usually ground handled task.
CASS	The cargo accounts settlement system
Code share	An agreement whereby an airline sells capacity on another carrier's service (generally applicable only to passenger services)
Combination carrier	An airline that operates both passenger and cargo services
Consignee	The person or organization to whom cargo is being sent
Consolidation	When the cargo from two or more shippers is carried in a single container
CTK	Cargo-tonne-kilometre – a key airline performance indicator
Curfew	Those hours, usually at night, when flights to and from an airport are banned or restricted
Dangerous goods	Cargo that can only be carried under strictly regulated circumstances and on specific flights
Door-to-door	The movement of cargo from consignor to consignee by a single operator (usually an express operator or integrator)
Dry lease	Lease of an aircraft, with the lessee operator providing its own crew, maintenance and insurance

e-AWB	Electronic air waybill
EDI	Electronic data interchange
FAA	Federal Aviation Administration (US)
FF	Freight forwarder
Flag carrier	The national airline of a country (often government-owned)
GHA	Ground handling agent
GSSA	General sales and services agent
HAWB	House air waybill
Hub-and-spoke	The route network where smaller aircraft feed cargo into a main hub which in turn is linked to other main hubs around the world by big long-haul aircraft
IATA	International Air Transport Association
ICAO	International Civil Aviation Organization
Integrator	An air express operator, usually with its own hub-and-spoke network
JIT	Just-in-time
KPI	Key performance indicator
MAWB	Master air waybill
MTOW	Maximum takeoff weight
Multimodal	The use of more than one transport mode, such as air, sea, road or rail
Noise footprint	The sound map made by an aircraft, usually when landing at or taking off from an airport in built-up areas
Offline	A destination not served by a scheduled airline
Oversize cargo	Cargo that will not fit in a standard container, or in a specific aircraft
Pallet	A ULD on which cargo is placed prior to being loaded into an aircraft
Reefer	Refrigerated vehicle or container
RFS	Road feeder service
Split charter	Where two or more consignors share space on a chartered aircraft
Tech stop	Where an aircraft lands at an airport prior to arriving at its destination airport, usually for refuelling purposes
TIACA	The International Air Cargo Association
Tonne	Metric weight measurement, equal to 1,000 kg
Traffic rights	Inter-governmental agreements stating which airlines may fly on specific routes between two countries
ULD	Unit load device
WCO	World Customs Organization
Wet lease	See ACMI and Dry lease

Index

Note: page numbers in *italic* type refer to figures.